Campus Rules and Moral Community

ISSUES IN ACADEMIC ETHICS

General Editor: Steven M. Cahn

Campus Rules and Moral Community

In Place of *In Loco Parentis*

David A. Hoekema

ROWMAN & LITTLEFIELD PUBLISHERS, INC.

ROWMAN & LITTLEFIELD PUBLISHERS, INC.

Published in the United States of America
by Rowman & Littlefield Publishers, Inc.
4720 Boston Way, Lanham, Maryland 20706

3 Henrietta Street
London WC2E 8LU, England

British Cataloging in Publication Information Available

Library of Congress Cataloging-in-Publication Data
Hoekema, David A.
Campus rules and moral community : in place of in loco parentis /
David A. Hoekema.
p.   cm.—(Issues in Academic Ethics)
Includes bibliographical references.
1. College discipline—United States.   2. College students—United
States—Conduct of life.   3. Student-administrator relationships-
-United States.   4. College students—Legal status, laws, etc.-
-United States.   5. Educational surveys—United
States.   I. Title.   II. Series.
LB2343.H64   1993   378.1'81'0973—dc20   93-26957   CIP

ISBN 0–8476–7688–9 (cloth: alk. paper)
ISBN 0–8476–7689–7 (pbk.: alk. paper)

Printed in the United States of America

∞ ™ The paper used in this publication meets the minimum requirements of
American National Standard for Information Sciences—Permanence
of Paper for Printed Library Materials, ANSI Z39.48–1984.

Issues in Academic Ethics

Academic life generates a variety of moral issues. These may be faced by students, staff, administrators, or trustees, but most often revolve around the rights and responsibilities of the faculty. In my 1986 book *Saints and Scamps: Ethics in Academia* (Rowman & Littlefield), I set out to enumerate, explain, and emphasize the most fundamental of these professorial obligations. To do justice to the complexities of academic ethics, however, requires the work of many scholars focused on numerous areas of investigation. The results of such an effort are embodied in this series.

Each volume concentrates on one set of connected issues and combines a single-authored monograph with reprinted sources chosen by the author to exemplify or amplify materials in the text. This format is intended to guide readers while encouraging them to develop and defend their own beliefs.

In recent years philosophers have examined the appropriate standards of conduct for physicians, nurses, lawyers, journalists, business managers, and government policymakers but have not given equal attention to formulating guidelines for their own profession. The time has come to observe the Delphic motto "Know thyself." Granted, the issues in need of critical examination are not exotic, but as the history of philosophy demonstrates, self-knowledge is often the most important to seek and the most difficult to attain.

Steven M. Cahn

For
Ruth Brink Hoekema
and in memory of
Anthony A. Hoekema

whose lives as teachers, writers, and parents
have exemplified the meaning
of moral and religious community

It is enacted that all the heads, fellows, and scholars of all colleges, as well as all persons in holy orders, shall dress as becomes clerks. Also that all others (except the sons of barons having the right of voting in the Upper House of Parliament, and also barons of the Scotch and Irish peerages) shall wear dresses of a black or dark colour, and shall not imitate anything betokening pride or luxury, but hold themselves aloof from them. Moreover they shall be obliged to abstain from that absurd and assuming practice of walking publicly in boots.

It is enacted, that scholars of all conditions shall keep away from inns, eating-houses, wine-shops, and all houses whatever within the city, or precinct of the University, wherein wine or any other drink, or the Nicotean herb, or tobacco, is commonly sold; also that if any person does otherwise, and is not eighteen years old, and not a graduate, he shall be flogged in public.

It is enacted, that scholars and graduates of all conditions are to keep away during the day, and especially at night, from the shops and houses of the townsmen; but particularly from houses where women of ill or suspected fame or harlots are kept or harbored, whose company is peremptorily forbidden to all scholars whatever, either in private rooms or in the citizens' houses.

—William Laud, Archbishop of Canterbury and Chancellor of Oxford University, *Laud's Code,* a compilation of rules drawn up in 1636.

Contents

Preface

This study was launched by an unexpected telephone call from Steven Cahn, editor of the series of which it is part. He told me he was working on an anthology on issues in academic ethics and asked if I would consider writing an essay on student behavioral rules and the passing of the *in loco parentis* model.

I protested that I had nothing particular to say about the topic. My philosophical work has been chiefly in the areas of punishment, coercion, and the morality of war and nonviolence. I had no more involvement with or knowledge of campus disciplinary rules and procedures than has the average faculty member. Perhaps so, Cahn replied, but he had extended his invitation because he was confident that, if I did take up the issues of student conduct and its regulation from a philosophical perspective, I would have interesting things to say.

The consequences of this shameless flattery include not only the requested contribution to the anthology (see Hoekema 1990) but the present project as well. As a result of that telephone inquiry, I have spent a substantial portion of my time during the past three years examining student conduct codes and assessing their intended purposes and functions. The project has proven more involved and more time-consuming than I imagined at the outset, for it quickly became evident that in order to offer any satisfactory account of the ethics of student behavior I would need to gather a broad base of information from campuses and review court decisions that have substantially affected institutions' powers to regulate student conduct. Whether the conclusions I have reached are sufficiently interesting to warrant the effort—as Cahn had hoped—I leave for readers to judge.

The research for this study and most of the manuscript were completed during a partial sabbatical leave granted to me by the American Philosophical Association in the academic year 1990–91, supplemented by a one-course sabbatical reduction granted by the University of Delaware in the fall of 1990. This sabbatical leave was the first ever granted to an APA Executive Director. I am deeply grateful to the Board of Officers of the APA, and in particular to Joel Feinberg and Robert Turnbull as chairs of the Board, for having provided a substantial reduction in my responsibilities for the year in order to make such a research project possible.

Two members of the APA staff, Publications Coordinator Diana Walls and Assistant Director Shirley Anderson lent invaluable assistance with the survey of colleges and universities that I conducted, the former in preparing and carrying out the mailing of the survey questionnaire and the latter in tabulating the responses and summarizing narrative comments. Furthermore, they conspired with the third member of the staff at our national office, Janet Sample, to place insuperable obstacles in the path of anyone who sought to encroach upon the time that had been granted me for research purposes. Their assistance in all of these forms has been invaluable.

To the forty-nine college and university administrators who responded to my request for information concerning student behavioral rules on their campuses I extend a word of thanks. Many indicated in their responses that they looked forward eagerly to seeing the results of my study, and I hope that my observations and recommendations will prove as useful in their work as were their responses and suggestions in mine.

I owe a special debt to Frank Dilley, Chair of the Philosophy Department at the University of Delaware, for his numerous, if indirect, contributions to this project. Not only did he lend essential assistance in making arrangements for my partial sabbatical; he also accepted the Board of Officers' appointment as Acting Executive Director of the APA to take up some of the duties that I set aside for the year. My colleagues in the Philosophy Department also responded with helpful comments and criticisms when I presented portions of the last section of the book to them in a departmental colloquium.

Susan Hoekema's careful reading of the entire manuscript has led to numerous improvements in clarity, organization, and content. I am grateful also to the librarians at Pepper, Hamilton, and Scheetz, the law firm where she is employed, who graciously permitted me to consult the firm's legal library on several weekends. The reference staff of the law library at the Delaware College of Law also lent invaluable aid in locating some nineteenth-century legal decisions on microfilm.

David A. Hoekema
Swarthmore, Pennsylvania

Note: In the period during which the manuscript of this book was in the editing process, I left my position at the University of Delaware and the American Philosophical Association in order to accept an appointment as Academic Dean and Professor of Philosophy at Calvin College, from which I was graduated twenty years earlier. This career change puts some references to Calvin in the text in a different light, but this seems to me no reason to excise them. In general, my experiences at an institution that is both familiar and unfamiliar to me have persuaded me even more strongly of the wisdom of addressing student behavior in the context of campus communities and institutional identity, themes that are developed in Chapters 6 and 7.

DAH
Grand Rapids, Michigan

Introduction

Campuses in the News for All the Wrong Reasons

There was a time within living memory when the nation's campuses figured prominently and regularly in the evening news and the daily papers. Strikes, demonstrations, and antiwar protests symbolized the deep division in the body politic over a costly war in Indochina, a division that deepened and hardened in the late 1960s and early 1970s as public awareness grew but the cause of the United States and its allies seemed increasingly hopeless. These campus scenes made for dramatic television footage as unkempt students, and some of their only slightly less disheveled professors, chanted slogans and carried placards. Occasionally police moved in and made arrests for trespassing or blocking roadways, or counter-demonstrators shouted patriotic slogans and waved flags—all of this a boon for the cameramen, a painful irritant to legislators and to the trustees of private colleges.

By the late 1970s, the war had ended with a whimper rather than a bang with the withdrawal of American forces and the subsequent collapse of South Vietnam. The campuses became quieter, the students more intent on career preparation than on political demonstrations. The Reagan and Bush administrations ushered in a new economic order in which deficits soared while social programs dwindled. Institutions of higher education suffered both from cutbacks in federal support and from a broad current of popular suspicion directed toward intellectual elites. Both the political atmosphere and the uncertainty of future employment dampened campus protests. Moreover, diminished opportunities for academic employment induced younger faculty members as well as students to concentrate on their careers

1

more than on the state of the world. A regular viewer of television news was seldom reminded that colleges and universities existed, apart from an occasional September interview with incoming freshmen on a well-groomed lawn, or a few snippets from commencement speeches by politicians each May. In these images, the lawns are always flawless, the flower beds filled, and the buildings scrubbed clean of graffiti.

Campus activism did not vanish entirely. But its recent manifestations have become much smaller in scope, and more focused in their concerns, than were the widespread protests of an earlier era. One cannot find on any campus today large numbers of students ready to heed the call to the barricades in the cause of political and social revolution, but one can find, on nearly every campus, a small group dedicated to environmental education and lobbying, another that focuses on Central American concerns, and either formal or informal caucuses of feminists and black students. Their small-scale efforts, however, seldom make the news.

In the 1990s, however, it is not political agitation but misbehavior that has brought the reporters back to the quad—something in which trustees and public relations officers can take little comfort. Within the space of a few months, for example, national news media carried stories reporting the following incidents:

• A Brown University student was expelled for a series of incidents of rowdiness, culminating in his return to a residence-hall courtyard late one evening in a state of advanced drunkenness, when he shouted epithets and insults directed against blacks, Jews, and homosexuals.[1]

• Local police raided three of the most popular social fraternities at the University of Virginia, resulting in the arrest and conviction of several students on drug-trafficking charges and the seizure of the fraternity houses by the federal government, under the terms of a law permitting seizure of property used in drug sales.[2]

• A Stanford University professor was dismissed after he disclosed in a letter to the head of federal drug enforcement programs that he regularly uses illegal drugs for recreational purposes in the company of students.[3]

• Upperclassmen at Skidmore College protested an administrative decision to ban beer kegs from a residence-hall complex many of whose residents are of legal age.[4] In contrast, a much stricter policy governing on-campus parties where alcohol is served was ratified by the student government at Bryn Mawr and appeared to enjoy broad student support.[5]

• Three students at St. John's University were brought to trial on charges arising from a March 1990 party at the house where they were living. A female student charged that they had forced her to engage in oral sex, coerced her to drink a potent alcoholic beverage, and then taken advantage of her after she passed out. The men were acquitted by the court but expelled by the university.[6]

• A University of Rhode Island student testified in court that she had been raped by a fellow student at a fraternity party while at least five other men watched. One of the men accused of being present during the rape committed suicide hours before he was scheduled to meet with state police to offer his account of the incident.[7]

• At a sorority keg party at the University of Hartford, campus security officers called in local police to assist in restoring order, but students greeted the police with a shower of rocks and bottles. The conflict spilled from the sorority onto the university commons, and a melee involving an estimated one thousand students and police officers from four cities resulted.[8]

• A male Bennington College student accused a male professor of sexual harassment, citing an incident in which the professor demanded sexual favors as a condition for a passing grade, and the professor was promptly dismissed from a tenured position he had held for eighteen years. The professor sued the college, claiming that the only ground for his dismissal was the uncorroborated and inaccurate testimony of the student.[9]

In response to incidents such as these, many people on and off campus wonder what has been going on during all the years of comparative quiet on the campuses. Are college students losing any sense of civility, of decency, of respect for others who differ from themselves or who simply stand in their way? Have colleges abandoned any effort to shape character? More generally, are the campuses of the 1990s still institutions where critical issues facing society are deliberated and leaders of tomorrow learn to hold themselves to the same high standards they observe in the lives of their mentors, or are they instead protected enclaves where students eschew all responsibility for their actions and their society's future, while faculty and administrators stand idly by?

According to the official story told by presidents and admissions officers to anxious parents and prospective students, the stories cited above are merely isolated incidents, blown up out of proportion by news media more interested in the salacious and scandalous than in balanced reporting. And they are manifestations more of the excesses of irresponsible youth than of problems specific to the campus. Drunkenness, assault, and sexual exploitation are equally common among high school graduates who have not gone on to college, but they become newsworthy only when they occur inside the campus gates.

Even college presidents, when they are candid, acknowledge that the problems are more than superficial. In a recent survey conducted by the American Council on Education and the Carnegie Foundation for the Advancement of Teaching, for example, more than half of the presidents responding to the survey said they are more concerned about the quality of campus life today than they were a few years ago. Nearly eighty percent identified alcohol abuse as a serious problem on their campus, and fifty percent said theft had become a serious problem. Sixty-eight percent of research university presidents, and twenty-eight percent of liberal-arts college presidents, reported serious problems arising from racial tensions on campus. The authors of the report summed up their findings thus: "We conclude that the idyllic vision so routinely portrayed in college promotional materials often masks disturbing realities of student life."[10]

Isn't it time, some now ask, to reimpose some of the controls that once restrained wayward students? When students engage in date rape, racial slurs, drug dealing, and flagrant drunkenness, should not the institutional parent put the institutional foot down? Isn't it high time, in other words, for the colleges and universities to resume their position *in loco parentis*, "in the place of the parent," that they abandoned a generation or more ago?

That model of the relationship between institution and student has long been considered dead, a victim both of student demands for greater autonomy and of institutional reluctance to meddle in students' private affairs. In the introduction to several colleges' student discipline handbooks, one can find an explicit statement that although the college of a generation or two ago thought of itself as standing in the place of the parent, such a position is utterly untenable today.

But changing patterns of behavior, heightened attention to student misbehavior, and changing expectations on the part of parents and others seem to be bringing the more directive and moralistic stance back from its presumed grave. Some campuses have tightened restrictions on alcohol, diminished student discretion in matters of residence and hours, and supplemented general statements about student responsibilities with specific behavioral rules. Students themselves have sometimes taken the lead, like children impatient with inattentive parents, in re-establishing single-sex residence halls, restricting visiting hours, and imposing harsher punishment for disorderly behavior.

Is a return to the stance of the institution *in loco parentis* desirable? Is it even possible? Or has the college's claim to act in place of the absent parent been irrevocably nullified by developments both in student life and in the law? If the parental model of student discipline is irretrievably lost, what—if anything—has replaced it?

These are the central questions that I address in this study. I will not dwell on any of the specific incidents cited above, which differ from those on a hundred other campuses only in that, for arbitrary reasons, they have been highlighted in the news media and in that some have become the subject of endless debate. To debate such individual cases would only distract attention from the underlying issues.

Nor will it be my purpose to put forward a blueprint for successful regulation of student conduct on a typical campus. Any attempt to do so would undervalue, and might undermine, the particularity and the rich diversity that are among the greatest strengths of American higher education. A discipline system that fits Amherst College cannot be exported to the University of Texas, or even to the University of Massachusetts right next door, without extensive changes dictated by different institutional histories and present situations. A set of basic rules and procedures that proves highly effective at Baylor University might be utterly disastrous at Rice.

Instead my purpose will be to review the present state of student behavioral regulation in order to discern its principal features, its major achievements, and its most serious shortcomings. Against this background I will recommend both overall aims and specific strategies that might make for a more successful system of rules of conduct.

I emphasize at the outset that I undertake this task from the standpoint of a philosopher and a concerned member of the academic community. My observations and recommendations would without doubt be different in many ways if I were in a position to reflect on personal experience as an administrator in the area of student life. My own responsibility in these areas has been no more than that of any responsible member of the faculty of a college or university—viz., to deal with student conduct and residence life problems as they affect students enrolled in my classes or entrusted to my advisement.

My lack of experience in student life administration seems to me no reason to demur from addressing the issues of student life. Indeed, I am convinced that the silence of the faculty on matters of student life is one of the principal obstacles to an effective and consistent approach to these matters. Yet I have no doubt that others with more experience in this area will be able to correct my observations, and refine my recommendations, at many points. I have nothing but admiration for administrators in the area of student affairs who are conscientiously seeking to translate the ideals of mutual respect and mutual responsibility into practice in their institutions, and I hope the present study may prove useful in their daunting task.

Included in the present volume as appendices, in addition to the text of the questionnaire used in my survey and a bibliography, are two sorts of background materials. First, I provide the text of a number of court decisions affecting college discipline and its enforcement, enabling readers to examine the reasoning behind decisions that are cited briefly in Chapter 2. Second, I also include a representative sample of student conduct policies from a variety of institutions. The inclusion of these longer excerpts, several of which are mentioned and briefly cited in the text, will serve both to augment that brief discussion and to provide models for comparison with other codes.

I identify the institution that is the source of each of the rules quoted in the text or reproduced in the appended materials, with the permission of the administrators who sent them. Many could be taken as models by any institution seeking to revise its codes of conduct. Others are an embarrassing testimony to carelessness and inattention. The university whose extensive and helpful plagiarism policy is itself plagiarized, and the college that declares its intent to help students make a responsible decision whether to use drugs will not be happy to find their policies highlighted here. My purpose, however, is not to assign praise or blame but to suggest goals and policies that can guide any institution seeking to draw the lines of student rights and responsibilities more clearly.

Footnote references will be made in abbreviated form throughout, and full publication information can be found in the appended bibliography. References to newspapers, periodicals, and reference works will appear in full in the footnotes, since these materials are not included in the bibliography. Campus discipline codes, identified in the text only by institution, are listed in a section of the bibliography.

Notes

1. "Student at Brown is Expelled Under a Rule Barring 'Hate Speech,' " *New York Times*, February 12, 1991, p. A17. Subsequent accounts in the same

newspaper corrected the misleading impression given by this headline that the principal ground for expulsion was a single incident of racial slurs. In fact the individual had previously been cited for several disciplinary violations, and expulsion was imposed not for the single incident featured in the story but for a series of infractions of University policy. See, for example, Anthony DePalma, "Battling Bias, Campuses Face Free Speech Fight," *New York Times,* February 20, 1991, p. B9.

2. "Drug Raids on 3 Fraternities Force University of Virginia to Re-Examine its Traditions and Relations with Students, *Chronicle of Higher Education,* April 24, 1991, pp. A33, A35; "Virginia Student's Sentence on Drug Charge is Cut," *New York Times,* July 30, 1991, p. A10.

3. "Stanford Faces Sanction in Drug Dispute," *New York Times,* April 23, 1991; "Threatened with Loss of U. S. Funds, Stanford Suspends Instructor in Drug Case," *Chronicle of Higher Education,* May 1, 1991, p. A1.

4. "Ban on Kegs Opposed by Those of Drinking Age," *New York Times,* April 28, 1991.

5. "New Rules Lead Some Drinkers to Go Off Campus," *New York Times,* February 10, 1991.

6. "Three Men Ousted by St. John's in Sex Assault," *New York Times,* October 10, 1991, p. B1.

7. "A Fraternity Party, a Rape Charge and a Tragedy," *New York Times,* November 12, 1990.

8. "Hartford Students and Police Clash at Party," *New York Times,* March 4, 1991, p. B6.

9. "Professor Ousted on Sex Charge Disputes Policy," *New York Times,* May 17, 1991, p. B17.

10. "Quality of Life Said to Have Diminished on U. S. Campuses," *Chronicle of Higher Education,* May 2, 1990, pp. A1, A32.

Chapter One

Living on Campus After the Revolution

Imagine that a young friend, a woman of nearly twenty who has come to the United States from abroad and succeeded in obtaining a temporary work visa, appears at your door in a state of high excitement to report on the outcome of her search for an apartment. She is delighted that her search has been successful, but she is puzzled by some peculiarities of the housing she has obtained.

She has found a furnished apartment, a third-floor walkup. It is very small, a single room of about two hundred square feet, but the other tenants seem exceptionally friendly, and the location is very convenient to her new job. The building is well maintained and the grounds around it are well kept. But the furnishings in the room—two straight chairs, two simple wooden desks, a bookcase, and two twin beds—are not only sparse but rather deteriorated from use. Tattered curtains hang at the windows, and bits and pieces of old posters and bumper stickers cling to the walls and furniture.

There is no bathroom in the apartment. Down at the end of a long hallway is a women's toilet with several toilet stalls and lavatories but no shower or bath facilities. At the other end of the hallway is the men's toilet. Your friend tells you that she bumped into another female tenant who was emerging from the men's toilet clad in a robe and a towel. Seeing your friend's surprise, the other woman told her that the women on the third floor generally use the shower stalls in the men's bathroom. If she is not comfortable with that, the other tenant added, she can use the showers in the women's toilet on the fifth floor.

There are no cooking facilities in the apartment, and there would be no room for them anyway. It is required of all residents, however, that

9

they sign up and pay in advance, four months at a time, for at least two meals a day in a nearby cafeteria run by the building's owners.

Your friend's uneasiness about the apartment building was multiplied, she adds, when she returned from work on her second afternoon after she moved into the apartment to find another woman moving her own clothing and books into the same room. The latter cheerfully informed your friend that she was her new roommate. "I'm sure we will get along fine," said this stranger. "I looked through your books and tapes this afternoon and I see we have lots in common. It looks as if you don't smoke, and I don't smoke cigarettes either—only a couple of joints in the evening. I moved your books to the top two shelves. Is it OK if I take the bed by the window?"

Is this usual, your friend asks? Is this the way most apartment buildings in the United States work? Is it customary to have shared showers and mandatory cafeteria meals?

You are puzzled. What sort of a facility has your friend found? Obviously it is not an ordinary apartment building. No tenants would tolerate the intrusiveness of the living arrangements, least of all the assignment of roommates. The city housing authority would move quickly to shut down any apartment building that lacked private bathrooms and kitchen facilities and that arbitrarily assigned two strangers to share one small room.

There are only two possibilities that enter your mind. Perhaps your friend has unwittingly checked into the novitiate of a religious order. The roommate's breezy avowal of a drug habit seems to count against that hypothesis, though one can never tell. The presence of men on the floor, however, clinches it. Her building cannot be a convent.

There is only one remaining possibility. The apartment building—yes, this has to be it!—is a university residence hall. Now it all makes sense. The intolerable conditions that your friend has described are simply the normal conditions of undergraduate life. She has unwittingly undertaken to live like a college student.

In what other imaginable context would any adults put up with the conditions that are imposed on college students who live on campus? Young and unformed as they may appear in the eyes of their professors, college students are nearly all of legal age. Those who have not reached eighteen by the time of matriculation usually pass that milestone during their first year. Were they to seek housing off campus, they would demand what every adult would expect: adequate living space, a private bath, a minimally equipped kitchen, and the right to choose whether and with whom they wish to share their quarters.

Because they are students, however, they are expected to forgo these minimal conditions.

An apartment building that opened in any American city and imposed the conditions of college residence halls would not remain open long. In the unlikely event that it attracted tenants, it would soon be closed by city inspectors. But because residence halls are on campus—because, in effect, they are steeped in a long tradition that places college students in a special category separate from all other adults—we seldom take notice of the peculiar conditions under which their residents live, unless it is made as explicit as in the story I have been telling.

And the conditions of college housing become even more peculiar the more closely one looks at them, assuming that one can reasonably credit the veracity of accounts from student newspapers and the personal experiences related to me and to a number of colleagues. Some students can request to share a room with a designated person, it is true; but others must accept the luck of the draw and share a room with a stranger. Not infrequently three students are crammed into a room that was designed to be barely adequate for two. When a student complains about a roommate's behavior—whether it be drug use, drunkenness, or just general rudeness—a new roommate may be assigned, or the student may merely be counseled to be more tolerant and less judgmental. "Learn to appreciate others' lifestyles," students may be told—no matter that the lifestyle they are thus asked to value involves violation of federal and state controlled-substance laws.

When a roommate hosts a party or invites a boyfriend or girlfriend over, the other tenant is expected to find another place to sleep. Noise and booze are often inescapable. Those who had imagined that their rooms would afford a refuge for quiet study find their illusions quickly shattered. On one state university campus, a student has told me, Monday, Wednesday, Friday, Saturday, and Sunday evenings are customarily devoted to parties. More academic pursuits are considered appropriate, or at least tolerated, on the two evenings remaining.

Such horror stories can be multiplied without end—as they frequently are by conservative critics of the present atmosphere on campus. They are emblems of the disrespect for authority and for each other, the laziness and lack of personal industry, and the weakness of character that infected the post-Vietnam student population—so goes the critique. The students of the 1950s worked hard and behaved properly. The students of the 1960s and 1970s were so caught up in politics that they neglected their studies as well as their hygiene, and their professors helped them trash the curriculum. Today's students want the benefits, the untrammeled freedom, of an era that is past. They want to enjoy the fruits of the revolution that their predecessors began. What they have forgotten is that the revolution failed.

Such diatribes are tiresomely familiar, and yet they contain an element of truth. It is true that the far-reaching social and political revolution that activists of the Vietnam era dreamed of has never arrived. Some of the changes they sought—from the local, such as greater student involvement in campus governance, to the global, such as an end to American involvement in Vietnam—were soon accomplished. But the prophecy of a dawning Age of Aquarius, an age in which old animosities and entrenched inequality would blow away like chaff before the fresh breezes of democratic socialism, proved to be unrealistic. Instead, idealism itself has been pushed aside by more practical and self-interested goals, both on campus and in American society at large.

But what the conservative critics fail to see is that another sort of revolution actually has occurred on the campuses in the past thirty years, one that has dramatically changed the lives of students and will shape the future course of American society. It is a revolution in modes of student life and in the relationship between students and the institution. It is a revolution not of political or economic upheaval but of altered roles and expectations, and it has created a new social and moral order on campus. If the significance of these changes has largely escaped our notice, that is only because they have occurred so gradually.

Prominent in Greek mythology are the stories of son killing father. Sometimes patricide is committed in anger, but unknowingly, as when Oedipus slew the man who insulted him on the highway. Other stories recount tragic error, like that of Theseus's grief-stricken father, who leaped into the sea in response to a signal that he mistook for an announcement of his son's death. In Mary Renault's retelling of the story of Theseus, these myths are woven into a universal pattern, encompassing not only human society but even communities of animals, in which a new generation can come to the fore only on the death of the king, the supreme figure of the father.[1] Scholars—particularly Freudians and feminists—have traced this theme through many windings in Western myth and literature.

The essence of the revolution on campus has been the death of the father, or more generally of the parent. For decades the college or university claimed a place in students' lives *in loco parentis*. Like a parent, the college set the limits of students' freedom—in dress, in deportment, and in curfew hours. Like a parent, the college strove to be flexible yet firm, benevolent but not indulgent. Also like a parent, the college commonly found that its benevolent concerns elicited resentment, grudging compliance, and frequent circumvention.

The model of the college *in loco parentis* endured longer at liberal-arts colleges than at larger universities, and it died last of all on church-related campuses. I attended one of the last category, where the parental model was very much alive even in the early 1970s, after its demise everywhere else. I remember vividly some of the concrete manifestations of the college's role, such as the knot of couples that gathered just before 11:00 P.M. on weeknights, 1:00 A.M. on weekends, in a hundred-yard semicircle centered on the entrance to each women's dormitory, seizing what little privacy the darkness and the low shrubbery afforded. The attentions mutually bestowed ranged from a friendly kiss to entanglements limited only by the necessity of being fully and more or less plausibly clothed in time to dash inside before the doors were locked. Or so it seemed. No one paid much attention to what others were doing, because the aversion of eyes was the only privacy available.

The scene I have described will strike contemporary college students as an exotic vignette from a far-distant time and place. At most institutions today, curfews and visitation hours have long been abandoned. Tactics for leaving back doors unlocked and evading resident advisors no longer figure among students' basic life skills. For the college as parent, the university that stands *in loco parentis*, has all but vanished from today's academy. The institutional father is dead.

Perhaps the most striking concrete evidence of the revolution on campus can be found in the disappearance of the women's and men's dormitories about whose doors students once courted. Indeed, the very term that I have just used has fallen from favor. There are no longer any "dormitories" on campus: Students now reside in "residence halls."

When I have made the mistake of referring to the present status of "dormitories" in speaking with student-affairs administrators, I have been rebuked in a tone of moral reproof, rather as if I had referred to women students as "girls." Perhaps the term has become improper because it suggests the image of a bedroom in the family house—even if few students know enough Latin to understand the reference. Anglophilia may also have been a motive in relabeling dormitories "halls," as in Oxbridge usage. Whatever the reason, American students no longer live in the institutional father's house: They do not sleep in dormitories but instead reside in halls. And in those halls, departing sharply from earlier tradition, men and women mingle freely and informally. The extent of this change was made very clear by the responses I received to a survey, some of whose other results are described in Chapter 3.[2]

I mailed an extensive questionnaire on student behavioral rules and practices to the chief student-affairs officers at seventy-five colleges and universities across the country, and I received responses from forty-nine of them. The responses to three questions about on-campus housing today document a dramatic shift over the past two decades.

Fifty-six percent of the institutions accommodated all resident students in single-sex men's or women's residence halls in 1969–70. Ten years later, the percentage had dropped by more than half, to twenty-two percent. Today only eleven percent of institutions have only sex-segregated residence halls.

Even these numbers understate the rapidity and extent of the change, because they include single-sex institutions. In 1970 such colleges accounted for twenty-six percent of the total; in 1980, nine percent. In 1990, only two institutions, six percent of the respondents, still admitted only men or only women. But these two, Westhampton and Richmond colleges, are the two undergraduate colleges of the University of Richmond, and in many respects they function as one coeducational college.[3]

If we take as the reference class responding institutions that admit both men and women, the shift noted above in housing patterns is even more pronounced: Seventy-seven percent had only single-sex residence halls in 1970 as compared with twenty-three percent in 1980 and ten percent in 1990.

Twenty years ago only one of the campuses surveyed had residence halls in which men and women occupied separate rooms or suites on the same floor. Six more accommodated men and women on alternate floors of the same buildings. Among the responding coeducational institutions, then, only twenty-two percent had mixed residence halls of either pattern.[4] Ten years later, forty-two percent of campuses had buildings in which men and women lived on alternate floors; thirty-five percent had buildings with men and women in alternate rooms or suites on the same floor. By 1990 the percentage of institutions with halls mixed by floor remained essentially the same, forty percent, whereas the number of institutions with men and women in adjacent rooms or suites had grown to forty-nine percent. The number of campuses with coeducational residence halls, in other words, increased more than threefold in two decades.

The change from single-sex to coeducational residence halls is only one of several important changes in campus life during the past two decades. I will point more briefly to three other broad changes, linked elements in what can fairly be called a revolution on campus. These have to do with the changing student population, with shifts in student interests, and with heightened concern for privacy and legal rights.

Taking up these changes in turn, we note first far-reaching shifts in the college population—most obviously in its size, which has grown steadily and significantly. It is true that growth has been concentrated principally in a few types of institutions, such as large state universities and community colleges, whereas enrollment at many liberal-arts colleges has remained unchanged. Aggregate increases in the college population have had an effect even on students at small colleges, for they, like their counterparts at state universities, form part of an increasingly influential segment of society, constantly courted by advertisers, merchants, banks, and book clubs.

More important than increased numbers have been changes in the character of the student population. Two are especially significant: the continued expansion of opportunities for higher education for students whose parents had no aspirations beyond high school, and the steady and continuing growth in the numbers of students older than traditional college age. Both of these have necessitated departures from the traditional role of the institution in student life.

First-generation college students are less likely than are their classmates to feel a part of traditional campus culture, with its peculiar synthesis of moralistic rules and indulgent enforcement practices. Students whose parents completed only limited secondary education cannot rely on Dad's stories as a model for their own fraternity parties. Older students, who bring to their college endeavors more experience

Table 1-1: Residence Halls for Men and Women Students

Housing for Men and Women	1969 - 70	1979 - 80	1989 - 90
Separate men's and women's dorms	77%	23%	10%
Alternate floors	19%	41%	40%
Alternate rooms or suites	3%	36%	50%

Note: Percentages are for coeducational institutions only.

at making their way in the world, are more likely to understand the need for controls on student behavior. But they are also more likely to resent any system of control that assumes students' immaturity.

Another major area of change lies in shifting student interests and self-perceptions. National statistics show that there has been a steady decline in numbers of students choosing a major in the core disciplines of the liberal arts and a corresponding increase in interest in more directly career-related fields. In 1970–71, for example, 8,146 students received the bachelor's degree with a major in philosophy or religion; that number increased slightly in the early 1970s but then declined steadily until it stood in 1987–88 at 5,959. In the social sciences, including history, the number dropped from 155,236 in 1970–71 to 91,461 in 1983–84, then climbed modestly in the next few years. Mathematics majors dropped from 24,801 in 1970–71 to 15,888 in 1987–88—all of these declines occurring during a period when the total number of undergraduate degrees increased by more than 150,000. The increase occurred in fields such as business and management, in which the number of majors climbed from 114,865 to 243,344, and health sciences, which rose from 35,190 to 60,095.[5]

These shifts reflect growing practical concern with the use to which education can be put. An era of seemingly unlimited economic expansion has ended, and in times of economic uncertainty it is only prudent to bear future employment prospects in mind when selecting a major field. Furthermore, students have frequently heard their professors complain that jobs are too few and salaries too low. Students want to make themselves readily employable, or at least choose an undergraduate course of studies that will serve them well in subsequent professional education. A professoriat that feels overworked and underpaid does not offer an attractive role model.

The shift in student interest also reflects a deeper shift, impossible to quantify, in students' perception of how college fits into their lives. Two decades ago, students typically thought of their college years as a time for intellectual, social, and political exploration and experimentation—a time to probe the depth and resilience of inherited religious beliefs, of accepted modes of politics, and of conventional understandings of oneself. Only a minority of students actually participated in the most visible manifestations of this spirit, from antiwar demonstrations to the open use of mind-altering drugs, and many, indeed, wanted nothing to do with them. Yet the culture of the campus encouraged, even demanded, an engagement with profound questions of value and identity.

On today's campuses such explorations continue, but they assume much less visible forms. Students' conversations in the corridors and in the weekly columns in student newspapers are more likely to turn to student loans and job possibilities. The heightened concern with the future is not merely a turn away from idealism but also carries with it a stronger sense of responsibility for one's own future prospects. Students who choose each course, even each instructor, with an eye to law school admissions and career prospects are taking onto their own shoulders greater accountability for their education and their progress. They rely less on either parents or faculty members to direct their studies or their lives. The readiness to make critical career decisions on the basis of prudent assessment of their own options may indeed reflect not so much the loss of ideals as the achievement of greater personal maturity.

Finally, on nearly every campus, concern with issues of student privacy and autonomy has been greatly heightened in the past generation or two. Students are less willing than were their forebears to defer to purportedly benevolent professors and administrators. Lawsuits for wrongful disclosure of information from confidential academic or personal records, and the organization of lesbian and gay student organizations across the country, are just two of many indications of students' concerns for their rights. These rights are articulated and protected by a growing body of law defining the limits of the institution's responsibility and supervision, as we will note in Chapter 2.

Seen in light of these broad changes, the metaphor of the death of the parent may be misplaced but not far off the mark. What has occurred is not patricide but rather the child-student's coming of age. Students typically matriculate just as they have passed or are approaching the threshold of legal majority. They are liable for their debts and contractual obligations, exempt from requirements for parental consent for medical treatment, and eligible to vote. Nearly the only respect in which they are now denied legal majority is in the purchase and consumption of alcoholic beverages—and many act as if they were already of age in this respect as well.

Each of the changes that I have pointed to—the shift to coed housing, increased numbers of nontraditional students, less philosophical and more practical concerns in choice of field, and heightened concern for privacy and for individual rights—is a token of an underlying change in students' conception of who they are, a change that can without exaggeration be considered a revolution. Students have thrown off the yoke of subservience to an institutional parent and claimed for themselves the right to make choices about living quarters, personal relationships, and studies, not following the familiar paths of their professors or older siblings but rather shouldering the responsibility to form their own lives.

The level of autonomy and maturity that students now claim makes the conditions of residence-hall life particularly onerous and absurd. Students of an earlier generation were content to live under the restrictions that a minor child expects to endure while living at home, because they regarded themselves as dwelling in a fictive extension of the family. But students who see themselves as adults are understandably impatient with the conditions imposed on them on campus. Is it any wonder, when young adults are compelled to live together under the conditions of the "apartment" that were imposed on the overseas visitor we imagined at the beginning of this chapter, that conflict and behavioral excess are commonplace? To compel a thousand or more young women and men, proud of their newly achieved adulthood, to live together like minor children, or like novitiates in a religious order, is to invite the most capricious and potentially uncontrollable forms of misbehavior.

The political activists of the 1960s were never a majority on campus, always a minority. The revolution that they dreamed would transform American society seems even more distant today. Yet there has been a revolution—one in which students have claimed their own majority, their own status as adults in shaping their lives and their futures. It is for just this reason that the model of the institution as standing *in loco parentis* has collapsed. The institution can no longer expect the obedience that minors owe their guardians but must deal with them as adults. The model of parental benevolence that once guided institutional administrators can no longer serve its purpose. Other models—other conceptions of the relationship between institution and student—must take its place.

What other models are available? The lack of any clear or satisfactory answer to this question, from any source, is precisely the motivation of the present study. For in most of American higher education—to anticipate in a few words a conclusion that will be supported in the chapters to follow—the death of *in loco parentis* has spelled the end of any clear or coherent understanding of the college's responsibility for students' moral and social life. Unable to play the role of the parent, no longer prescribing bedtimes or enforcing a moral code, the institution has effectively withdrawn from the field of morality and character formation. Even to suggest that universities bear responsibility not only for the academic achievements but also for the character of their graduates has today a ring of anachronism and nostalgia.

This retreat from responsibility, I shall argue, is both unnecessary and unjustified. There is a place for colleges and universities in the moral and social as well as the intellectual lives of students. Both students and institutions suffer when that place is left vacant. Just what that place is will emerge as we examine present practices on campus and the ways in which they are established and administered.

Notes

1. Mary Renault, *The Bull from the Sea* (New York, Pantheon Books, 1962).
2. The text of the survey instrument and a complete tabulation of the results are contained in Appendix C.
3. Nearly all of the single-sex institutions in the United States today are women's colleges, if we disregard paired men's and women's colleges such as Westhampton and Richmond. Since the Rose-Hulman Institute of Technology opened its doors to women in 1991, the only remaining all-male private colleges in the United States are Wabash College, also in Indiana, and Hampton-Sydney College in Virginia. Only two state-governed military institutions, the Virginia Military Institute and the Citadel, remain male-only. The numbers of women's colleges are larger, running into two figures, but their ranks are also diminishing; cf., "College to End a 117-Year All-Male Tradition," *New York Times*, October 7, 1991, p. A10.
4. In this and the following paragraph and in Table 1-4, the percentages cited exclude single-sex institutions from each group. Percentages are of institutions responding and may in some cases total more than 100, as the respondents on campuses where some residence halls are segregated by floor and others by room or suite checked two answers to the relevant questions.
5. National Center for Education Statistics, *Digest of Education Statistics 1990* (Washington: U.S. Department of Education, 1991), Table 225: "Bachelor's degrees conferred by institutions of higher education, by discipline division: 1970–71 to 1987–88."

Chapter Two

Institutional Parenthood: The Doctrine of *In Loco Parentis*

Before we can formulate new models of the relationship between colleges and universities and their students, we must first have a clear picture of the doctrine that such models would replace. The present chapter, therefore, offers a brief survey of the doctrine that institutions stand *in loco parentis*. Our focus will be on the legal decisions that once defined that doctrine and more recently eroded its force.

In thus limiting the scope of this chapter, I do not intend to suggest that other aspects of the doctrine—its invocation in the rhetoric of college handbooks, for example—are unimportant. The opinions of the courts, however, form an essential background for our discussion. The courts' backing of institutions when they acted as legal parents was once a key support for institutional control, and the progressive withdrawal of that legal authority in recent decades has been one of the most potent forces working to change institutional policies regarding student conduct and discipline.

The legal doctrine that educational authorities at every level act *in loco parentis* once provided the foundation for a broad range of regulations over student conduct. At one time, for example, it was a common practice for a school district to prohibit school attendance by married students, with the intent of discouraging marriage before school completion—like a strict father who would not grant his daughter's hand to a suitor until graduation.

In 1928 the school superintendent of a Mississippi high school learned that a female student planning to enroll in his school was married. He denied her admission, citing a school-district ordinance barring married persons from the schools because "the marriage relation brings about views of life which should not be known to unmarried children." The student challenged the ordinance, which was overturned by the state supreme court with the droll observation that "marriage is a domestic relation highly favored by the law."[1] The Mississippi district's regulation now seems hopelessly misguided. But the invalidated policy reveals how broad was the extent of local authorities' presumed right to exercise the control of a parent over student behavior sixty years ago.

The practice of excluding married students from school has long been abandoned, as a result both of legal decisions and of changing social attitudes. The more familiar practice of excluding pregnant students or segregating them in special classes survived much longer, but it was successfully challenged in a number of court cases in the 1960s and 1970s. Both state and federal courts rejected school authorities' claims that the presence of pregnant students would either disrupt other students' education or constitute approval of immorality.[2] The somewhat narrower policy of excluding married students from participation in extracurricular activities, allowed by the courts as late as the 1960s as a reasonable exercise of the school's authority to regulate student conduct, was also invalidated in the 1970s, first by federal courts and then by state courts, on the ground that the school district's authority to act *in loco parentis* must yield to the students' rights to an education and to marital privacy.[3] Thus in one particular area—exclusion of students because of marriage or pregnancy—the courts have decisively rejected the schools' claim of quasiparental authority.

Legal Cases Invoking the Doctrine

In broad outline, to say that an institution may act *in loco parentis* is to assert an authority over students analogous to that of a parent over a child. To define the legal doctrine more precisely we need to trace it back to some key decisions in which its implications were spelled out. In this chapter we will take brief note of several cases that have marked, first, the meaning and, second, the diminishing force of this model. In the last section of the chapter we will also review some legal developments not directly linked to the parental model that alter the institution's relationship to its students. In Appendix A several of these cases are cited in full or at greater length.

The *in loco parentis* doctrine was succinctly invoked by the Court of Appeals of Kentucky in its 1913 decision in *Gott v. Berea College*. "College authorities stand in loco parentis concerning the physical and moral welfare and mental training of the pupils," the court wrote.[4] The same doctrine had been articulated fifty years earlier in *People v. Wheaton College* in the following terms:

> A discretionary power had been given [to college authorities] to regulate the discipline of the college in such manner as they deem proper; and, so long as their rules violate neither divine nor human law, we have no more authority to interfere than we have to control the domestic discipline of a father in his family.[5]

The terms that the Illinois court chose are revealing, not only of an extremely traditional model of the family as governed by the father but also of the explicit linking of the standards of care required in the family with those required of others who stand *in loco parentis*. By implication, the authority of institutions to act as they please by invoking parental authority can extend no farther than the authority of natural parents to control their children. Where formerly "neither divine nor human law" was seen to bar severe physical punishment of children, the legal system today is frequently used to block domestic abuse. By implication, an institution's authority under the *in loco parentis* doctrine is also limited by considerations of fairness and the prevention of harm.

Even at the turn of the century, before *Gott v. Berea College* was decided, this doctrine had come under attack in both legal and educational circles. At the inauguration of Rush Rhees as president of Rochester University in 1900, for example, William Rainey Harper, then president of the University of Chicago, delivered an address entitled "The College Officer and the College Student" in which he explicitly called for the rejection of the model of institution as parent. "The college professor today is not an officer *in loco parentis*," he stated, employing "college officer" and "college professor" as synonyms, as befitted an era in which the faculty, by and large, was also the college administration. He explained:

> No, the college instructor is not a parent, nor does he have the authority of a parent. Parents in these days are themselves wise enough to know that at the college age the time has come when the young man or the young woman will not brook objective or institutional authority. . . . For

the college community is a real democracy. All men, even in a democracy, are not equal although all deserve equal privileges.[6]

The *in loco parentis* doctrine has continued to exercise a pervasive influence in this century, in rhetoric if not in actual effect, even while its legal force has been steadily eroded. Precisely what does the doctrine imply, in legal terms? The familiar phrase is defined concisely in *Black's Law Dictionary*: "In the place of a parent; instead of a parent; charged, factitiously, with a parent's rights, duties, and responsibilities."[7] Another law dictionary borrows its definition from the body of case law:

> Latin: in the place of a parent; "according to its generally accepted common law meaning, refers to a person who has put himself in the situation of a lawful parent by assuming the obligations incident to the parental relation without going through the formalities necessary to legal adoption. It embodies the two ideas of assuming the parental status and discharging the parental duties." The term is commonly used with reference to the relationship between a minor and a residential institution such as a boarding school.[8]

To place a college or university *in loco parentis*, then, is to grant to it the powers of a parent to supervise the life of students as well as the responsibilities of a parent for their welfare. The two complementary elements of the relationship are of equal importance, and each serves to justify and ground the other. Because the college has a special duty to ensure students' welfare, it is granted extensive permission to enact and enforce policies directing and restricting their behavior. Conversely, because the college presumes in the place of the parent to set guidelines for behavior, it also assumes the responsibility of a parent to use this power in a benevolent manner.

Characteristically, the doctrine has been applied especially to the institution's disciplinary authority over students, as is evident in the cases cited above and in the classic statement contained in *Blackstone's Commentaries*:

> A parent may also delegate part of his parental authority, during his life, to the tutor or schoolmaster of his child; who is then *in loco parentis*, and has such a portion of the power of the parent, viz. that of restraint and correction, as may be necessary to answer the purposes for which he is employed.[9]

But the scope of the doctrine reaches farther than disciplinary matters alone. A 1968 Illinois court decision, even while grounding the doctrine in its familiar application, points to a much broader responsibility.

Teachers . . . shall maintain discipline in the schools. In all matters relating to the discipline in and conduct of the schools and the school children, they stand in the relation of parents and guardians to the pupils. This relationship shall extend to all activities connected with the school program and may be exercised at any time for the safety and supervision of the pupils in the absence of their parents or guardians.[10]

A similarly broad reading of the doctrine can be traced through many decisions that have invoked it in recent decades.[11]

But even when the doctrine itself has been upheld, in decisions of the past half-century, the scope of teachers' authority has gradually diminished, particularly in the public schools—elementary, secondary, and post-secondary—that have come to share the place in American society once occupied almost exclusively by private institutions. Public school teachers can be construed as agents of the state, and hence as subject to stricter control than are teachers in private schools, who act more directly in place of parents. Recent court decisions have placed less and less emphasis on the distinction between private and public educational institutions, however, and have applied to teachers in public and private schools and colleges essentially the same standards of both care and liability.

The school's authority to act in place of the parent has never provided a blanket authorization for arbitrary action, even where it has protected school officials in the reasonable exercise of disciplinary supervision. Exclusion of students from school, whether by temporary suspension or permanent expulsion, is explicitly permitted by statute, but even in this area the freedom of institutions to act *in loco parentis* is not unlimited. Students are entitled to be informed of the rules that will be applied to them, and when serious disciplinary action is defended only by invoking vague rules of conduct, any sanction imposed is likely to be disallowed by the courts.[12]

To what extent must the rules of conduct be spelled out in detail in order to be enforceable? The courts' decisions provide no general answer but only a flexible standard of reasonableness. Three examples from the 1970s illustrate the point. In a 1976 Pennsylvania case, a federal district court ruled that rules against "flagrant disregard of teachers," "loitering in areas of heavy traffic," and "rowdy behavior" were sufficiently specific to provide grounds for suspension of students found to have violated them.[13] On the other hand, in a 1975 decision the Supreme Court of Connecticut invalidated a state statute authorizing expulsion of students found to be guilty of "conduct inimical to the best interests of the school." Without a clear account of what sorts of behavior this statute prohibited, the court ruled, it was so vague as to be unenforceable.[14]

All the same, behavior that is flagrantly disruptive may be the basis for sanctions even in the absence of any specific rule. Thus, the expulsion of two students for a vicious attack on a fellow student with fists, feet, and scissors was upheld in 1974 by an Arkansas court, even though no specific statute could be cited to warrant the sanction.[15]

Many aspects of the *in loco parentis* doctrine are by their very nature applicable only to the situation of secondary-school students. Compulsory school attendance, for example, has been interpreted as an element in the state's quasiparental care for students. In this context, the legal authority of the fictitious parent and of actual parents have come into direct conflict over the legality of home schooling.[16] Parental beliefs and preferences, and the interests of the state in children's welfare have also collided over the issue of vaccinations.[17] In both of these areas there is a substantial body of legal precedent. But neither area is of direct relevance to postsecondary education, where attendance is not legally compulsory and students themselves are responsible for medical decisions such as consent to receive a vaccination.

The authority of schools has also been tested with respect to the regulation of student dress and appearance, an area that was once regulated by colleges as well as secondary schools but is now of comparatively little concern even on the lower level. A legal reference book written in 1976 noted that more than a hundred court cases regarding student hair length had been litigated in the preceding ten years. In general, regulation of hairstyles and other issues of personal appearance had been found to be unconstitutional except in cases where school authorities had offered positive proof that the practices they wished to discourage were disruptive, unsanitary, or dangerous. "Much to the relief of the judiciary and others," the author noted, "the hair style issue has ceased to be a significant issue for litigation."[18] In this and certain other areas of personal choice, the authority of the school as fictitious parent has yielded to the right of students to self-expression.

If areas such as compulsory attendance, vaccination, and dress are of little importance at the college level, what are the major applications of the *in loco parentis* doctrine at that level? In what ways have colleges and universities acted—or attempted to act—in the place of parents? What privileges and responsibilities have colleges assumed over students' conduct, in keeping with this doctrine?

It has already been noted that the *in loco parentis* doctrine invests the institution with both the privileges and the responsibilities that normally fall to parents. This statement cannot be taken in its full literal force. High schools and colleges assume no responsibility for buying clothes and meals for their students, nor is there any legal or moral duty on the part of universities, or private schools at any level, to pay their charges' tuition. Schools have no legal authority to grant consent *in loco parentis* for the medical treatment or marriage of minor students. The relationship is limited, by legal precedent and common sense, to a few areas.

Four Elements of the Doctrine

The import of the *in loco parentis* doctrine, in its full force, can be summarized as incorporating four related but distinct powers or immunities. First, the institution had the *authority to direct the behavior* of students. It could enact rules concerning personal behavior and responsibility to the community. Its authority, like a parent's, was not without limits. Arbitrary and pointless rules were regularly invalidated by the courts, and students have long been granted protection in the exercise of certain basic freedoms. All the same, the authority of the institution acting *in loco parentis* to set behavioral rules went far beyond that of most other social institutions.

Second, as a consequence, the institution had the *authority to punish* rule violations, albeit once again within limits. Students are entitled to be informed of the rules they are expected to follow, and they have the right to be told of the charges and the evidence against them. But the institution's authority was not subject to the same limits as that of the police. Like a parent, the institution's representatives could set procedures for gathering and evaluating evidence at their discretion, within broad bounds of fairness.

Third, the institution's position *in loco parentis* carried with it a special *responsibility of care* for students. Schools and colleges were held to a higher standard of care for their students than were corporations for their customers or employees. The institution's policies and practices had to uphold the best interests of the students and promote their welfare.

Fourth, the college or university also enjoyed, to a certain degree, an *exemption from limits on searches* carried out in conjunction with the enforcement of school rules. Once again the exemption was only partial. An intrusive search of a student's person or room for no cause was impermissible. But because the campus environment was more like that of a family, in the eyes of the law, than like ordinary civil society, the administrators of a school or college were permitted some discretion to look for evidence of wrongdoing in some circumstances in which the police, for example, could not. Furthermore, the legal rule invalidating evidence gathered illegally was not binding on institutional disciplinary procedures.

These four headings sum up the effect of the doctrine that the school or college stands *in loco parentis*, and they summarize the overall effect of the court decisions cited above. This doctrine underlay most of the court decisions regarding student discipline and conduct from the nineteenth century well into the middle of the twentieth. One reference book on education law published in 1961, for example, stated simply, "The college stands in the same position to its students as that of a parent—in loco parentis."[19]

The Retreat from *In Loco Parentis*

In recent decades the very notion that the institution holds parental duties and privileges has come increasingly under attack. The reasons for this are several. In the first place, it has been increasingly difficult to uphold the fiction of the institution as parent with respect to college students, who are for nearly all purposes adults in the eyes of the law once they reach the age of eighteen. A majority of college students, it is true, still depend upon their parents in some of the ways characteristic of minor children. Most are financially dependent, for example, and many reside at home between terms. Moreover, relatively few seem to have reached a sufficient stage of adulthood to be capable of doing their own laundry. All the same, all but the youngest college students are legally entitled to vote, to sign contracts, to marry without parental approval, and to purchase firearms and pornographic magazines, if not beer. The college's fictitious parental role has been greatly eroded by these legal developments.

Numerous legal cases questioning a college's authority to set behavioral rules were brought during the 1960s and early 1970s, when the campus culture demanded student independence in both political and practical realms. The plausibility of the *in loco parentis* model was eroded each time a student successfully challenged institutional control over student publications or public demonstrations.

Perhaps the most decisive blow to the remnants of the former doctrine was dealt by the Third Circuit Court in its appellate judgment in the case of *Bradshaw v. Rawlings* in 1979.[20] A student at Delaware Valley Community College had been injured in an automobile accident after becoming intoxicated at a sophomore class picnic. He brought suit against the college and its administrators, alleging that they were negligent in supervising the class picnic, and persuaded the trial court to award him damages. On appeal, however, the U.S. Court of Appeals, Third Circuit, decisively refuted the claim of negligence, and in doing so it sounded an eloquent obituary for the legal notion that the college stands *in loco parentis*.

> Our beginning point is a recognition that the modern American college is not an insuror of the safety of its students. Whatever may have been its responsibility in an earlier era, the authoritarian role of today's college administrations has been notably diluted in recent decades. Trustees, administrators, and faculties have been required to yield to the expanding rights and privileges of their students.[21]

The appeals court cited several legal developments that had in effect overruled the former doctrine concerning the legal status of college students:

> By constitutional amendment, written and unwritten law, and through the evolution of new customs, rights formerly possessed by college administrators have been transferred to students. College students today are no longer minors; they are now regarded as adults in almost every phase of community life. For example, except for purchases of alcoholic beverages, eighteen year old persons are considered adults by the Commonwealth of Pennsylvania. They may vote, marry, make a will, qualify as a personal representative, serve as the guardian of the estate of a minor, wager at racetracks, register as a public accountant, drive trucks, ambulances, and other official fire vehicles, perform general firefighting duties, and qualify as a private detective.[22]

The opinion explicitly invoked, and discarded, the doctrine that has been our focus in this chapter.

> There was a time when college adminitrators and faculties assumed a role *in loco parentis*. . . . But today students vigorously claim the right to define and regulate their own lives.[23]

The Court of Appeals considered the question of whether, even in the absence of a quasiparental relationship, there might still exist a special relationship between the institution and the individual that creates a duty of care and thereby could support a claim of negligence. To this question it responded: No, there is no such duty in the circumstances of the case. The behavior of the students was not sufficiently foreseeable to create a duty to prevent it, nor did the existence of college rules against abuse of alcohol establish a special duty either to take extraordinary measures of enforcement or to avert possible harms resulting from its violation.

> A college regulation that essentially tracks state law and prohibits conduct that to students under twenty-one is already prohibited under state law does not, in our view, indicate that the college voluntarily assumed a custodial relationship with its students.[24]

Numerous subsequent cases have cited these pronouncements in rejecting any appeal to a quasiparental model of institutional responsibility. Thus the District Court of Pennsylvania observed curtly in 1982, citing *Bradshaw*, that "the principle of *in loco parentis* appears no longer to apply to college students."[25]

A similar case involving injury to an intoxicated student, in this case due not to an automobile accident but to a fall suffered on a class trip, drove yet another nail into the coffin of the doctrine. The student in this case claimed that her injury resulted from inadequate supervision by the faculty organizer of the trip and further claimed, no doubt in order to avoid a direct appeal to the *in loco parentis* doctrine, that the university's sponsorship of the field trip created a special duty whose breach constituted negligence. In its opinion in the case, *Beach v. University of Utah*, the Supreme Court of Utah unequivocally rejected the attempt to substitute a new form of custodial responsibility for the old.

> The students whose relationship to the University we are asked to characterize as "custodial" are not juveniles. Beach was twenty years of age at the time of the accident. She may have been denied the right to drink by Utah law, but in nearly all other respects she was entitled to be treated as an adult. She had a constitutional right to vote, she was to to be chargeable on her contracts, and if she had committed a crime, she would have been tried and sentenced as an adult. Had she not been a college student, but an employee in industry, she could not argue realistically that her employer would be responsible for compensating her for injuries incurred by her voluntary intoxication during her off-hours while traveling on company business. We do not believe that Beach should be viewed as fragile and in need of protection simply because she had the luxury of attending an institution of higher education.
>
> Not only are students such as Beach adults, but law and society have increasingly come to recognize their status as such in the past decade or

two. Nowhere is this more true than in the relations between students and institutions of higher education.[26]

The court dismissed in a truculent footnote the notion that individuals whom the Congress has judged old enough to vote "are so immature that they should be considered wards of their particular institution of higher education."[27]

Thus the special relationship that was once both legally and socially recognized is no longer determinative of the privileges and responsibilities of colleges with respect to control of student behavior. Some writers have suggested that the *in loco parentis* doctrine has reemerged in a new form with recent court decisions concerning liability in supervision of student activities.[28] As evidence they cite student demands for services such as placement assistance, financial aid, and counseling as well as claims for compensation in cases of physical injury incurred in college-related activities. But in none of these instances do the four characteristics identified above come into play. The courts have issued their rulings by reference to students' rights as consumers of educational services, to contractual obligations of both institutions and students, and to general standards of negligence and liability. But in numerous cases in which the *in loco parentis* standard was discussed in recent years it has been explicitly rejected as a basis for liability.[29]

The doctrine that colleges act *in loco parentis*, then, has ceased to operate as the guiding metaphor in the legal system, even as it has also fallen from favor in the popular mind. Whatever role the college or university plays in students' lives today, it is no longer that of a parent in the once-familiar context—the authority empowered to set rules and enforce them, exempted from the usual limits of liability and of investigative tactics, and broadly reponsible for their welfare.

Recent Legal Developments

If the legal doctrine of *in loco parentis* is now commonly seen as inapplicable to college students, what legal relationship between institution and student now occupies its place? In the concluding section of this chapter, we will note several cases that delineate a new model, one that inherits some but not all of the defining characteristics of the former doctrine.

The number of suits brought against colleges and universities for failing to exercise adequate supervision of student activities has grown steadily, reflecting a growing tendency to look to litigation to resolve many social conflicts once left to informal negotiation. Positing a duty of care by the university over broad aspects of student life, students have sued universities because another student who was intoxicated assaulted them; because the university failed to cancel classes in bad weather and the student slipped and fell on ice; and because of an injury sustained while playing touch football during orientation. In still another case, the family of a student who collapsed and died after participating in an informal student-organized footrace sought damages from the university.[30]

Suits alleging institutional negligence in connection with accidental injury inflicted by intoxicated students are numerous. A Montana high-school student in a summer program at the state university, for example, was injured in a motorcycle accident on his way back to campus from an off-campus party where alcohol was served and charged the university with negligence.[31] In the incident that gave rise to another suit, a Rutgers student who had smuggled a grain-alcohol-and-Koolaid punch into a football game, and consumed it liberally, leaped over what he took to be a low retaining wall, only to plummet thirty feet to the concrete below. He argued, in suing the university, that its policies against alcohol created a duty to protect football spectators, including those who had become intoxicated, from any dangers that might result from consumption of alcohol in the stadium.[32]

Summaries published regularly in the *Journal of Law and Education* recount even more far-fetched suits involving alcohol and other controlled substances. An Ohio school bus driver, for example, sought reinstatement on the ground that the school district dismissed her, after learning that her driver's license had been revoked for a drunk-driving conviction, without first conducting a disciplinary hearing.[33] In an Arizona case, a student sought a court injunction to restore his eligibility to play basketball, which had been withdrawn by the school after he was convicted of burglary and incarcerated for nine months. The student claimed that, although his four years of eligibility had expired, he should be given an additional year because he committed burglary to support a cocaine habit, and his time behind bars should therefore be counted as absence due to illness and not as part of the period of eligibility.[34]

All eight of the cases just cited have one common feature: All of the students lost their suits, and each case was decided in the school's favor. Increased levels of litigation do not necessarily translate into increased numbers of judgments against institutions. It may yet be true that cases such as these reveal too great a readiness to rush to court when something goes wrong; yet their disposition has had minimal effects. Court decisions have clarified the line between duties that colleges and universities are actually required to fulfill, and whose breach constitutes negligence, and exaggerated standards of care that the courts will not uphold.

A suit involving injuries sustained on a fraternity trampoline at the University of Denver initially yielded a judgment of more than $5 million against the university for failing to exercise adequate supervision over student use of the trampoline, which was located in the front yard of the fraternity house. The student plaintiff had been jumping on the trampoline at midnight, in the midst of a fraternity party, and had suffered severe neck injuries that rendered him quadriplegic. In the lower courts, the university was held liable for his injury because it had done nothing to prevent a highly risky activity that it could have known was likely to occur.[35]

This ruling was reversed by the Supreme Court of Colorado, however. In its decision, the Supreme Court emphasized that the alleged negligence of the university involved not positive action but failure to act. This distinction "strongly militates against imposition of a duty on the University," because no one has a legally enforceable duty to prevent another from injuring a third party in the absence of a special relationship, such as that of parent to child or innkeeper to guest, and the plaintiff had not shown that any such relationship existed.[36]

Similarly, in a 1990 Pennsylvania case involving an intoxicated minor student at Bucknell who allegedly set fires that caused $400,000 of property damage to a fraternity house, the Supreme Court of Pennsylvania declined to hold the University liable because it had no special duty of care that could have been breached through inaction. The Court noted, "clearly, in modern times, it would be inappropriate to impose an *in loco parentis* duty upon a university."[37]

In circumstances where there is a specific duty of care, either failure to act or positive action may constitute negligence. Thus in several recent cases students have successfully sought compensation for injuries suffered on campus or in institutionally sponsored activities. In a Massachusetts case, for example, a student who had been sexually attacked on college grounds by a nonstudent alleged that college authorities had been negligent in failing to undertake security measures that would have prevented the attack, and both the lower court and the the Supreme Court of Massachusetts agreed. In its opinion the latter court noted:

Of course, changes in college life reflected in the general decline of the theory that a college stands *in loco parentis* to its students, arguably cut against this view. The fact that a college need not police the morals of its students, however, does not entitle it to abandon any effort to ensure their physical safety. Parents, students, and the general community still have a reasonable expectation, fostered in part by the colleges themselves, that reasonable care will be exercised to protect resident students from foreseeable harm.[38]

The college's lax security measures, in an urban setting, provided crucial evidence in support of the plaintiff's allegation of negligence.[39]

A Pennsylvania court, refusing to hold a university liable for the harm suffered by a student who climbed on a rail car on campus and contacted overhead wires, stated succinctly that a university has no special duty to protect students from the consequences of their own volitional acts.[40] But universities are liable, according to a 1989 California case, for preventing foreseeable crimes.[41] Cases such as these demonstrate the courts' increasing tendency to apply established standards of care derived from other contexts—from the duties of landlords and landowners, for example—to questions concerning the university's legal duties.

Earlier we noted four legal elements of the *in loco parentis* doctrine: (1) a broad authority to direct student behavior, (2) the authority to punish infractions of disciplinary rules, (3) a special responsibility of care for the welfare of students entrusted to its charge, and (4) a legal exemption from some of the legal requirements of due process in carrying out its disciplinary procedures. With respect to each of these elements, we may note both the eclipse of the former model of institutional authority and the persistence of some of its implications in considerably altered form.

The first of these four elements, the authority to set rules and to direct student behavior in a broad range of areas, has probably been least eroded by the legal developments I have described. The prerogative of the institution to set and enforce rules that are in its judgment necessary to maintain good order and an appropriate atmosphere for educational purposes has been reaffirmed time and again in the courts at every level. The Supreme Court's 1972 decision in *Healy v. James*, frequently cited in subsequent cases, in turn quoted with approval the earlier pronouncement of the Court of Appeals, Eighth Circuit,

that a college has the inherent right to promulgate rules and regulations; that it has the inherent power properly to discipline; that it has power appropriately to protect itself and its property; that it may expect that its students adhere to generally accepted standards of conduct.[42]

In the words of a Michigan federal district court, "it is axiomatic that school officials have inherent power to promulgate and enforce regulations."[43] This axiom has not been overturned, even if universities themselves have gradually altered their own interpretation of which "generally accepted standards of conduct" they aspire to enforce.

The courts have consistently deferred to the institution's decisions concerning appropriate standards, and with regard to their procedures for enforcement, universities are "entitled to a presumption of honesty and integrity, absent a showing of actual bias, such as animosity, prejudice, or a personal or financial stake in the outcome," in the words of a federal court in Illinois.[44] A Colorado federal court made the point even more forcefully in a 1990 decision:

> Because the university must remain independent and autonomous to enjoy academic freedom, the federal courts are reluctant to interfere in the internal daily operations of the academy which do not directly and sharply implicate basic constitutional values.[45]

Institutional authority to set and enforce rules must be restrained, however, by the legal rights of students. The Michigan court whose decision was quoted earlier added this caution—in one of the rare moments of wit in the entire body of legal opinion bearing on these matters:

> If it is axiomatic that school officials have inherent power to promulgate and enforce regulations, it is also axiomatic that this comprehensive authority must be exercised consistently "with fundamental constitutional safeguards." Students have constitutional rights which must be respected. Students are no longer members of what Graham Greene's Secret Police Captain called the "torturable class."[46]

The Michigan case involved a warrantless search of student dormitory rooms for illegal drugs. The court refused to admit evidence seized in the search on the ground that "the plaintiff's dormitory room is his house for all practical purposes, and he has the same interest in the privacy of his room as any adult has in the privacy of his home, dwelling, or lodging."[47] This case does not directly bear on the authority of the institution to set rules, but—relevant to the second and fourth implications of the *in loco parentis* doctrine—it constrains the manner in which rules against conduct judged undesirable, even conduct specifically proscribed by law, may be enforced.

The area of free speech is one in which institutions' desire to maintain mutual respect and good order has regularly come into conflict with individual rights. The Supreme Court took note of this potential conflict and its importance in its decision in *Healy v. James*, quoted above, noting that "vigilant protection of constitutional freedoms is nowhere more vital than in the community of American schools."[48]

This battle between legitimate regulation and free speech has been regularly fought in recent years in the context of campus regulations banning "hate speech." I will have more to say about this application of constitutional rights in Chapter 4, below; and another volume forthcoming in this series of studies in academic ethics will be devoted wholly to that topic. Leaving this topic aside, I will note here only two decisions that have also clarified the extent of student rights to free speech and association. Both are cases that arose at Southern universities in which, overruling lower court decisions, appeals courts have struck down institutional attempts to regulate student social and political associations.

In the first of these cases, a newly organized gay and lesbian organization at the University of Missouri persuaded a federal appeals court to overturn a trial court ruling in the university's favor. The court acknowledged that university officials may impose "reasonable regulations" that go beyond what a government may required of citizens, but it added that "the First Amendment must flourish as much in the academic setting as anywhere else."[49] In response to the university's dubious claim that recognition of the group would tend to encourage homosexual activity, which is illegal under Missouri statute, the court asserted that even credible evidence to this effect could not override the students' First Amendment rights.

The same issues were raised, nearly simultaneously, at the University of Texas, whose administration refused recognition to a social organization formed in order to provide the campus community with "information concerning the structures and realities of gay life" and "a forum for the interchange of ideas and constructive solutions to gay people's problems." The university defended its refusal on grounds similar to those invoked in Missouri. The lower courts accepted the University's grounds, but the Court of Appeals of the Fifth Circuit overturned the ruling, observing that when rights of free expression are at issue only the most compelling considerations of good order or public safety can override them.[50]

In the family, and in the quasifamilial campus atmosphere of another era, paternalistic control over the expression of disfavored views may be taken for granted and exercised routinely. On today's campus, as these decisions demonstrate, the situation has changed, and the balance is tilted decisively toward the recognition that students are entitled to the rights of adults.[51]

The second of the four elements of the *in loco parentis* doctrine, the institution's authority to punish infractions of rules, is implied by the authority to direct behavior. To the extent that institutions retain the power to enact rules of conduct, they retain the authority to punish violators. The limits on institutional control mandated by students' rights to privacy and free speech also imply limits on means of enforcement. All the same, institutions still enjoy a broader freedom to set their own disciplinary proceedings and rules than do municipal authorities and the police.

A number of recent lawsuits have sought to challenge the institution's imposition of academic discipline and withholding of academic rewards. The courts have long refused, however, to interfere in matters pertaining to the essential educational functioning of colleges, universities, and professional schools, and complaints of arbitrary or unfair treatment in these areas have usually found that the law turns a deaf ear toward them. To cite one representative example: A student at the University of Montana sued to obtain a degree denied him because he had not met a new requirement added after his matriculation, alleging that the university had breached an implied contract, but the District Court ruled for the university.[52]

This principle draws support from an important Supreme Court decision handed down in 1978 in *Board of Curators v. Horowitz*, in which the Supreme Court declined to intervene in the academic evaluation process of a medical school. A student denied permission to graduate, after her surgery skills had been judged insufficient in several internal reviews, alleged that her constitutional rights had been violated because she was never given a formal hearing at which she could rebut the charge of incompetence. The Court noted that "a school is an academic institution, not a courtroom or administrative hearing room," and its own procedures therefore deserve to be respected so long as they are fundamentally fair.[53]

In a 1983 decision, the U.S. Court of Appeals, Fourth Circuit, cited the *Horowitz* decision in dismissing the claim of a University of Virginia student that the provisions of the Honor Code are unfair because they do not provide for a full hearing on the judicial model. The requirements of due process are more stringent in disciplinary than in academic matters, the court observed, but even in the former case full adherence to the judicial model is by no means required.

> The clear implication of *Horowitz* is that disciplinary proceedings require more stringent procedural protection than academic evaluations, even though the effects of an adverse decision on the student may be the same. Labeling a school proceeding disciplinary in nature, however, does not mean that complete adherence to the judicial model of decision-making is required.[54]

In particular, a rule barring attorneys from the university's disciplinary proceedings, the Court ruled, did not invalidate the university's procedures.

The *Henson* decision, in the paragraph just quoted, cited two key Supreme Court decisions that have defined due process in the academic setting. The first of these, *Dixon v. Alabama State Board of Education*, is of historical as well as legal interest, as it concerns the summary expulsion of a group of students at Alabama State College after they participated in a lunch-counter sit-in to protest segregation laws. The Court refused to accept the argument of the college president, or of the Board of Education in his support, that good order and public safety demanded the students' immediate expulsion, without notice and without a hearing. On the contrary, it observed:

> In the disciplining of college students there are no considerations of immediate danger to the public, or of peril to the national security, which should prevent the Board from exercising at least the fundamental principles of fairness by giving the accused students notice of the charges and an opportunity to be heard in their own defense.[55]

The Court went on to describe in some detail what measures are necessary in order to provide students with just such constitutional protection. These requirements were succinctly summarized in a later Supreme Court case, *Goss v. Lopez*, as follows:

> . . . Due process requires, in connection with a suspension of 10 days or less, that the student be given oral or written notice of the charges against him and, if he denies them, an explanation of the evidence and an opportunity to present his side of the story. . . . Longer suspensions or expulsions . . . may require more formal procedures.[56]

In the third area of traditional discretion for colleges regarded as standing *in loco parentis*—the admissibility of evidence seized in a warrantless search—the recent record is ambiguous. A federal court in Michigan ruled in the case of *Smyth v. Lubbers*, quoted earlier, that drugs seized in a warrantless room search could not be used as evidence in college disciplinary proceedings. A district court in New York, however, stated specifically in a 1976 case that the exclusionary rule is not applicable to institutional disciplinary hearings.[57]

In other respects the courts have consistently granted a broad range of discretion in the implementation of the principle of procedural fairness. Note, for example, the broad language in which the Court of Appeals, First Circuit, upheld the procedures employed at the University of Rhode Island in a 1988 decision:

> Generally, in examining administrative proceedings, the presumption favors the administrators, and the burden is upon the party challenging the action to produce evidence sufficient to rebut this presumption. Gorman has not met this burden of proof in this case. . . . A major purpose of the administrative process, and the administrative hearing, is to avoid the formalistic adversary mode of procedure. . . . Hence, on review, the courts ought not to extol form over substance, and impose on educational institutions all the procedural requirements of a common law criminal trial.[58]

There remains one more element of the traditional *in loco parentis* model: the special responsibility of care, like that of parent for child, that grounds a special concern for student welfare and whose breach constitutes negligence. Whether a special relationship of care exists is crucial for any finding of negligence against a college, because there can be no negligence unless a duty has been breached.[59] We noted earlier several cases in which no such relationship was found to exist, as well as one in which, the court observed, a "self-evident" threat to women students in an urban setting was enough to ground a negligence claim.[60] The decline of the doctrine of *in loco parentis* in no way diminishes the college's duty to take reasonable precautions for its students' protection, acting not as their fictive parent but rather as their landlord and building supervisor. Indeed, in a similar case decided by the Court of Appeals of North Carolina in the same year, the court appealed explicitly to the model of landlord-tenant relations as the basis for a claim of negligence.[61]

Summary

A 1986 decision by the Court of Appeals of Indiana, First District, succinctly sums up the demise of the *in loco parentis* model in current law. The case concerned injuries suffered by a woman student when an automobile driven by a fraternity member was involved in an accident, after an evening of heavy drinking by both driver and passenger. The passenger alleged that Wabash College was liable for its student's irresponsible action. The court disagreed.

> College students and fraternity members are not children. Save for very few legal exceptions, they are adult citizens, ready, able, and willing to be responsible for their own actions. Colleges and fraternities are not expected to assume a role anything akin to *in loco parentis* or a general insuror. . . . In her attempt to reach the proverbial "deep pocket," [plaintiff] Campbell asks us to extend the duty to control the conduct of others to an absurd extent. We decline the invitation.[62]

The model of the university or college as fictive parent, clearly, no longer operates in the legal context. Some of the elements of the college's special legal status remain, all the same. The institution is still permitted a broad range of discretion in the regulation of student conduct and in procedures for adjudication of disciplinary violations. But its realm of legitimate control is strictly bounded by the rights of students to freedom of expression, freedom of association, and due process. In the eyes of the law, students are adults, not minors subject to the supervision of an institutional guardian. The university has no special duty of parental care toward them, and it can expect no exemption from the law's scrutiny if its concern for their welfare leads it to infringe their constitutional freedom.

Many observers have noted, often with alarm, the rapid growth in lawsuits filed against colleges and universities.[63] The enhanced legal status of students is in itself a powerful brake on such litigation, diminishing the likelihood that a student will prevail against an institution except in circumstances that would also constitute unfair treatment or negligence outside the institutional setting. The pattern of decisions rendered in recent cases seems clear: Institutions that are careless and inattentive to student welfare are highly vulnerable to legal action, whereas those that impose behavioral controls and disciplinary sanctions in a consistent way have little reason to worry about lawsuits.

One finding of the survey that will be reviewed in the next chapter supports this point. Among the items of information that I requested from administrators was the number of lawsuits that had been filed against their institution in the past five years, either based on claims of negligence in supervising student activities or with regard to disciplinary matters. About fifteen percent reported having been the target of one such lawsuit in the former category, thirteen percent in the latter, while nine percent more, in each case, reported more than one case. Yet when I asked the administrators to describe the ways in which legal action or its threat had changed disciplinary policies or practices, a large majority responded that there had been no change at all. Those who reported that changes had been made described minor adjustments in their procedures, such as sending proposed rules to the university counsel for review before they are formally enacted.

If colleges and universities now leave unregulated many of the areas of student conduct that were once subject to strict scrutiny, it is their own changing values and priorities that have brought this about. They cannot claim that the courts have made them do it.

Notes

1. *McLeod v. State*, 154 Miss. 468, 475, 122 So.737,738 (1929); quoted in Dutile 1986, 169.
2. Hudgins and Vacca 1978, pp. 217–19.
3. Bolmeier 1976, pp. 151–61.
4. Kemerer and Deutsch 1979, p. 67.
5. *People v. Wheaton College*, 40 Ill. 186 (1866); quoted in Szablewicz and Gibbs 1989.
6. William Rainey Harper, "The College Officer and the College Student," in Fulton 1926, pp. 368–69.
7. Henry Campbell Black, *Black's Law Dictionary*, 5th ed. (St. Paul, Minn.: West, 1979), p. 708.
8. Stephen H. Gifis, *Law Dictionary*, 2nd ed. (Woodbury, N.Y.: Barron's Educational Series, 1984), p. 233.
9. Blackstone 1886, p. 453.
10. *Woodman v. Litchfield Community School Dist. No. 12*, 242 N.E.2nd 780 (Ill. App. 1968); quoted in Bollmeier 1976, p. 10.
11. See Bolmeier 1976, Ch. 2; Hudgins and Vacca 1979, Ch. 10; and Szablewicz and Gibbs 1987; and the cases there cited.
12. See, for example, *Knight v. Board of Educ.*, 38 Ill. App. 3d 603, 348 N.E.2nd 299 (1976); *Dorsey v. Bale*, 521 S.W.2nd 76 (C. A. Ky. 1975).
13. *Alex v. Allen*, 409 F. Supp. 379 (W.D. Pa. 1976).
14. *Mitchell v. King*, 363 A.2nd 68 (Conn. 1975).
15. *Fortnam v. Texarkana School Dist.*, 514 S.W.2nd 720 (Ark. 1974).
16. See Bolmeier 1976, pp. 14–18; Hudgins and Vacca 1979, pp. 194–99.
17. See Bolmeier 1976, pp. 18–24; Hudgins and Vacca 1979, pp. 199–200.
18. Bolmeier 1976, p. 26.
19. Blackwell 1961, p. 104.

20. *Bradshaw v. Rawlings*, 612 F.2d 135 (3rd Cir. 1979), *cert. denied* 100 S. Ct. 1836 (1980). See Appendix A for the text of the decision.

21. *Bradshaw v. Rawlings*, at 138.

22. *Bradshaw v. Rawlings*, at 138–139.

23. *Bradshaw v. Rawlings*, at 140.

24. *Bradshaw v. Rawlings*, at 141.

25. *American Future Systems v. Pennsylvania State University*, 553 F. Supp. 1268 (D. C. Pa. 1982). The decision, which had to do with commercial activities in residence halls, was reversed in federal courts on grounds unrelated to the lower court's summary rejection of *in loco parentis* considerations (752 F.2d, 854).

26. *Beach v. University of Utah*, 726 P.2d 413 (Utah 1986), at 418; cites omitted. See Appendix A.

27. *Beach v. University of Utah*, at 418, n. 4

28. Szablewicz and Gibbs 1989; Gibbs and Szablewitz 1988; see also references cited by Richmond 1990, n. 21.

29. In addition to *Beach v. University of Utah* and *Bradshaw v. Rawlings*, see also *Campbell v. Board of Trustees of Wabash College*, 495 N.E.2d 227 (Ind. Ct. App. 1986).

30. The examples are, respectively, *Crowe v. State*, 1990; *University of Texas at Arlington v. Akers*, 1980; *Drew v. State*, 1989; and *Gehling v. St. George's University School of Medicine*, 1989; all are cited in Thomas 1991.

31. *Graham v. Montana State University*, 767 P. 2d 301 (1988); cited in *Journal of Legal Education* 18:4, p. 625.

32. *Allen v. Rutgers*, 523 A.2d 262 (N. J. Super. A. D. 1987); summarized and discussed in Richmond 1990.

33. *Patton v. Springfield Board of Education*, 40 Ohio St. 3rd 14, 531 N.E. 2d 310 (Ohio 1988); summarized in *Journal of Legal Education* 18:3, pp. 473–74.

34. *Clay v. Arizona Interscholastic Association*, 157 Arizona 350, 757 P. 2d 1059 (1988); summarized in *JLE*, 18:1, p. 153. The summary does not explicitly state, but the context of other cases cited alongside it implies, that the case concerned a high school student.

35. *Whitlock v. University of Denver*, 712 P.2d 1072 (Colo. Ct. App. 1985); *reversed*, 744 P.2d 54 (Colo. 1987). See Appendix A.

36. The Colorado Supreme Court observed: "The University's very limited actions concerning safety of student recreation did not give Whitlock or the other members of campus fraternities any reason to depend upon the University for evaluation of the safety of trampoline use. . . . Therefore, we conclude that the student-university relationship is not a special relationship of the type giving rise to a duty of the University to take reasonable measures to protect the members of fraternities and sororities from risks of engaging in extracurricular trampoline jumping." 744 P.2d 54, at 57–58.

37. *Alumni Association v. Sullivan*, 572 A.2d 1209 (Pa. 1990), at 1213.

38. *Mullins v. Pine Manor College*, 389 Mass. 47, 449 N.E.2d 331 (1983), at 335–36.

39. In a similar California case, a community college was held liable when a student was sexually assaulted in the college parking lot. The college had a duty, the court observed, to exercise due care for the safety of students, and it had failed to do so. *Peterson v. San Francisco Community College*, 36 Cal. 3rd 799, 685 P.2d 1193 (1984).

40. *Heller v. Consolidated Rail Corp.*, 576 F. Supp. 6, affirmed 720 F.2nd 662 (D.C.Pa. 1982).

41. *Figueroa v. Evangelical Covenant Church*, 879 F.2d 1427 (C.A. 7,Ill.), rehearing denied.

42. *Healy v. James*, 408 U.S. 169 (1972), at 192; quoting *Esteban v. Central Missouri State College*, 415 F.2d 1077 (8th Cir. 1969), at 1089, cert. denied 398 U.S. 965. See Appendix A.

43. *Smyth v. Lubbers*, 308 F. Supp. 777 (D. C., W. Dist., Mich. 1975), at 785.

44. *Holert v. University of Chicago*, 751 F. Supp. 1294 (N.D.Ill. 1990), at 1301.

45. *Wirsing v. Board of Regents of University of Colorado*, 739 F. Supp. 551 (D.Colo. 1990), at 553. The case involved not student discipline but the university's authority to require a faculty member to distribute an evaluation form to students in her classes. But the decision was based on reasoning as applicable to student rules as to faculty policies.

46. *Smyth v. Lubbers*, at 785. Cites (to several cases and to Graham Greene's *Our Man in Havana*) omitted.

47. *Smyth v. Lubbers*, at 786.

48. *Healy v. James*, at 180.

49. *Gay Lib v. University of Missouri*, 558 F.2nd 848 (8th Cir., 1977) *cert. denied*, 434 U.S. 1080, rehearing denied 435 U.S. 981 (1978).

50. *Gay Student Services v. Texas A&M University*, 737 F.2d 1317 (C. A. 5th Cir., 1984).

51. The right of free speech has also been established in a series of cases of "commercial speech" in which students have challenged institutional bans on commercial activity and the selling of products in dormitories. In its ruling on one such case in 1988, the United States Supreme Court drew the boundaries of protected speech very widely. A New York State court had ruled that universities could prohibit commercial activity in residence halls, but the Supreme Court reversed the decision on the ground that students may not be deprived of any free speech rights that they would enjoy off-campus unless the institution can show that its educational mission would be seriously disrupted by the exercise of those rights. *Fox v. Board of Trustees of State University of New York*, 841 F.2nd 1207, on remand 695 F. Supp. 1409, cert. granted 109 S.Ct. 52, reversed 109 S.Ct. 3028 (C.A.2d (N.Y.) 1988).

52. The *Journal of Law and Education* noted in its summary of the case that the "principle of no interference with school officials' discretion in matters

that are conferred to their judgment, unless clearly abused, guided the court."
Bindrim v. University of Montana, 766 P.2d 861 (Mont. 1988); "Recent Developments in the Law," *Journal of Law and Education* 18(4): 626 (Fall 1989).

53. *Board of Curators v. Horowitz*, 435 U.S. 78, at 88.

54. *Henson v. Honor Committee of U. Va.*, 719 F.2d 69 (C. A., Fourth Cir.), at 719; cites omitted.

55. *Dixon v. Alabama State Board of Education*, 294 F.2d 150 (1961), at 157.

56. *Goss v. Lopez*, 95 S.Ct. 729 (1975), at 740, 741. The case concerned expulsion from secondary school, but the Court's succinct summary of procedural rights has been held applicable to higher educational institutions as well.

57. *Ekelund v. Secretary of Commerce*, 418 F. Supp. 102 (D.C. N.Y. 1976).

58. *Gorman v. University of Rhode Island*, 837 F.2d 7 (1st Cir., 1988), at 14, 16.

59. A standard reference on tort law includes as elements of any cause of action for negligence "(1) A duty or obligation, recognized by the law, requiring the actor to conform to a certain standard of conduct, for the protection of others against unreasonable risks. (2) A failure on his part to conform to the standard required. . . . (3) A reasonably close causal connection between the conduct and the resulting injury. . . . (4) Actual loss or damage resulting to the interests of another." Prosser 1971, p. 143.

60. *Mullins v. Pine Manor College*, 449 N.E.2d (Mass. 1983), at 335.

61. *Brown v. North Carolina Wesleyan College*, 309 S.E.2d 701 (N.C. App. 1983), at 702.

62. *Campbell v. Board of Trustees*, 495 N.E.2d (Ind. App. 1st Dist. 1986), at 232–33.

63. See, for example, Gaffney and Moots 1982, p. 92.

Chapter 3

Two Views of the Present Situation: A Survey and a Field Study

"To form a college atmosphere, there should be free intercourse among the students."[1] Many present-day Stanford students would agree with this statement, put forward in 1903 by their university's first president. But what they mean by it would have horrified David Starr Jordan.

President Jordan went on to offer remarks on the relationship between college spirit and intercollegiate athletics. Some of his observations about sportsmanship and the conduct of a gentleman would draw only hoots from his university's present-day students:

> When a Yale batter strikes a foul and returns to his base, he finds the Harvard catcher handing him his bat. That a man may play a strenuous game, the fiercest ever seen on the gridiron, and yet keep the speech and manners of a gentleman, is one of the lessons Harvard may teach us, and we of the West cannot listen to any better lesson in college spirit. . . .

Yet the warning he sounded against colleges' willingness to compromise academic standards for athletes might have been written for an editorial page in the 1990s.

> The athletic tramp should receive no academic welcome. The athletic parasite is no better than any other parasite. The man who is in college for athletics alone, disgraces the college, degrades athletics and shuts out a better man for his place on the team. In tolerating the presence of athletes who do not study, the college faculty becomes party to a fraud. Some of our greatest institutions stand disgraced in the eyes of the college world, by reason of the methods employed to win football victories.[2]

45

The history of higher education provides an effective antidote for the impression that today's problems are unprecedented.

The solution to such problems, Jordan suggested, lay in fostering a strong sense of college spirit, for which he placed responsibility with "the girls as well as the boys," on the doubtful ground that "to create the sense of manly duty is largely women's work." Women students, he believed, needed to show themselves to be "worthy of their opportunity, as the vast majority are." He counseled them:

> Don't behave as if you needed a guardian. . . . If there are too many balls in college society and they last too long, have the courage to refuse to go, the courage to refuse to stay after it is time to sleep. . . . Do not be put into false positions. Young men value young women more when their society is not to be had too easily.[3]

President Jordan did not need to add that when the young women decided that it was time to leave the ball, they would sleep alone. Gentleman that he was, President Jordan came no nearer to mentioning such matters than to quote a student's sage observation that "when a girl's name is bandied about the campus, it is a hard proposition for her to live it down."

This glimpse of campus life early in this century is a vivid reminder of how greatly the atmosphere has changed. Compare the advice that President Jordan bestowed concerning social relations, for example, with the following excerpt from an insider's account of life on a state university campus today:

> Older college authorities had been sure they knew exactly what late-adolescent college females and males would get up to if they were given the chance, if they were not carefully sequestered from one another. In the 1980s, the students were living the unsupervised private lives that the older authorities had feared. And the authorities had been right in their premises if not in their judgments that adolescent sex was immoral and corrupting. Rutgers students in the 1980s did have a great deal of sexual fun with each other. Sexual fun, in fact, could be said to be at the very core of college life as the students defined it in the late twentieth century.[4]

The author, Michael Moffatt, is an anthropologist who conducted his first extended field study in a small village in South India and chose for his next subject of ethnographic study the residence halls of his own university. The resulting study—entitled *Coming of Age in New Jersey*, in homage to Margaret Mead—has been widely read, on campus and off. The author claims to offer a uniquely revelatory and unbowdlerized version of student life. By spending a night a week in the residence halls during two extended periods, he was able both to observe student behavior firsthand and to gain the trust of students as "native informants" on their subculture.

Moffatt's study provides one perspective from which to assess the present state of student life, especially the social life of men and women, and it deserves our attention for that reason. Before highlighting some of Moffatt's findings, however, I will describe the findings of a survey of student-life administrators that I conducted for this study. The two perspectives thus afforded—that of administrators responsible for the enforcement of discipline codes and that of a researcher attempting a field study of his own institution—will together provide a broad picture of the present situation on campus. To provide yet another perspective, in the chapter following I will sketch the principal features of the student conduct codes and procedures that are now in effect on a variety of campuses, using materials sent to me by the administrators who responded to the survey.

Administrators' Perceptions: Results of a Survey

In the course of this study, I mailed an extensive questionnaire to the chief student life officers at seventy-six colleges and universities across the United States. The institutions were selected not as a random sample of institutions of all kinds but rather as a group representative of the institutions that play a leading role in American higher education. They included selective liberal arts colleges, large and small state universities, and religiously affiliated institutions.[5] There are more liberal arts colleges, and more of the most prestigious institutions in each category, than a random sample would contain. Statistical extrapolation of the results of this survey to all institutions would therefore be inappropriate. But this somewhat selective group provides an indication of the current practices of the nation's leading institutions, whose example is likely to be influential on others.[6]

I received forty-nine completed questionnaires, yielding an overall response rate of sixty-four percent. Among the responding institutions, fifteen classify themselves as research universities and twenty-nine as liberal-arts colleges.[7] In size they ranged from very small to comparatively large. Two (4%) report enrollments of fewer than 1000 full-time undergraduate students, fifteen (33%) between 1000 and 1999, fourteen more (30%) between 2000 and 3999, ten (22%) between 4000 and 7999, and five (11%) more than 8000. Six of the responding institutions

(13%) are state universities or colleges, thirty-eight (84%) are privately controlled, and two (4%) describe themselves as "church-related institutions whose sponsoring church plays a significant role in governance." The responding institutions represent a cross-section of American higher education.

The questionnaire was divided into two sections.[8] I shall begin with the second part, in which respondents were asked for narrative responses to several broad questions. Difficult as they are to summarize, the answers provided in this section provide valuable insights into the present state of affairs on campus.

The first of these questions was, "What is *the most significant change that has occurred* in the rules and procedures governing student conduct on your campus in the past few years?" One respondent succinctly summarized his campus's policy—and the theme of the entire present study—in his observation, "We are gradually moving away from *in loco parentis*, educating trustees and students to issues of personal responsibility and accountability."

By far the most frequently cited change was a tightened policy on alcohol use. This reflects the change of the legal drinking age to twenty-one in states that until recently set a lower threshold age and the need to comply with federal law, in particular the Drug-Free Schools and Communities Act Amendment of 1989. Indeed, one institution had had no regulation at all regarding alcohol, and had a drug policy prohibiting only drug sales and distribution, until that act forced a drastic change.

Not all of the respondents saw these changes as salutary. One described both the higher legal drinking age and the federal mandates as "counterproductive," and another reported that a principal result of the twenty-one-year-old drinking age has been to increase student drinking in the residence halls, where the law cannot be as effectively enforced as in public places such as bars and restaurants. Others, however, reported that recent years have seen "more alcohol awareness in self-governance of students." Several institutions have instituted stricter policies regarding open alcohol use, with more consistent enforcement. Thus one respondent cited "the virtual elimination of alcohol at scheduled events," and another stated, "We have managed to control (a little better) the abuse of alcohol in fraternities."

Several respondents cited institutional changes, such as the adoption of a wholly new or extensively revised code of conduct. Some credited this undertaking with a positive contribution to the campus atmosphere, but others judged the process "very contentious and time-consuming.'' Several respondents noted that students have become more involved in disciplinary policies and their enforcement and judged this a very important change. In the words of one: "Students now play a major role in the establishing of rules and procedures as well as in their implementation and evaluation. They take much more ownership in the entire process.''

An area of student conduct not specifically surveyed in the questionnaire but cited by several respondents is that of sexual harassment and assault, for which several institutions have recently adopted new policies. One institution reports that its newly adopted policy provides "greater protection for complainants of sexual assault and harassment,'' and another has instituted a "Sexual Assault Hearing System.'' One respondent cited as the most significant recent change "greater enforcement of rules—I call it 'taking back the night.' ''

One weary dean responded to this first question simply by citing "more restrictions, tighter enforcement, more bureaucracy.'' One of his or her colleagues, referring specifically to a tightened alcohol policy, deftly summarized the ideal toward which all those concerned with student conduct are striving: "the continuing attempt to write a policy which is realistic, workable, and legal.''

Student affairs administrators were asked next to identify the area in which, in their judgment, their institution "is *now most successful in encouraging responsible student conduct.*'' The brief responses given to this question fall under a few broad headings. Most commonly cited was the area of academic honesty and integrity, achieved either through the adoption or resuscitation of an honor code or through better dissemination and enforcement of disciplinary policies.[9] Second most frequently cited was alcohol abuse, which several campuses reported to be more nearly under control than was the case a few years ago. Other areas of noteworthy success, each cited by at least four respondents, included the development of a sense of community and mutual responsibility in residence halls; greater respect for others and toleration of diverse lifestyles; diminished problems with drug use; and greater awareness of issues of sexual harassment and exploitation. Two respondents cited the growing involvement of students in self-government and rule enforcement, and two reported that once-rampant vandalism on campus has been effectively stopped.

When asked to identify the *areas of least success*, respondents mentioned several of the same areas, most notably alcohol abuse. Indeed, alcohol was cited more than six times as often as any other area of student behavior in response to this question. One respondent who had cited "diminished alcohol consumption" as a success also identified "patterns of alcohol consumption (binge drinking by some students)" as the most significant problem. Another noted: "Alcohol policy remains the most ambiguous. We do not and will not supervise student behavior in private rooms. Therefore underage drinking does exist; however, common room and party situations have clearly defined rules which are enforced." The institution's dilemma, noted another, is "continued frustration over inconsistent messages from our society regarding alcohol use—how to make student adhere to laws which are inconsistent and laughed at."

Academic honesty was cited as a continuing problem by several respondents. Others mentioned a lack of sense of community and respect for others. Some cited fraternities in particular, others an atmosphere of racial tension, still others the campus atmosphere in general. "We have far to go on the racial and ethnic road to real and comfortable pluralism," wrote one respondent. Another cited the need for "interpersonal and intergroup relations of cohesion, civility, and tolerance."

Surprisingly, only one respondent mentioned drug use as a serious problem, and only one identified sexual harassment. Several, however, mentioned the need to help students build stronger personal relationships. One cited "responsible human sexuality" as the principal problem area. Another wrote, tellingly: "We are least successful in developing positive and healthy relationships between men and women students."

Asked to describe *ways in which the threat of legal action has compelled changes* in rules of conduct and modes of enforcement, a large majority observed little or no effect. One noted cynically, "No impact. The lawyers come after you no matter what you do." A more nuanced negative answer, from another respondent: "We specifically avoid making changes based on legal threats. Any changes we make are based on looking at the principles and deciding whether changes are needed."

Among those who credited legal developments as having some effect, most cited recent state and federal laws governing alcohol and drug use. Several more observed that the growth in lawsuits against colleges and universities has led to greater explicitness and clarity in promulgating regulations. The law "clearly affects our thinking," wrote one respondent, "especially in trying not to write regulations that are unenforceable. Continually, we must measure what is, and what is not, our responsibility." Another noted that, while the substance of college policies has not changed, "we are clearer in all our publications about our policies and procedures."

Issues of due process and proper conduct in disciplinary action were cited by several respondents. "We have been more attentive in our training of resident staff to issues of liability," wrote one respondent, and another stated that the possibility of legal action has affected his campus "chiefly in making us even more vigilant about due process."

The last two questions solicited respondents' judgment concerning *faculty and student involvement* in rules of conduct and their enforcement. A majority professed to be satisfied with faculty involvement. One added, "I wish they were more pro-active in spotting and referring students they believe are in trouble with substance abuse." Several noted that faculty involvement varies widely—one person decried the unhelpful example of "those who serve alcohol to underage students"—and others lamented the lack of interest of most faculty. One evidently beleaguered administrator responded to the question with the comment, "Get real!"

A majority also reported satisfaction with student involvement, many expressing appreciation and admiration for students' contributions. "The students involved have been mature and responsible, completely committed to the mission of the college," wrote one, and another observed: "By and large the students are extremely responsible. They have always participated fully in the formulation and enforcement of policies. They continue to feel that the alcohol policy is ambiguous—but then so do I."

Some respondents reported great difficulty in enlisting student cooperation. "Many students tend to be short-sighted and to see merely the trees and not the forest," wrote one, and for that reason "leadership and productivity has come from staff, not students." But others blamed institutional barriers, such as a "very dean-centered" institution where "no one figures to be the 'heavy' except an administrator," for student apathy.

Overall, the responses to this section of the survey show that the deans and vice presidents responsible for student affairs believe they have attained a reasonable degree of success in maintaining discipline on campus, even though alcohol abuse persists, and students and faculty members are less concerned or involved with such matters than they might be. The same conclusion is supported, and filled out in more detail, by the results of the first section of the survey, which focused on statistical and numerical data. I will summarize some of the principal results, supplementing them by tables as appropriate.

Readers interested in a more complete summary of the results may consult the full tabulations in Appendix C.

The information that I gathered on student housing on campus has already been summarized in Chapter 1, and Table 1-1. At institutions that admit both men and women, the patterns of housing have shifted rapidly from separate residence halls for men and women to buildings that house both sexes on alternate floors or in adjacent suites or rooms. Only eleven percent of the responding institutions (excluding single-sex institutions) maintain separate men's and women's buildings today, compared with twenty-three percent a decade ago and seventy-seven percent two decades ago.[10] The "women's dorm" and its accompanying rituals—from afternoon tea with the dean of women to after-hours panty raids—are distant memories on most campuses.

Turning to the rules governing major areas of student conduct, the responses reveal that not one of the forty-nine institutions prohibits student alcohol consumption.[11] Fifteen percent prohibit student drinking on campus, and another fifteen percent limit drinking to functions with faculty or staff present or to designated sites. One campus has no stated alcohol policy. The remainder of the responding institutions, seventy-four percent, indicate that "responsible use by students of legal age is permitted," typically in the private rooms of students of legal age and, in somewhat less than half the institutions, in common areas of residence halls. These policies and those governing several other areas of conduct are summarized in Table 3-1 (p. 64).

Respondents were asked how many students had been subject to formal disciplinary procedures for alleged violation of student rules in each area during the academic year 1989-90. It will surprise no one who has set foot on a college campus that cases involving alcohol were by far the most frequent (see Table 3-2 [p. 64]). More than forty percent of campuses report twenty or more alcohol-related discipline cases. Still, at nineteen percent of the responding institutions there were no such cases—whether as a result of self-restraint by students in their habits of consumption, or of self-restraint by administrators in their habits of enforcement, I cannot tell.

Respondents were also asked about policies concerning student use of tobacco products. Most permit smoking only in designated areas, but a substantial minority, twenty-eight percent, have no stated policy. As in the case of alcohol, no institution forbids student smoking. No campus reports more than five disciplinary cases regarding smoking in the past year, and only nine percent report even one such case. The tolerance granted to smokers does not extend to other habit-forming and addictive substances, however. Every responding institution prohibits student use of controlled substances such as marijuana, cocaine, amphetamines and other drugs. Violations of drug policy accounted for a substantial number of discipline cases, although thirty-six percent of institutions report no such cases, and only one institution reported twenty or more.

Only two institutions (4%) reported that their rules prohibit sexual relations among unmarried students, and only four more (9%) report a policy of strong discouragement. Seventy-nine percent of the respondents characterize their institution's policy as permitting nonmarital sex, while six percent report that they have no stated policy. About one-third have some visiting-hour restrictions for at least some residence halls (see Table 3–3 [p. 64]). In response to the question "Does your institution's residence-hall. policy permit a student to invite a person of the opposite sex as an overnight guest?" thirty-six percent of the respondents answered simply "yes," twenty-eight percent said "yes, with restrictions (e.g., explicit permission of other students sharing a room or suite)," and thirty-four percent said "no." Same-sex visitors are permitted on every campus, with restrictions such as those described above in about half the cases. Even though visitation policies are relatively permissive, a majority of campuses report at least one discipline case for violation of visitation rules.

Much media attention has recently been focused on the problems of abusive and derogatory speech and writing on campus, especially when directed against minorities and gay and lesbian students. Two-thirds of the responding institutions report that they now have or are actively considering a policy prohibiting racist or antihomosexual speech and writing. About half of these institutions (31% of the entire sample) report that such a policy was adopted for the first time in the past two years. But these policies appear to be enforced infrequently. Seventy-one percent of the responding institutions reported no discipline cases in this area in the past year.

All but three institutions (93%) reported at least one discipline case involving academic dishonesty, by contrast.[12] Thirty-nine percent reported five cases or fewer, twenty-two percent reported ten or more.[13]

Table 3–4 (p. 64) summarizes the response to three questions concerning procedures for enactment and enforcement of rules. For each of three areas—the enactment of rules, the disposition of cases, and the hearing of appeals—respondents were asked to indicate the composition of the responsible committee. These procedures were difficult to sort into categories, and an unusually large number chose "none of the above." Among the significant results: The two most common legislative sources are a committee of administrators only and a committee in which faculty, administration, and students are all represented but no group has a majority. The former is more commonly assigned to hear cases, by a margin of more than three to one over the next most common option, whereas appeal routes are more varied. At none of the three stages, on any campus, are faculty members alone empowered to enact or enforce rules.

Student-life officers were asked to supplement these facts with their personal judgment—confidentiality assured—concerning the areas of student behavior surveyed. Asked to characterize their institutions' implementation of alcohol policies, thirty-one percent responded that "they are enforced consistently and strictly," and a substantial majority, sixty percent, indicated that "minor violations are frequently overlooked; flagrant violations are dealt with strictly." Responses with reference to drug use were similar, except that the proportions in the first two categories were reversed. For both alcohol and drugs, only one institution (2%) reports that "enforcement is irregular and arbitrary," none that policies "are not enforced."[14]

A majority skipped the question on sexual relations among students because their institutions have no stated policy. If we set aside the thirty-one institutions that have no rules of conduct regarding sexual relations or chose "none of the above," ten institutions remain. Enforcement is judged to be strict at four campuses, selective at two, irregular and arbitrary at three, and nonexistent at one.

The respondents were also asked to state whether, in their judgment, enforcement of student behavioral rules had changed significantly in the past decade. An overwhelming majority report stricter alcohol policies, but in other areas little has changed. Only in the case of drug policies, which are stricter at one-third of the institutions, did as many as ten percent report any change.

The remaining section of the survey solicited data concerning the institution's way of communicating expectations to students and its experience with legal challenges to its disciplinary authority. In many other situations, institutions fearful of liability claims have sought to limit their exposure by requesting individuals to sign waivers or contracts spelling out institutional rules and limiting subsequent liability. One might expect that the same concerns would lead institutions to request formal student consent to disciplinary codes. This is not a common practice, however.

Respondents were also asked whether in the past five years they have been subject to legal action of either of two kinds: a challenge to the institution's authority to enforce behavioral rules, or a claim of negligence in overseeing student behavior. The former type of proceedings would arise if a student sought to invalidate a rule for whose violation he or she was disciplined, whereas the latter would be typical of a liability claim for an injury suffered on campus or in an institution-related activity. Only a small minority reported having experienced legal challenges of either kind.

From these factual data and from the narrative responses summarized earlier, we gain a sense both of how much has changed on campus in a generation and of how persistent are many of the problems of maintaining order. Problems of alcohol abuse and academic dishonesty are the most frequent grounds for disciplinary action, and administrators voice their frustration not only with student irresponsibility but with faculty inattention. Having abandoned the attempt to impose quasiparental control over student behavior, those responsible for discipline are seeking new ways of communicating the sense of shared responsibility. For another indication of the degree to which these measures succeed, and of the atmosphere on campus as students perceive it, I will turn in the last section of this chapter to the field study of residence-hall culture that was quoted at the beginning.

An Anthropologist's View: Results of a Field Study

In the women's residence halls of an earlier era, a man admitted during visiting hours was customarily preceded by a sort of floor crier, calling out "Man on the floor!" to warn residents to put a robe on before dashing to the shower. I can imagine that the students in the Rutgers building where Michael Moffatt spent one night each week during his field study might have adopted a similar cry: "Anthropologist on the floor!"

Moffatt's report on the culture of the residence hall quickly dispels the popular image that coeducational residence halls have become dens of incessant and untrammeled fornication. Romantic or sexual relationships between residence-hall neighbors were rare, he found, and the students took pains to preserve what little privacy remained in their cramped quarters. "Women and men," he observes, "did not usually walk around in front of each other in their underwear, let alone naked."[15] Students considered it necessary to be at least minimally decent even when dashing to the bathroom or taking a telephone call late at night. Students of either sex who tried to slip from the showers back to their rooms wrapped in a towel faced a chorus of hecklers if their path took them past a lounge. The following description, like much of Moffatt's study, shows his special concern (one might almost say obsession) with sexual behavior but also notes patterns that have a broader application.

> Considering the potential, the late-adolescent women and men who lived together on most coed dorm floors maintained remarkably discreet, self-monitored sexual codes among themselves without adult supervision. In the dorms and in the student body more widely, a significant minority of both sexes were probably sexually inactive at any given time, either out of choice, out of lack of opportunity, or out of ineptitude. And most of the students who were sexually active were guided by the same sexual moralities that most middle-class Americans under the age of forty-five followed or preached in the 1980s.[16]

There was no effective "adult supervision" of life in the residence halls where Moffatt lived, whatever the assurances to the contrary that may have been given to anxious parents. His floor's resident "preceptor" made no attempt to guide student behavior unless it became wantonly abusive or destructive, and it seems never to have occurred to the students who lived on the floor to consult their preceptor for moral or personal advice. The principal effect of the preceptor's presence in the hall seems to have been simply to shift the wildest parties to weekends when he was away.

There was once a time when "house mothers," acting *in loco parentis* in the most literal sense, scrutinized visitors carefully and shooed them away at the end of visiting hours. No more. One of the preceptors at Rutgers, in an ironic turning of the tables, quit his job and moved out of the dormitory largely because the students teased him about the girlfriend who shared his room.

Moffatt's study is by no means solely a study of sexual practices, despite the impression given by its jacket.[17] It is true that the index lists more than a column of references under "sex," whereas there are no entries for "ethics," "morality," or "values."[18] But Moffatt actually devotes a considerable amount of attention to students' personal codes regarding sex, which he categorizes under four headings: There are the "neotraditionalists," the men and a few women who uphold some version of the familiar double standard; the "romantic men," who reject the double standard and are closer to what are traditionally women's views concerning relationships; the "liberals" of both genders who have "attempted the higher synthesis: casual sex without guilt *and* the deeper pleasures of romance;" and a few "sexual radicals," including women who view sexuality in a feminist frame.[19] Apart from all of these factions stood the gay and lesbian students, who felt alienated in many ways but increasingly made their presence known on campus.

What is most troubling in Moffatt's account, and casts doubt not just on his motives but on the reliability of his conclusions, is the mingling of two very different sources of information that ground his account of student sexual moralities and practices. The first consists of his conversations with and observations of students in the residence hall. The second—the source of the prurient appeal of Moffatt's book—is a set of "sexual autobiographies" submitted by students as an anonymous, ungraded course assignment, submitted at the student's option in place of a critical paper on an assigned book. In content and language, they seem to run the gamut from the disciplined introspection of a literary journal to the smutty salaciousness characteristic of the purported letters columns of pornographic magazines. Moffatt uses these anonymous student reports to supplement—indeed, in many cases to take the place of—the information he gathers from other sources. Virtually all of the evidence that some students fall into the category of "experimentalists" and "sexual radicals," for example, comes from these anonymous reports.

Flying the banner of the bold new sexual openness, Moffatt spices his exposition of student behavior with liberal doses of student essays from both the Proustian and the Penthousean mold. How much weight can reasonably be placed on freeform essays submitted anonymously in a course that is, by Moffatt's account, deliberately designed to liberate students from their own culture's moralism concerning sex? To take them as a source of reliable information about contemporary student behavior and mores challenges credulity.[20] If we bracket these as less reliable than Moffatt's direct observations, however, we can still draw a reasonably informative picture of student social and sexual life from the rest of his evidence. The picture thus drawn has implications for the other areas of student conduct as well.

Clearly, the number of students who regarded sexual relations as permissible only in wedlock was extremely small. Moffatt observes shrewdly that many students regarded sexual satisfaction as something having almost the status of a human right. One male student, expressing regret at his own lack of experience, added, "I consider sex a basic need in life, comparable to food and shelter."[21] Few students seemed troubled either by moral scruples or by whether present affairs would lead to, or on the other hand would preclude, a permanent and monogamous commitment in the future. Moffatt claims that "perhaps two-thirds of the men and half the women overtly or tacitly promoted some version of the Playboy ethic, the obvious goodness of sexual pleasure for all persons."[22] The proportion may be overstated, and it has diminished with increasing worries over AIDS, whose effect was only beginning to be felt during Moffatt's study. But the mentality he identifies is surely present on nearly every campus.

The anonymous student self-reports, Moffatt writes, showed that only about twenty percent of the students, male and female, were virgins. Among them, he reports, only three individuals remained so by intention.[23] "By the time I turned twenty I was growing anxious about my virginity," wrote a female student. "I was ready to get rid of it but nobody wanted the damn thing."[24] Some skepticism is warranted with respect to these numbers as well, as Moffatt's own direct observations of the behavior of students living on his floor suggest a lower estimate of the level of sexual activity. All the same, it is evident that many students regarded sex as appropriate and mutually beneficial in relationships on campus or off.

Is this situation peculiar to Rutgers, a large state university that draws most of its students from major Eastern urban areas? Not likely. Students at a thousand campuses, from small private colleges to large state universities, read the same books and magazines, listen to the same music, and watch the same films and television shows. The nationwide student culture propagates itself through conversations with friends and siblings on other campuses and through concert tours. Even when its effects are much tempered by strong local traditions, as in the more conservative church-related colleges, some of its manifestations remain. Dress styles, student slang, and musical tastes seem to travel from campus to campus across the country at something approaching the speed of light.

The increasingly unified student culture generally endorses two dogmas widely held in contemporary society: that every life should contain good sex, and that whether sex takes place within or without marriage has little to do with whether it is good sex. Both these dogmas—however controversial their explicit formulation—are nearly universally assumed by the guardians of our societal heritage: popular novelists, scriptwriters, filmmakers, television producers, and popular musicians. It is unrealistic to expect that a fundamentally opposed morality could somehow be instilled in students on any campus, either by rigid enforcement of restrictive rules or by moral exhortation.

It is prudent, therefore, to assume as a background to any discussion of institutional regulation of student personal life that a great many students are now and will remain sexually active, in relationships that may be only an evening in duration or may lead to lifelong commitment. The level of sexual activity, no doubt, varies widely from campus to campus, in response to students' religious and social backgrounds, the degree of privacy available to students, the extent of control imposed by the institution, and the moral attitudes communicated by fellow students, faculty, and administrators. At Rutgers—as Moffatt depicts it—none of these factors exerted any effective restraint on students' search for sexual fulfillment. The lives of the students he studied are probably typical of those of their age group whose behavior is essentially self-governed.

At small private institutions, at least at those that retain close ties either to a sponsoring church or to a local community, student experimentation with sex is likely to be substantially less frequent and far less open than at a state university. But no one who has lived in a campus environment can seriously entertain the hypothesis that even the strictest campus rules, rigorously enforced, can bring about celibacy.

In this, students are following trends equally evident off campus. One historical study has concluded that levels of premarital intercourse among young adults in the United States increased substantially in the 1920s, remained essentially unchanged for forty years, increased in the late 1960s and early 1970s, and then leveled off once again.[25] A recent study of sexual activity and sexually transmitted diseases among young women conducted by the Centers for Disease Control, on the other hand, found that the number of young women aged fifteen to nineteen who report that they have had premarital sex nearly doubled during the past two decades. In 1970, 28.6 percent of young women indicated that they had had sex. In 1988 the figure had climbed to 51.5 percent, rising by age bracket within the entire population studied from 25.6 percent of fifteen-year-olds to 75.3 percent of nineteen-year-olds.[26]

The same trend is evident on campus, where figures are available. College officials interviewed about a sexually transmitted disease by a reporter for the *Chronicle of Higher Education* in 1989 had little to offer in the way of comprehensive statistics, but the comment of one student-health officer who reported being "deluged with new cases" was a typical response.[27] A Gallup poll conducted in 1989 looked specifically at sexual behavior of college students, and the researchers were startled to find that nine percent of the women students surveyed reported having had at least one abortion. Fifteen percent of the men surveyed reported that at least one of their sexual partners had had an abortion. Four percent of the respondents reported having been treated for a sexually transmitted disease.[28]

Even in the era when college administrators retained their role as moralists *in loco parentis* and dealt sternly with students caught in sexual affairs, the enforcers of strict policies knew that such activities were far more widespread than they dared acknowledge openly. If there has indeed been a substantial increase in sexual activity among unmarried young adults in the past few decades, there has at the same time been a much more dramatic change in the attitudes of popular media and society at large toward such activity. According to a recent study, for example, afternoon and evening programming on American television networks incorporates an average of twenty-seven "sexual messages" each hour, including nine kisses, five hugs, ten sexual innuendos, and three references to sexual intercourse and other sexual practices.[29] In such an atmosphere one can hardly expect the campuses to be oases of monastic chastity.

Moffatt's depiction of the freewheeling sexual morality of the campus, therefore, draws support from a variety of quantitative studies, not of college students alone but of their age group as a whole. Moffatt himself puts the point succinctly in a telling footnote—one that usefully links several themes of the present study.

> It may be deceptive to say that the colleges abandoned *in loco parentis* in the 1960s, as is generally said. What the colleges actually did was to stop trying to exercise increasingly archaic kinds of parentlike authority. For, with the rapid shifts in sexual norms and youth culture that were occurring in the sixties, American middle-class parents themselves were no longer able or willing to supervise their own late-adolescent children according to older Victorian norms. In this sense, the colleges were simply going along with the parents.[30]

Conclusion

Campuses today are neither the paragons of community spirit and intellectual curiosity depicted in their promotional literature nor the pits of chaos and lawlessness decried by their critics. Discipline problems are real, and in some respects growing more severe. The dominant mentality expressed by the administrators is not the traditional *in loco parentis* stance but rather a complex amalgam whose elements include respect for students' privacy and autonomy, concern for the harm that they may do to themselves and to others, and responsibility for good order in the institution.

Many of the problems of student conduct—excessive drinking, cheating, and sexual exploitation—have existed for generations and will doubtless plague future generations of administrators in their turn. But the task of countering improper behavior has become more complex, as student rights to privacy and autonomy have come to be more generally recognized at the same time that the responsibility for setting and enforcing policies has become concentrated more and more in the hands of administrators. The help of the faculty in both setting and enforcing conduct standards has never been more urgently needed—and it has perhaps never been less frequently offered.

The present study is offered as an installment on the debt owed by faculty members to their administrative colleagues. It is my hope that faculty members who read it will be motivated to become more closely involved in the oversight of student behavioral rules on their campuses, and that administrators will be assisted in articulating the goals of student-life policies and in setting procedures and practices accordingly.

Notes

1. David Starr Jordan, "College Spirit," in Fulton 1926, pp. 400–9, at 402.
2. Jordan, pp. 405–6.
3. *Ibid.*, p. 406.
4. Moffatt 1989, p. 48.
5. A list of the institutions to which the survey was sent and of those that responded can be found, together with the text of the questionnaire, in Appendix C.
6. The comparative underrepresentation of state universities in my sample is less significant than it may initially appear, for two reasons. First, neither the responses to the survey questionnaire nor the published materials I received provide any reason to believe that disciplinary practices correlate predictably with institutional size and type—as is clearly the case, in contrast, on matters such as teaching load and research support. Second, institutional influence is not symmetrical. In other words, when a discipline code is under revision, it is far more likely that a state university or a small college will adopt

or adapt the policies now in effect at Stanford, Yale, or Princeton—all of them included in my survey—than that the borrowing will go in the other direction.

7. Two institutions fit neither category, and three more skipped this question.

8. The text of the questionnaire is contained in Appendix C.

9. The differences between these two distinct models are described in Chapter 4.

10. This figure includes a few institutions that checked this category as well as one or more others. Thus the percentage of institutions now offering *only* single-sex campus housing, among responding institutions, is less than eleven.

11. None of the responding institutions falls into a category in which complete prohibition is common, such as colleges of the Mormon or Seventh-Day Adventist churches or colleges linked to the more conservative strands of the Methodist or Baptist traditions.

12. Respondents were instructed to count only incidents brought before an administrator or committee for adjudication, not those dealt with solely by the course instructor.

13. A review of the responses in comparison with demographic categories shows that, as one would expect, the institutions reporting large numbers of disciplinary cases are for the most part large state institutions. At the same time, other institutions of comparable size report fewer problems in one or more of the categories surveyed, and some smaller colleges report nearly as many disciplinary cases as do the largest universities. I have not attempted to correlate reported discipline problems with either size or location, however, because the small numbers involved, and the isolation of a single year, might yield misleading results. Moreover, cross-tabulations of responses to the questionnaire, given the small numbers of responding institutions in each category, might in effect permit readers to identify particular institutions, violating my assurance to the respondents that the information they provided would be reported in aggregate form only.

14. A typographical error in the survey instrument caused some confusion in responses to this question: Respondents were asked to choose from the same responses as previously but were wrongly directed to a much earlier question. The larger-than-usual number who did not respond to this question may reflect this confusion—as well as the sensitive nature of the question. Percentages, here as elsewhere, are with reference to those who did respond.

15. Moffatt 1989, p. 182.

16. Moffatt 1989, p. 49.

17. "With Kinseyesque diligence [Moffatt] catalogues the sexual habits and fantasies of his students," leers the *New York Times Book Review* in the back-cover copy of the paperback edition. Has any other academic tome ever attracted such a blurb, the stuff of the dreams of the marketing department? Never mind that the sentence is lifted from the middle of the fifth paragraph of

a full-page review whose overall tone is by no means salacious. Rand Richards Cooper, "No Orgies, Please, We're Studying," *New York Times Book Review,* April 30, 1989, sec. VII, p. 27.

18. The only arguably moral topic is a page reference under "guilt, sexual," which proves to denote a passage in which Moffatt expresses his admiration for students who have escaped from the burdens of this tiresome and antiquated notion.

19. Moffatt 1989, pp. 202–25.

20. Moffatt expresses his own reservations about relying on these purportedly factual accounts as a source of anthropological data. He cannot be sure of the "honesty" of these papers, he admits, and many of them obviously imitate familiar models either of clinical sex research or of popular fiction. All the same, he maintains, "Most of them sounded true, or they appeared to be *fictional* in the constructive sense of the term: they employed well-known writing genres to construct and to comprehend experiences that their writers themselves considered to have been real" (p. 189). But these abstruse literary musings do not prevent him from relying heavily on the essays in describing patterns of student morality.

21. Moffatt 1989, p. 195.

22. Moffatt 1989, p. 196.

23. Moffatt 1989, pp. 195–196, 248.

24. Moffatt 1989, p. 196.

25. Hildebrand and Abramowitz 1984.

26. "More Females Have Premarital Sex Earlier," *Philadelphia Inquirer,* January 5, 1991, p. 4C.

27. Michele N-K Collison, "Dramatic Increase in Genital-Warts Disease Among Students Worries College Health Officers," *Chronicle of Higher Education,* May 31, 1989, p. A23.

28. Courtney Leatherman, "Nearly 1 in 10 Female College Students Has Had Abortion, Gallup Survey Finds," *Chronicle of Higher Education,* May 31, 1989, p. A23.

29. Eleanor Blau, "Study Finds Barrage of Sex on TV," *New York Times,* January 17, 1988, p. C26; cited in Moffatt 1986, p. 233 n. 4.

30. Moffatt, p. 63, n. 3.

Tables

Table 3-1:   Summary of Disciplinary Policies

	Alcohol	Tobacco	Drugs	Sex	Hate Speech
Banned, or banned on campus	15%	0	100%	13%	58%
Permitted with restrictions	15%	59%	0	79%	0*
Responsible use permitted	74%	11%	0	6%	0*
No policy/other	2%	30%	0	2%	42%

* The second and third options are inappropriate to regulation of hate speech; respondents were simply asked whether there is a policy against it.

Table 3-2:   Number of Discipline Cases in the Past Academic Year

	Alcohol	Tobacco	Drugs	Sex	Hate Speech	Plagia- rism
None	19%	91%	36%	42%	71%	70%
1–5 students	13%	9%	47%	29%	24%	39%
6–9 students	8%	0	11%	6%	2%	13%
10–19 students	21%	0	4%	8%	2%	15%
20–39 students	15%	0	2%	6%	0	13%
40 or more	25%	0	0	8%	0	9%

Table 3-3:   Alcohol and Visitation Restrictions

	Yes	No
Drinking permitted in student rooms?	90%	10%
Drinking permitted in common areas?	40%	60%
Restricted visiting hours in all dorms?	26%	74%
Restricted visiting hours in some dorms?	32%	68%
Opposite-sex overnight guests permitted?	65%	35%
Same-sex overnight guests permitted?	100%	0

Note: Figures provided may represent sums of two or more responses; percentages are of those answering the questions.

Table 3-4:   Make-up of Legislative and Judicial Bodies

Composition of committee:	Legisla- tion	Adjudi- cation	Appeal
Administrators only (or an administrator)	28%	50%	22%
Faculty only	0	0	0
Students only	5%	8%	2%
Administrator majority	2%	0	2%
Faculty majority	12%	8%	20%
Student majority	9%	11%	11%
Mixed committee	28%	11%	26%
None of the above	14%	24%	13%

Chapter 4

The Content of Student Codes: Thou Shalt Have No Large Refrigerators

The most reliable authority concerning the present practices of colleges and universities is the stated policy of institutions as revealed in printed material—handbooks, judicial codes, honor codes, and the like—that is distributed to students. I asked each survey respondent to send me copies of such materials, and thirty-one of the forty-nine respondents did so. Six declined permission to quote from the materials, and in those cases I have been able to use the policies only to corroborate or refine general conclusions.[1]

I received policy statements on the major areas of student life and, in most cases, codes of procedures for handling their violation. Fifteen of these twenty-five institutions whose policies I will cite are liberal-arts colleges, and the other ten include both small universities in which the undergraduate college is the largest element and large state universities.[2]

Both the numerous similarities and the occasional sharp differences that emerge from studying the documents I received are instructive. Drug policies, for example, are substantially similar across all institutions. But visitation and cohabitation policies differ sharply at different institutions. A sample of twenty-five does not tell us how representative each of these patterns is, but it does provide the basis for identifying several distinct models and discerning their motives and goals. In this chapter I include brief excerpts from several codes of student conduct. These are supplemented by a few representative policy statements, quoted in their entirety, among the appended resource materials.

No Cooking in the Kitchenette and Other Curiosities

If all that one knew of student behavior came from student handbooks and disciplinary codes, one's impression of the life of the contemporary college student would be bizarre. Certainly one would not mistake today's campus for the restrictive and moralistic domain of a benevolent dean acting *in loco parentis*. Today, the handbooks seem to imply, the problems of sexual exploitation and drug abuse pale to insignificance in comparison with the threat posed by extension cords.

At my home institution, the University of Delaware, the official student handbook—imaginatively entitled "The Official Student Handbook"—runs to one hundred fifty pages. In it a student will find only one short and enigmatic sentence on the issue of cohabitation: "The University does not condone members of the opposite sex staying overnight in a residence hall." On extension cords, however, there are three columns of detailed rules and specifications, with fourteen numbered subsections. The student handbook of another college says little more concerning alcohol use than that the laws of the state regarding underage drinking will be enforced, but it delineates in far greater detail the student's right to a written notice of alleged electrical cord violation, the grace period during which the violation may be corrected, and the procedures for confiscating offending cords.

Students at Carleton are warned, "Any person who installs a dimmer switch will have it removed by the College and will have to pay a fine of $50" (Carleton, p. 22).[3] This falls under the heading of "Electrical Appliances and Dimmer Switches," one of fifty-odd headings in the student code. Davidson's residence hall regulations prohibit air conditioners, hotplates, changes in room wiring, and "any applicant which in the judgment of college authorities is either undesirable or dangerous" (Davidson, "Honor Code and Code of Responsibility," p. 28). Excluding undesirable applicants, one would think, is the responsibility of the admissions office. (The context suggests that "appliance" was intended.)

Many institutions specify precisely the maximum allowable dimensions for an in-room refrigerator. But the most puzzling rule in any of the handbooks is that of Mount Holyoke College, which includes in a long list of electrical appliances whose "keeping and use" in student rooms "is *strictly prohibited*": "*Household-size and apartment-size refrigerators* measuring approximately 16 by 19 by 18 inches" (Mount Holyoke, p. 81; italics in original). Refrigerators whose dimensions differ from this specification, evidently, are permitted. One imagines the resident adviser dutifully advising one of her charges to get rid of her small refrigerator and replace it with a large side-by-side model. The Mount Holyoke handbook leaves no doubt that the prohibition on "cooking equipment" is to be interpreted inclusively: It specifically "includes, but is not limited to: toasters, toaster ovens, hotplates, frying pans, broilers, microwave ovens, hamburger makers, crock pots, woks, immersion heaters, quickheat pots, fondue pots, and percolators" (p. 81). Why should any college, particularly a women's college eager to shed old gender stereotypes, be so peculiarly obsessive about defining the category of "cooking equipment"? At neighboring Smith College the rules are much simpler: "food preparation utensils and appliances (except for corn poppers and coffee pots that have UL approval) are . . . banned from college housing" (Smith, p. 52).

Smith's handbook states that ironing boards are provided in all residence-hall kitchenettes and that irons are to be used only in these locations. Back at Holyoke, the subject of kitchenettes brings forth a remarkable example of administrative casuistry: "Cooking is prohibited in kitchenettes."[4]

No doubt good order in the residence hall as well as the capacity of the electrical system are under threat from the multiplication of electrical devices. Perhaps statistical evidence would even show that more students suffer lasting injury from use of substandard extension cords (University of Delaware students, please consult section III.J.2.c.: use minimum 16 gauge, minimum rating 13 amperes) than from binge drinking or casual sex.

A colleague who studies medieval monastic life has told me that the disciplinary codes of the several orders provide an illuminating and invaluable indicator of the kinds of misbehavior that regularly occurred. A future historian might justifiably draw the conclusion that the most persistent threats to good order on campuses in the 1990s came from small appliances.

I will forgo further analysis of campus regulation of extension cords, refrigerators, hot plates, dimmer switches, lofts, picture hangers, window screens, permissible holiday decorations and means of affixing them to walls and doors, or the placement of plants on window ledges—all of them discussed in depth in some of the handbooks. The principal topic of this chapter is the application of discipline codes to weightier matters such as plagiarism and drugs. But before taking up these areas of content let us first take brief note of the procedures that have been established on various campuses for adjudicating alleged infractions of rules.

Procedures for Enactment and Enforcement

We noted in Chapter 2 that recent legal decisions have drawn increasingly sharp boundaries around the zone of discretion within which each institution is free to set its own procedures for the enforcement of campus rules. The courts have ruled that certain minimum procedural standards, including the right to notice of charges and the right to examine and challenge evidence, are guaranteed to students. Initially posited in the context of state-supported universities, these protections have come to be applied to private institutions as well. Every one of the twenty-five responding institutions states these rights explicitly in its student discipline code. Most institutions also permit a student to bring an advisor or advocate to a disciplinary hearing, but lawyers are, in some instances, specifically barred. This, too, is in keeping with legal decisions that mandate basic procedural fairness but do not require replication of a juridical model.

The stated procedures used on different campuses are strikingly similar. The two summaries of procedural rights that are reproduced in Appendix B are from two institutions that differ in almost every way: One is a small, religiously affiliated institution in the Midwest that identifies itself primarily as a liberal-arts college; the other is a very large urban branch of a state university. Yet their disciplinary procedures are nearly interchangeable.

On a typical campus, the process of adjudication for alleged rule violations can be analyzed as involving up to ten distinct stages:

1. A complaint or charge of a disciplinary violation is registered.
2. The accused student is notified of the charge.
3. A hearing is scheduled either with an administrator or before a disciplinary committee, frequently at the student's option. If serious legal charges are involved, the institution may skip directly to step 9.
4. Evidence of the alleged violation is presented.
5. The student is given the opportunity to challenge the evidence and present a defense.
6. The administrator or adjudicatory body issues a finding of guilt or innocence on the basis of the evidence presented. If innocence is the finding, the process jumps to step 10.

7. Appropriate sanctions are imposed for a finding of guilt, taking into account not only the evidence of the present proceeding but also the record of any previous infractions. If neither party exercises the option in step 8 or 9, the process jumps to step 10.

8. The student may elect to lodge an appeal with an administrator or, more commonly, a committee empowered to assess the fairness of the original proceeding and to overturn the previous finding of guilt.

9. The institution may elect to request the involvement of the local police and prosecutor, for adjudication in the courts. This may be pursued in addition to or in place of steps 1 through 7.

10. Records of completed disciplinary proceedings are normally destroyed after a short interval if the student has been acquitted; added to a student's permanent file if the student has been found guilty.

The details of the procedure and the identity of the individuals or committees responsible for each stage vary from institution to institution. But the overall pattern of initiating charges, presenting and countering evidence, and rendering judgment is invariant.

On every campus, a great majority of all infractions of behavioral rules are dealt with in ways that do not even reach the first step enumerated above, the formal registering of a charge or complaint. One of the marks of a skillful staff member or administrator is the ability to maintain good order through admonition, example, and personal reprimand for minor infractions. Yet if serious or repeated infractions of a rule elicit nothing more than informal sanctions such as these, students will soon conclude that the institution is not serious about the rule. This is not uncommonly the case with respect to student alcohol abuse and on campuses that promulgate rules against cohabitation in residence halls but tolerate it in practice. Under these conditions students quickly learn that they are not really expected to live up to the stated rules.

Disciplinary proceedings may be initiated by an administrator, a faculty member, or a fellow student. Some college codes also make explicit provision for acceptance of a complaint by a nonstudent—the neighbor of a fraternity house that throws noisy parties, for example. Others limit participation in campus disciplinary actions to those formally affiliated with the institution as students, faculty or staff, leaving it to the local police to deal with allegations of misconduct initiated by others.

Even a case that originates on campus may eventually be handed over to the police and courts—step 9 in the outline above—if the alleged misconduct is so serious as to require both the more severe sanctions and the extended procedural safeguards of the legal system. No campus disciplinary council should attempt to adjudicate charges of murder, rape, or embezzlement. Several institutions also state that alleged violations of drug laws on campus, particularly the sale of hard drugs, will be immediately handed over to the police.

A majority of the procedural codes sent to me provide explicitly for possible institutional sanctions following conviction by a court of law. In some instances the likely sanctions are enumerated: expulsion for conviction of a felony, or a felony of a certain class; suspension or probation for conviction of a misdemeanor; and so forth. Other codes simply state that the college or university reserves the right to impose its own disciplinary measures as appropriate.

Such policies need to be applied with caution. Suppose, for example, one student is convicted of a misdemeanor involving drug use on the testimony of a classmate who avoids prosecution only by testifying against him. In this case, a policy of adding institutional sanctions when and only when the courts have rendered a guilty verdict would compound the arbitrariness of the legal outcome.

Whatever the origin of a complaint that a student has violated campus disciplinary rules, formal charges of rule violation are most often brought by an administrator, such as a residence-hall supervisor or a dean. But there is an important exception: Some colleges require that complaints for certain offenses be lodged directly by students. Typically such a requirement forms an integral part of a comprehensive honor code, the focus of which is about issues of academic honesty but whose scope may be much broader.

At the University of Virginia, for example, a student who suspects another of violating the honor code is required to enlist the aid of one or more other students, to consult with a specially trained student "honor adviser," and then to meet face to face with the accused student in what is described as a "confrontation." "The purpose of the meeting," explains this institution's honor-system handbook, "is to provide a confidential forum for the investigating students to explain the reasons for their suspicions and to ask the student for an explanation of his behavior."

The subsequent steps in resolution of alleged honor violations include stages analogous to each of those described above. But the procedure as described in the handbook is reminiscent less of a criminal trial than of the elaborate code by which gentlemen of an earlier era challenged each other for breach of the aristocratic social code. The beginnings of the University of Virginia honor system date back more than a century, and at various times violations have included cheating at cards, drinking on the day of a dance, gambling with first-year students, and insulting a lady. These social sins are no longer punishable, but something of their spirit remains.

The second stage, giving the student notice of the charges, is essential under the guidelines established by the courts for fundamental procedural fairness. It is usually specified that such notice must be written, must state the nature of the alleged infraction, and must offer the student the opportunity to rebut the charges at a hearing.

Out of concern for the damage that may result when groundless accusations are aired in public, a number of institutions close disciplinary hearings to all except the members of the responsible discipline committee, administrators and witnesses directly involved, the accused student, and a fellow student or faculty member selected by the student. Some codes add that a hearing may be opened to others with the consent of all parties.

But closed hearings heighten the danger that the institution will take advantage of the student's highly vulnerable position. Publicity is an essential protection against arbitrariness in civil and criminal proceedings. Its absence in this context makes other measures of procedural protection, such as keeping an official record for possible review, all the more important.

A very few institutions mandate open hearings as the routine rather than the occasional exception, with the proviso that any party may request a closed hearing instead. Such a policy allows the student to weigh the risks of publicity against the dangers of a closed session.

The sanctions that may be applied for a guilty finding commonly range from either social or academic probation, which has little effect unless other infractions follow, to permanent expulsion from the institution. The sanction of withdrawing eligibility for specified extracurricular activities is seldom imposed by campus disciplinary boards; but the rules governing intercollegiate athletics frequently mandate harsh penalties for drug and alcohol offenses. For intramural sports and other cooperative activities, similar rules are made and enforced by on-campus supervisors. Members of organizations ranging from intramural teams to college choirs often accept willingly the informal jurisdiction of student or staff supervisors for codes of conduct whose demands may extend well beyond the specific activity.

I will argue in the closing section of this study that the patterns of expectation and enforcement that characterize informal groups on campus are at least as important to the overall ethos of the campus as are its more formal disciplinary procedures. Students learn what is expected of them and what they can expect of each other more directly by playing bassoon in the college orchestra and right field in the residence-hall softball league than by studying the all-campus discipline code. Our focus in these chapters, however, is not on these informal networks but on the formal rules of permissible and impermissible student conduct.

What is it that these rules seek to prevent? In the next section I turn to what is in many ways the least controversial and the most successful example of the enforcement of rules for student behavior, namely, the prevention of academic dishonesty.

Plagiarism and Academic Dishonesty

Cheating on campus is hardly news, but it occasionally makes the news. In the spring of 1991, for example, national media carried a report on seventy-three students at the Massachusetts Institute of Technology who were caught cribbing assigned work in a computer programming course. An eight-month investigation found that some students had submitted as their own work done in groups, some had pulled others' work from wastebaskets, and some had broken into other students' computer accounts.[5]

Clearly, to leave matters of academic honesty solely to student discretion—following the policy that many advocate in an area such as cohabitation—would open Pandora's box in the classroom. The problem is not that everyone would cheat. Many students would continue to submit honest work—just as most citizens obey the law, out of habit or honor, or both. But the unscrupulous would take advantage of the scrupulous, and the system of academic evaluation would then reward theft as highly as diligence.

Let us engage for a moment in a thought experiment. Imagine a college or university campus where honesty is left to each student's conscience, and faculty members make no special efforts to prevent or punish cheating. Professors routinely leave the room during examinations, leaving students on their honor. If a student is found to have cheated, the professor warns him or her not to repeat the offense, requires resubmission of the test or assignment, and imposes no further sanctions.

What would be the result? In some contexts, such as upper-level seminars in which only departmental majors enroll, dishonesty might not be a problem at all. Small numbers, close contact among students and professor, and the nature of independent research projects would all work together to make cheating easy to detect, difficult to accomplish, and extremely embarrassing to the student if detected. In many other classes, however, the opposite conditions would pertain: large numbers, limited contact, and common assignments. In a large introductory lecture course, under such an informal system, the occasional honest test might come as a pleasant surprise.

One result of the removal of specific sanctions for dishonesty, in short, would be a high level of cheating on tests and assignments. Another would be a decline in the credibility of course grades, particularly in large introductory courses. In response, some professors would no doubt undertake their own campaigns both to instill in students habits of honesty and to punish dishonesty. But anyone who mounted such an individual campaign would be waging a hopeless battle, so long as colleagues continued to tolerate cheating in their classes.

In nearly every academic context, it is possible to take unfair advantage by presenting others' work as one's own. No means short of twenty-four-hour surveillance of every student can ferret out every act of plagiarism or illicit borrowing. Yet most students, most of the time, resist temptation and submit honest work. There must be sanctions for dishonesty not because everyone would cheat if there were not, but because the presence of meaningful penalties both deters cheating in circumstances where it is easiest and protects honest students from being the victims of others' intellectual fraud.

When a student is tempted to cheat—whether by cribbing from notes during a test, borrowing a classmate's lab results, or copying from a reference work for a paper—his or her sense of personal integrity is the most crucial preventative. Yet this sense is both shaped and supported by many other factors. Simple tactics such as widely spaced seats and multiple versions of the same exam make cheating both more difficult and riskier. The sense of personal and intellectual engagement that accompanies advanced study in small classes, on a more abstract level, diminishes both the occasions for and the advantages of cheating.

Occupying a prominent and essential position on the middle ground, between administrative details of seating and intangible notions of personal responsibility, is a clearly articulated campus code of conduct in academic matters. The campus described above, where there is no such system, is purely imaginary. No campus that responded to my survey, and no other campus that I know of, is willing to risk the chaos that might result from a purely informal and implicit honor system. Many campuses go so far as to make plagiarism policies one of the required topics in first-year classes.

Responses to the survey cited in Chapter 3 indicate that plagiarism policies are not just stated but enforced on most campuses. At all but three institutions, there have been some disciplinary cases involving academic dishonesty in the past year. At nearly forty percent there have been ten or more such cases. At first glance these figures might appear to give evidence of the failure of institutions to enforce their policies regarding academic honesty. That there are substantial numbers of cases does not indicate that the rules have failed in their purpose, however, but is rather a sign of how powerful are the incentives that move many students to cheat.[6]

In this chapter we will look briefly at a few examples of campus policies in each area, beginning with plagiarism. The particulars of these policies add an important element, I believe, to a study whose emphasis is ethical and philosophical. To pass judgment on a social issue from a broad moral perspective without adequate attention to the daily routines through which the problem must be addressed is too common a failing in philosophical discussions of contemporary issues.

Policies regarding academic honesty and plagiarism fall into two broad categories. In the first are policies that state that plagiarism and academic dishonesty are strictly prohibited and that violations of the policy will be dealt with severely. In a second category are institutions where the issue of honesty is addressed by a comprehensive honor code to which all students are expected to subscribe.

Among institutions responding to my survey, the number holding to the disciplinary model is approximately equal to the number that rely on an honor code. In this instance my sample is patently not representative of all institutions of higher learning. Honor codes are commonest at private liberal-arts colleges of small to medium size, which compose a much larger share of my sample than of all institutions. At public institutions, large or small, the disciplinary model generally prevails.

The two models resemble each other in many ways, but three distinctive features mark the honor code. First, it is typical of institutions with honor codes that all students are expected explicitly to state their commitment to uphold the honor code. Sometimes their agreement takes the form of signing a formal document on matriculation; sometimes enrollment itself is taken as an implicit token of acceptance of the code. Students are usually also required to write a brief "honor pledge" on every piece of written work that is submitted for grading. Second, the responsibility for upholding and, when appropriate, revising the honor code is commonly placed either with students alone or with a committee on which students dominate. Third, it is characteristic of honor codes that students are expected not only to abide by them but also to report any violations by other students of which they become aware.

The honor code seems in many ways a survival from an earlier era in higher education, and indeed many of the institutions that now uphold such codes can trace them back several generations. But a few institutions have only recently put an honor code in place.

What form do the rules governing academic dishonesty take? Let us look first at two examples from institutions without explicit honor codes. The first, that of the University of Delaware, covers in the space of a few paragraphs a broad range of situations in which dishonesty may occur.

> The first law of academic life is intellectual honesty. Academic relationships within the University community should be governed by a sense of honor, fair play, and trust, and a readiness to give appropriate credit to the intellectual endeavors of others where such credit is due. . . .
>
> One form of academic dishonesty is plagiarism. Plagiarism is intellectual larceny, the theft of ideas or their manner of expression. The following are examples of plagiarism:
>
> A. Copying another student's test answers.
> B. Taking an essay from a magazine and passing it off as one's own work.
> C. Lifting a well-phrased sentence or two and including them without crediting the author using quotation marks.
> D. Passing another person's good ideas as examples of one's own.

The avoidance of plagiarism, it is added, requires acknowledgement of indebtedness whenever a student quotes another person's actual words; paraphrases another person's idea, opinion, or theory; or borrows facts, statistics, or other illustrative materials "unless the information is common knowledge" (Delaware, pp. 41–42).

The authors of this policy—disregarding their own counsel in the phrase just quoted—felt it necessary to cite three authorities, two college grammar handbooks and another University handbook, as the sources of their relatively elementary account of plagiarism. Their overscrupulousness was not shared by the authorities who prepared the section on "Use and Acknowledgement of Sources" in the Duke University handbook. After noting that cheating often results from inexperience with research and from careless notetaking, the handbook provides a detailed account of the nature of plagiarism, which begins as follows:

> The academic counterpart of the bank embezzler and of the manufacturer who mislabels his product is the plagiarist, the student or scholar who leads his reader to believe that what he is reading is the original work of the writer when it is not. If it could be assumed that the distinction between plagiarism and honest use of sources is perfectly clear in everyone's mind, there would be no need for the explanation that follows. . . . But it is apparent that sometimes people of good will draw the suspicion of guilt upon themselves (and, indeed, are guilty) simply because they are not aware of the illegitimacy of certain kinds of "borrowing" and of the procedures for correct identification of materials other than those gained through independent research and reflection. (Duke, p. 62)

This account continues, in considerable detail, for four pages, comparing a sample quotation from a secondary reference source—a dense paragraph from an introduction to Locke's *Treatise of Civil Government*—with representative examples of four distinct modes of improper borrowing: word-for-word plagiarizing, the "mosaic" of borrowed words and phrases interspersed with one's own, the paraphrase, and the lifting of "the apt term." It is added that "if instances occur which these examples do not seem to cover, conscience will in all likelihood be prepared to supply advice."

When I read this section, helpful and detailed as it is, I found the same mental alarm going off as when the tone and style of a student paper abruptly turns more formal and traditional—a warning bell to check source citations and be on the lookout for plagiarism.[7] The gears of the amateur detective began to turn in my mind, and I looked for clues.

Continuing to study the materials sent to me eventually yielded evidence confirming my suspicions. In the Wesleyan University "Blue Book" distributed to both faculty and students I encountered language that had an oddly familiar ring.

DEFINITION OF PLAGIARISM
By Harold C. Martin

The academic counterpart of the bank embezzler and of the manufacturer who mislabels his products is the plagiarist, the student or scholar who leads his readers to believe that what he is reading is the original work of the writer when it is not. If it could be assumed that the distinction between plagiarism and honest use of sources is perfectly clear in everyone's mind, there would be no need for the explanation that follows. . . . (Wesleyan, p. 86)

A footnote reference credits the four-page passage that follows—it is identical, word for word, with that reprinted without attribution in the Duke handbook—to a rhetoric handbook written by Harold Martin and two coauthors.[8]

How can it have happened that Duke University plagiarized its plagiarism policy—four entire pages reproduced verbatim without attribution? We can only surmise. The most charitable interpretation is that a Duke administrator with a perverse sense of humor wondered whether any reader would ever discover that the passage in question "illustrates the improper use of source material" in more senses than one.

Each of the statements quoted is accompanied by a brief summary of the procedural handling of allegations of dishonesty, which follows the stages enumerated earlier in this chapter. If cheating is found to have occurred, sanctions commonly begin with the imposition of a failing grade in the course in which dishonest work was submitted and range upward, for more serious or repeated offenses, through suspension to permanent expulsion. The inclusion of the most severe academic sanctions that can be imposed is no empty threat. Several institutions report that one or more students have been permanently expelled in recent years for flagrant and repeated dishonesty. And when students have challenged their academic dismissal through legal action, the courts have upheld the autonomy of colleges and universities in academic matters, so long as they have adhered to their own policies and procedures.[9]

At the University of Delaware, when a student fails a course for reasons of academic dishonesty, the transcript bears not only an "F" but an additional notation that the failure was due to academic dishonesty. Students who receive such a grade are required to complete a noncredit seminar on academic conduct, for which additional tuition is charged. On completion of the seminar, provided they have not been found guilty of any other similar offenses, they may petition for the removal of the additional black mark, but not the failing grade, from their permanent transcripts. This option to clear the record is not mentioned in any other of the policies I reviewed.

The examples cited convey both the substance and the style of typical plagiarism rules that follow the first model, that of a conventional discipline code. The stance is one of firm exhortation coupled with concern to instill an understanding of the nature and severity of the offense. Clearly, the universities are untroubled by doubts about their moral authority to prohibit plagiarism or about their competence to identify its occurrence. Plagiarism policies carry no apologetic prefaces explaining how reluctant the college is to presume to make moral judgments on behalf of students. The gravity of the offense and its direct threat to the health of the academic community are beyond dispute.

There remains one major alternative: the honor code. The language of such a code is typically more formal and categorical than that of the rules quoted above. The code itself may be very brief. Here, for example, is that of Davidson College, in its entirety:

> Every student shall be honor bound to refrain from cheating (including plagiarism). Every student shall be honor bound to refrain from stealing. Every student shall be honor bound to refrain from lying about official college business. Every student shall be honor bound to report immediately all violations of the Honor System which come under his observation; failure to do so shall be a violation of the Honor System. Every student found guilty of a violation shall ordinarily be dismissed from the college.

The brochure containing the code offers a brief definition of plagiarism, a procedural outline, and advice on papers and take-home examinations, and it concludes with a short homily:

> The habit of honor which is practiced here is unusual. Few other colleges have been able to maintain it. We do not live in a very honorable time; the academic competition, dishonesty among high officials, and the unwillingness to accept responsibility for one's deeds all serve to erode the habit of honor. Parents who do not wish their children to be held accountable are also an impediment. The Davidson community still believes the honor code is not just a convenience; it also develops the kinds of persons who will be trusted and respected after they leave Davidson.

This additional statement is typical of college honor codes. Nearly all of those sent to me included an assertion that, though everywhere else honor and trust have been sadly eroded, here on our campus it still flourishes, a precious and endangered flower.

Not all of these claims can be literally true, of course, for to accept one college's claim of uniqueness is to brand the rest liars. But such claims are not intended so much to make a factual claim as to create a moral atmosphere.

The honor codes are effective, when they are effective, because they appeal to students' desire to live up to a higher standard than that expected of them in ordinary contexts. The honor code that is solemnly read out at opening ceremonies—one of the features that makes this college a bright beacon amid the dark forces now at work in the world, and so on—may in fact employ the same phrases as do the policies being read at several dozen other colleges across the nation on the same morning. It serves its intended purpose, all the same, if it succeeds in appealing to students' pride in and commitment to their own academic community.

On several campuses, an additional factor reinforces students' sense of commitment to the high standards of the honor code: On these campuses it is the responsibility of students, not the faculty or administration, both to enforce the code and to revise it when necessary. The preamble to one such code emphasizes that it "has been written and implemented by students in a community of individuals which values integrity as a way of life." The preface to this honor code describes its enactment in 1893 as a result of the efforts of a group of students, since which time responsibility for its enforcement has been given to an undergraduate Honor Board (Wesleyan, p. 83).

Several characteristic rituals reinforce the independence of students from faculty monitoring. It is customary at many institutions governed by an honor code for instructors to leave the room during examinations, for example—indeed, at some colleges instructors are formally prohibited from being present. One honor code goes so far as to direct an instructor who needs to be present to show slides during an exam to obtain advance permission from the dean. Also characteristic is the inclusion of an honor pledge on each piece of academic work submitted for grading. If any work is submitted without a pledge, the instructor is commonly required to notify the student honor committee and to postpone grading of any students' work until the committee formally examines the student who submitted unsigned work and determines whether this was mere oversight or an indication that cheating was occurring.

Requiring pledges and empowering a student panel to enforce the code serve to protect students from retaliation if they report dishonesty. Equally important, they constitute rituals through which students reaffirm their commitment to the honor system. Where such systems are used successfully, they enlist students in the task of promoting honest work and preventing unfair competition.

The inherent difficulty of enforcement of the other model—the promulgation of rules and their enforcement by means like those employed in other disciplinary matters—provides a powerful argument for the honor system. The disciplinary model, by its very nature, is likely to snare the unpracticed at plagiarism, while the most skilled practitioners hide their tracks so well that they escape detection. Enlisting students as the primary agents of enforcement places the means of detection far closer to the actual occurrence of the offense, and it places in the hands of those most directly victimized by academic dishonesty both the responsibility and the means of preventing and punishing it. The honor code also precisely exemplifies the important truth—one on which I will elaborate in the closing chapters of this study—that behavior can be far more effectively shaped by the desire to live up to the standards of a community of which one feels a part than by the attempted enforcement of rules.

In the area of academic dishonesty, no institution refrains from making forceful and categorical moral pronouncements. Honesty in academic work is a necessary and indispensable virtue in university life, and its violation cannot be condoned. The judgment is categorical and objective, and it is clearly communicated either through disciplinary rules or through an honor code on every campus. Would that institutions could muster the same degree of clarity and forthrightness in addressing the problems of alcohol use or sexual relations, to which we turn next.

Drinking and Alcohol Abuse on Campus

On March 24, 1807, Francis Cummins, a senior at the College of New Jersey, was expelled for harassing townspeople after imbibing too freely at a local tavern. This incident had consequences far greater than could have been anticipated either by the offending student or by the college, which later became Princeton University. Student anger over this and two subsequent suspensions simmered for several weeks until, on the day before final examinations for the term, President Samuel Stanhope Smith was presented with a petition signed by one hundred sixty students demanding that he reconsider the suspensions. The signers represented a large majority of the two hundred students then enrolled in the college.

The president responded by inviting one of the college's trustees to speak on the following day at the required chapel services. But rather than listen to his sermon calling upon the protesters to "renounce the principle of uniting together to control the government of the college according to their humours," most of the students noisily walked out. They were immediately suspended.

When the students barricaded themselves inside the main college building, the president called in the local militia to force them out. The students beat them back with broken banisters and stones. Finally the president closed the college and agreed to negotiate with student representatives. Echoing the rhetoric of the recent American revolution, the students stood firm in demanding the right "to petition when we think ourselves aggrieved." To the trustees' dismissal of their rebellion as youthful excess, they responded in a printed broadside. "With due deference to the superior judgment and discrimination of the trustees," they wrote, "and without presuming to question their veracity or honor, we beg leave to correct a few mis-statements in their publication." They proceeded to offer their own self-exculpatory account of the sequence of events leading to their dismissal. But their protests had little effect. Only fifty-five of the suspended rebels ever returned to the college.[10]

The Princeton rebellion of 1807 inspired a New York newspaper to observe that the "same mental epidemick which has crazed Europe, and is extending its baleful ravages throughout the civilized world, has contaminated these young rights-of-boy politicians."[11] All this as a result of one rowdy student's walk back to the college from the local saloon.

A case might be made that one of the oldest traditions in the American college, older even than most honor codes and school songs, is that of wanton abuse of alcohol. Early college records demonstrate clearly that the alcohol-related problems that deans and residence hall directors face today—public drunkenness, vandalism and destruction of property, fights and assaults of all kinds—have existed on campus since the earliest days. Anecdotal evidence is added from time to time in the pages of alumni magazines, when octogenarian graduates write to the letters column to note that some drunken prank recently committed at the college was remarkably like the stunt for which the writer and his classmates were suspended decades ago.

A news item that appeared, oddly enough, in the philatelic column of the Sunday *New York Times* provides another reminder of the ubiquity of the problem. The item describes a "single folded letter" recently acquired by the columnist at auction, in which a Yale student relates to a friend in Maryland "an unpleasant affair that happened to some of our most promising votaries of Bacchus a few Sundays since." It seems that six students, having dined at a local hotel, and "supposing it necessary to have something to settle their stomachs, called for six bottles of wine, which being quaffed, they demanded six more, so that in about half an hour, they were most of them pretty well soaked." The sheriff was called in and brought them before the president of Yale for discipline, with the result that one student was dismissed, the others suspended. The year of this undated letter, a Yale archivist was able to determine from the university's disciplinary records, was 1827.[12] Evidently Yale is not an institution where disciplinary records are periodically wiped clean—not, at any rate, for a couple of centuries.

The dominant attitude of the college toward drinking until a generation or more ago—the tone that emerges from news accounts and administrators' admonitions stretching from the 1800s into the 1960s and 1970s—was one of official condemnation tempered by tacit toleration, even bemused admiration. Certainly no college or university of the nineteenth or early twentieth century condoned open and public abuse of alcohol. On every campus students were subject to discipline for public drunkenness or rowdiness, like the Princeton student whose suspension touched off a rebellion or the Yalies whose rowdiness attracted the sheriff. Yet the weight of unofficial tradition, and the difficulty of detecting violation, militated against any serious effort at enforcement. For this reason some advised against promulgating any rules governing student behavior in the tavern. Thus a dean of men observed, speaking before the National Education Association in 1910:

> Many college rules are virtually a dead letter because they are difficult or impossible of execution, and the existence of such regulations can do nothing less than bring the whole system of college statutes into ridicule and disrepute. I believe, for illustration, that it would be a most excellent thing if college students did not visit saloons, for I have known very few students who were not to a greater or less degree injured by such a practice. It seems to me, however, worse than useless, and in fact often harmful, for a college to make a rule prohibiting students from entering saloons, because it is so evidently a rule unlikely or impossible to be enforced.[13]

The attitudes of administrators toward student drinking and resulting misbehavior, it appears, were very much like those toward college pranks. Bringing a cow into the college chapel and running underwear up the flagpole seem to have evoked much the same response from deans of an earlier era as did a boisterous party in which drunken students destroyed a few windows and pieces of furniture. Sexual assault against women made pliable by drink is by no means an invention of the current generation of college students. But in an era when most colleges were all-male and their female guests were typically not students, colleges seldom acknowledged this or any other predictable consequences of student drinking as falling within the realm of their concern or responsibility.

Even the most vehement condemnations of students' behavior often included an indulgent wink toward the ineradicable appetite of young men for an evening's carousing. Consider, as an example, the following passages excerpted from the essay "College Spirit," written by Stanford's first president in 1903:

> I once heard a graduate of the Boston Institute of Technology make this plea to a body of students of another institution: "Never carry your colors into a saloon. If you must disgrace yourself, do it in the name of someone else. When we visited a saloon in Boston," he added, "we always gave the Harvard yell." You may not care for your own disgrace, but do not make your college party to it. If you must visit saloons to express your feelings, do not take your college with you. If you must scream, give the other fellow's yell. Perhaps if you do this, some other fellow may whip the breath out of you. Be a martyr if it must be, but rather die than disgrace your college.[14]

Broadened access and nearly universal coeducation have altered the campus environment profoundly, and the days when the student body consisted solely of young men from the best families are now far behind us. Moreover, two important developments of recent years have brought significant changes to campus alcohol policies. The first was the establishment in the 1980s of a uniform legal age of twenty-one for the purchase and consumption of alcoholic beverages in every state. The second, less dramatic but equally influential, has been an increased social awareness of the dangers of alcohol abuse, reflected both informally in community and parent expectations of colleges and formally in federal regulations.

At Princeton, where the expulsion of an inebriated Princeton student led to a minor revolution on campus nearly two hundred years ago, the battle between the college's desire for decorum and the students' for the freedom to party still rages. During the summer of 1991, the president banned kegs of beer from all university events. A few months later, under intense pressure not only from students but from alumni as well, he relented and approved a new policy that permits kegs at events sponsored by seniors, graduate students, or alumni.[15] Alcohol is in the news on many other campuses as well. I quoted earlier from a

New York Times report on new rules requiring hostesses of large parties at Bryn Mawr to submit their guest list in advance. Students interviewed by a reporter were generally supportive of the new policy, but some observed that the policy has simply driven the rowdier students off campus.[16] On another campus, a few months later, students were less willing to cooperate. A policy banning kegs from all campus housing at Skidmore College in New York state, even a named complex most of whose residents are over twenty-one, sparked a protest by more than three hundred students.[17]

In the disciplinary documents sent to me by colleges and universities, policies regarding alcohol differ widely in their manner of exposition. Some are elaborate, detailed, and specific, describing both proscribed conduct and the reasons for the proscription in detail. Others are extremely cursory—no more than a summary of state and local laws and a statement that the college will not condone their violation.

Differences from one campus to another in the matter of alcohol policy do not correlate directly with factors such as the character and size of the campus. Not even the religious character of the college is a reliable predictor of the strictness of alcohol policies. Among the forty-nine responding institutions, two describe themselves as "church-related institutions whose sponsoring church plays a significant role in its governance," and of these one prohibits and the other permits alcohol consumption on campus. Six other institutions that describe themselves as "private colleges or universities" but have no religious affiliation prohibit on-campus drinking.

At forty-two institutions, responsible use by students of legal age is permitted under some circumstances, provided that it occurs either in private residence-hall rooms or in designated common areas and does not lead to violent or destructive behavior. In some cases serving alcohol in common areas requires staff supervision. Other schools simply warn against excess. The line between responsible and irresponsible use can be drawn in several distinct ways.

Not one of the institutions forbids student drinking altogether. Such a policy was once common, yet it probably never was, and surely is not now, realistically enforceable. The abandonment of such restrictive rules even by most church colleges has meant the end of some forms of intercollege rivalry. A Carleton alumnus of forty years ago has told me of the unusual Marine-style haircuts that he occasionally observed on Saint Olaf College students, for example. In the taverns of the small town where both colleges are located, Carleton students would kidnap Saint Olaf students and shave their heads, confident that the victims would not report the incident because to do so, and thereby admit having visited the tavern, would be to invite expulsion from Saint Olaf.

There remain a number of institutions in the United States that prohibit student drinking under any circumstances, but none was among those responding to the survey. In every case that I am aware of, such a restrictive policy arises from religious traditions and standards. Each seems to fall into one of three classes: colleges closely tied to a conservative Protestant church, such as Asbury College in Kansas; colleges not directly church-governed but embedded in the more conservative strands of Protestantism, such as Wheaton College in Illinois; and colleges or universities of some of the American sects that have broken away from mainstream Protestantism, such as Andrews University in Michigan (Seventh-day Adventist) and Brigham Young University in Utah (Latter-day Saints). Informal discussions with faculty members and former students at several of these institutions suggest that the restrictive policies are generally if not universally respected—more from a voluntary sense of commitment to the values of a small community than from fear of penalties. Even the smaller and more socially conservative Catholic colleges, by contrast—Saint Anselm, for example, among the survey respondents—permit student drinking.

At the opposite end of the spectrum of regulation, Stanford is unique among the forty-nine responding institutions in that its student conduct handbook contains no statements or rules whatever concerning alcohol use, save to prohibit "drunk driving on campus in a way that presents a threat to the life or property of others" (Stanford, p. 4). (Careful and considerate drunk driving, apparently, is permissible.)

At every institution except Stanford, the student conduct handbook contains both rules regarding alcohol use, a reference to state and local laws, and an explanation for the institution's concern with this area of conduct. Typical is Yale's succinct statement:

ALCOHOL: The unlawful possession, use, or distribution of alcohol on University property or as part of any University activity is prohibited. (p. 7)

Another section of the Yale discipline code sets out the college's regulations on alcoholic beverages in greater detail, beginning with a summary of "general responsibilities of students":

Yale College recognizes its students to be responsible adults and believes that they should behave in a manner that does not endanger themselves or others and that is in compliance with State and local laws regarding the consumption and delivery of alcohol. Furthermore, students will be held fully responsible for their own behavior, even when acting under the influence of alcohol. Infractions of the alcohol regulations as well as any alcohol-related behavior that violates the Undergraduate Regulations will be subject to disciplinary action by the appropriate University officials. In such cases, the association of alcohol with problem behavior will not be seen as a mitigating factor and may be seen as an exacerbating factor. (p. 52; italics omitted)

The last two sentences, italicized for additional emphasis in the original, convey forcefully the abandonment of the public admonition and private wink that once characterized campus alcohol policies.

Among other provisions of Yale's policy is a requirement that Yale students obtain a special University identification card certifying that they are of legal age in order to be served any alcoholic beverages at campus functions. Citing state law, Yale also categorically prohibits the sale of alcohol on campus. Included in the scope of this ban are not only the "sale of chits, potato chips, set-ups, or any article which may be redeemed for liquor" but also admission fees for parties where alcohol is available. The hosts of every party must offer "nonalcoholic beverages and food of sufficient quality and in adequate amounts." It is not specified what precisely counts as "food of sufficient quality" for Yale students (Brenner's wafers and Brie, not Saltines and Velveeta?), but it is specified that "service of alcoholic beverages must cease if the supply of nonalcoholic beverages is exhausted" (p. 53).

Other institutions spell out parallel sets of rules and procedures intended to prevent alcohol abuse, even by students of legal age. Smith's requirement that all parties be "registered with the coordinator of social events six class days prior to the event" (p. 36) is typical of the rules imposed by several schools. Smith spells out a number of rules of conduct for parties: keep two people at the door to check IDs, keep liquor behind the bar so that only designated bartenders have access to it, and so forth. Its handbook also stresses the special responsibility of student leaders, such as head residents and officers of organizations, to identify both individuals and organizations that use alcohol irresponsibly. Students in such a position of responsibility are required either to take disciplinary action against offending groups or individuals or to assist in obtaining treatment when an individual shows signs of alcohol dependence (pp. 34–35).[18]

One college couples its enumeration of alcohol rules with an unusually frank admission of its inability to enforce them universally.

The college recognizes that it cannot guarantee that this policy or the alcohol-related laws will be honored by everyone. It must therefore rely on the good judgment of students, faculty, staff and other members of the college community to observe the laws and policies. Those who choose to violate them must be prepared to accept total responsibility for their individual or collective action and should understand that possible outcomes include disciplinary action, loss of party privileges, personal liability, fines and/or imprisonment. (Mount Holyoke, pp. 55–56)

The specific rules that follow are accompanied, as at several other schools, by a detailed summary of the relevant state statutes regarding alcohol consumption. This inclusion serves not only to inform students of the legal context for the college policies but also—and this is surely part of the motive—to remind them of the seriousness of alcohol offenses. A list of college-imposed sanctions probably instills less fear in students who read the handbook than does the recitation of the penalties for violation of state laws, such as the Massachusetts penalty of "a fine of $1,000 or six months' imprisonment, or both" for providing alcohol to a person under the legal age (p. 57).

The institutional penalties specified for alcohol abuse on some campuses, in contrast, are so light as to invite students to take the policies themselves lightly. Westminster College, for example, states that the punishment for a first offense against the alcohol policy will be a $50 fine; for a second offense, a meeting with the dean of students and a mandatory alcohol-education class; for a third offense, dismissal from college housing or, for off-campus students, a $100 fine. Richmond College mandates only a $25 fine for underage drinking or drinking in a public area. Such lenient penalties seem to imply that the college has little real interest in enforcing its policies against alcohol abuse. A fine that amounts to no more than the cost of a case of beer is unlikely to deter underage drinking.

Rules governing alcoholic beverages at parties range from the very simple to the very complex. Richmond College, for example, permits only wine and beer and prohibits all distilled liquor in residence halls. Richmond also bans kegs, "party balls," and other "large containers" of beer or other alcoholic beverages (p. 65). The University of California at Los Angeles has a somewhat more flexible but equally vague policy prohibiting "amounts for storage or use that are excessive under the circumstances for personal use" (UCLA Housing Handbook,

p. 29). Williams College, in contrast, leaves little to interpretation. Parties for seventy-five people or more may provide up to eight kegs, according to the student handbook.[19] Parties for 21 to 74 people may serve no more than two kegs, and parties for fewer than 20 may not order kegs at all (Williams, p. 71). Perhaps clarity in such matters must always be purchased at the cost of an element of arbitrariness. The arbitrariness in this case seems excessive, however. One can imagine the zeal with which Williams students roll out six more kegs from the basement the moment their seventy-fifth guest is spotted coming up the walk—and the dutiful reluctance with which they lock them up again when someone departs.

Many institutions require advance registration of all large parties with the security office. One college requires, in accordance with state law, that student hosts file a formal notice with the state liquor board a week in advance. A new policy put into place in 1990 at Columbia University even requires student party hosts to obtain a temporary beer and wine permit, for a $25 fee, from the New York Alcoholic Beverage Control Board, if the party is in a location not already licensed, and admission will be charged.

The task that institutions are addressing through these policies is the management of student drinking and its consequences, not its wholesale prevention. Every campus except the seven where on-campus drinking is forbidden tolerates the presence of alcoholic beverages at student social functions. And even the "prohibition" campuses know that their policy does not eliminate student drinking but, at best, reduces its frequency and openness.

Institutions where student drinking is permitted use a variety of measures intended to make alcohol an incidental feature, not the central purpose, of social gatherings. Among such measures are rules concerning the way in which social events may be advertised. Duke, for example, requires that "flyers, banners, and signs which advertise social events where alcohol is served must not overtly or covertly state or imply an invitation to participate in excessive drinking" (Duke, p. 49).[20]

The discipline codes of some smaller colleges are more hortatory. Illinois Wesleyan, for example, which describes itself as "a private institution with a religious affiliation," prohibits alcohol use on campus and adds that "the University has never encouraged or condoned the use of alcohol" (Illinois Wesleyan, p. 49). The same tone can persist even when the actual rules are more permissive. Southwestern College states that, "in keeping with its United Methodist heritage, Southwestern University supports abstinence from the use of alcohol," but it goes on to urge "responsible self-control" on those who choose to imbibe. Saint Anselm College permits moderate drinking in student rooms but warns that drunkenness in itself is a disciplinary violation. Are these policies enforced? No one who has spent a weekend evening in the vicinity of fraternity houses or residence halls can doubt that alcohol abuse is a serious problem on campus. Enforcement of alcohol policies, we have noted, was judged to be both strict and consistent at fewer than a third of the campuses responding to the survey—and this, coming from student deans, is probably an overestimate. One hardly needs survey results, in any case, to verify the serious problems with alcohol abuse on the nation's campuses. In recent years several students have died as a result of grossly excessive drinking on campus, and police raids on fraternities where underage students are being served are reported in newspapers regularly.

"Almost all administrators agree that state laws raising the drinking age to twenty-one have made it difficult to set campuswide policy, since some undergraduates can drink legally and others cannot," wrote a reporter for the *Chronicle of Higher Education* early in 1990.[21] In a major statewide study in Pennsylvania, a panel of thirty-five representatives of institutions across the state found that five to ten percent of college students drink to the point of intoxication once or twice each week and that "alcohol is an underlying influence in most acts of vandalism and violence, including rape, on college campuses, and the incipient cause of most traffic fatalities and other fatal accidents for college-age youth."[22]

In addition to their formal discipline codes, a few institutions sent me a copy of a published or unpublished report on the disposition of disciplinary cases in the past year. These reports emphatically confirm the impression that alcohol abuse is a major, if not the principal, behavioral problem on campus.

I have already noted that Stanford is the only institution surveyed that does not explicitly regulate student alcohol use. A five-year cumulative summary of disciplinary proceedings at that institution confirms that no student has been disciplined by the university for underage or excessive drinking. But the report's anonymous author adds this observation:

Nonacademic misconduct . . . continues to be highly associated with use of alcohol. All assaults prosecuted through the judicial system last year were triggered in one way or another by alcohol. (Stanford, judicial report, p. 2)

The disciplinary codes excerpted here, disparate as they are in some ways, are for the most part firm and specific in drawing the line between responsible social drinking and the abuse of alcohol. The problem, accordingly, lies not in lack of stated restrictions but in their implementation. To make any rules such as those that we have cited truly effective requires much more than simply proctoring parties and punishing violators. It is vital to communicate to students a sense of the importance and legitimacy of the rules themselves, because in this area, even more than in matters such as academic honesty, student behavior can be effectively controlled only by students themselves.

The opportunities for either clandestine or open abuse of alcohol are too numerous, and the tolerance of our society for alcohol abuse too high, to give any reason to hope that even the most vigorous enforcement of known violations will put an end to irresponsible drinking on campus. In the last chapters of this study, however, I will suggest a variety of means by which institutions can create an atmosphere in which such problems are less likely to arise.

Illegal Drug Use

In the related area of use of legally prohibited drugs, institutional policies are very similar, and our survey can be brief. The legal background sets the parameters for campus rules. In every state, nonprescription sale or use of drugs such as heroin, cocaine, LSD, marijuana, and amphetamines is illegal. In the eyes of the law there is no threshold, as in the case of alcohol, between responsible and irresponsible use of these substances, nor between permissible use by adults and impermissible use by minors. Federal legislation also mandates severe penalties for sale and distribution of such drugs. The ambiguities that attend alcohol policies therefore do not arise in the case of drug use. Colleges and universities are committed—explicitly, with one exception that will be noted below—to upholding these laws.

The link between federal and state law and college regulation was forged more tightly by pressure from the federal government during the Reagan and Bush administrations. The Drug-Free Workplace Act of 1988 and the Drug-Free Schools and Communities Act Amendment of 1989 required every institution receiving federal funds to document its policies and procedures for preventing drug use. Grant agreements with a number of federal agencies now incorporate similar provisions.

Several universities, we have already noted, cited these developments as a principal motive for newly tightened drug policies.

The motives of such legislative behavioral regulation are above reproach, but their implementation can lead to absurdity. I wondered just what was going to be expected of me, for example, when in early 1989, as financial administrator of a complex ten-year project to translate ancient Greek commentators on Aristotle involving collaborative work among several dozen scholars across Europe and America, I agreed to "maintain a drug-free work environment." This was a condition of the grant awarded to the American Philosophical Association by the National Endowment for the Humanities. Had I seen any sign that the new translation of Simplicius's commentary on the *De Motu Animalium* was being prepared in a drug-induced state, I would certainly have taken whatever steps I could to call a halt to the practice. It seems unlikely, however, that the threat of impounding a $100 honorarium would have been sufficient to bring about the moral reform, say, of a classical philologist in Utrecht or Toronto who has fallen into the depraved habit of smoking a joint with her husband on a Saturday evening.

The recent legislation was seriously intended, and there is no doubt that institutions receiving federal assistance take its requirements seriously. Witness the treatment of a Stanford faculty member, mentioned in the introduction to this study, who openly challenged federal antidrug policies by informing Bob Martinez, coordinator of federal drug policy, that he has used certain illegal drugs and has advised students to do so as well. Representatives of the federal government warned Stanford that it risked losing all federal aid, and the university responded by suspending the faculty member from teaching pending the outcome of an investigation.[23] Some colleagues protested the university's actions, arguing that due process and free-speech rights had been trampled in the university's zeal to show that it is not soft on drugs. But the university stood firm.[24]

Only one surveyed institution lacks a strict antidrug policy, so far as I could determine. Mount Holyoke's 165–page student handbook covers nearly every aspect of campus life in detail, from bicycles to plagiarism. Its lengthy and specific alcohol policy even incorporates a "Reference Guide to Massachusetts Alcohol Laws." But the handbook contains no policies at all related to drug use. Drugs are mentioned only elliptically in a description of the college's "Alcohol and Drug Awareness Project," whose purposes are "prevention, intervention, and continuous exploration of alcohol and drug-related issues."

The absence of any other mention of the subject from an otherwise comprehensive handbook is puzzling. Perhaps the topic slipped administrators' minds simply because there has never been any drug abuse at Holyoke. But of course that cannot be the actual reason. No campus is entirely free of drug abuse, when cocaine and various illicit pills are readily available in even the smallest communities. Not long ago five seventh- and eighth-grade students at my children's middle school, part of an excellent school system in a close-knit community near Philadelphia, were apprehended in a drug distribution ring. Drugs found in junior high schools surely cannot be difficult to obtain on any campus.

Yet student-affairs administrators do not consider drug use a major campus problem, according to the results of the survey. Nearly two-thirds of the respondents judged the enforcement of drug policy to be strict and consistent, more than twice as many as made the same judgment regarding alcohol policy. "Alcohol abuse" was cited six times as often as was any other problem area in student conduct; but drug use was mentioned only once.

These data are open to two quite different interpretations. Perhaps the era of widespread drug use has passed, and students, following the example of their elders, have turned to alcohol as their drug of choice. Or possibly, drug abuse on campus is widespread but is kept effectively out of sight and out of mind. Where alcohol abuse often leads to acts of vandalism, assault, and rape, use of other illegal substances seldom causes such conspicuously irresponsible behavior. The most serious social problems of drug use arise from lack of alertness in risky occupations—operation of heavy machinery or public transit vehicles, for example—and from theft and assault by addicts desperate to support their habits. Neither is likely to be a major problem on campus.

No doubt both of these explanations—that drug use has declined and that it is more effectively concealed—contain some truth. Whatever the reason, campus administrators seem unmoved by the stridency with which the universities' critics deplore student drug use in the media. When those least informed are most concerned, and vice versa, one must wonder whether the noisy debate is really about drug abuse or rather represents an attempt by critics to manipulate public distrust for political gain.

What specifically do colleges and universities tell their students about drug use? Several institutions cover the major recreational drugs of our culture, alcohol included, in a single policy. Two such policies are included in the appended documents. Davidson's includes a reference to alcohol in its brief statement of drug policy:

> Davidson College, as an institution, expects to operate in accordance with federal and state laws regarding the possession, sale, and consumption of certain drugs. The use of such drugs is potentially disruptive of the community and harmful to the user. The college disapproves of the illegal use of drugs and will not allow itself to become a sanctuary for legal offenders. The college will seek, by education and counseling, (1) to prevent the illegal use of drugs, including alcohol; (2) to prevent harmful legal uses of drugs, including alcohol; and (3) to help students suffering from undesirable effects of the abuse of drugs, including alcohol. Misuse of drugs by any student is grounds for disciplinary action by the college, ranging from warning to indefinite suspension. (Davidson, "Drugs and Alcohol," unpaginated)

This brief statement is followed by a summary of North Carolina liquor laws and an account of the nature and effects of several common drugs, including alcohol.

Several elements of the succinct Davidson policy are found in nearly every other institution's policies regarding illegal drugs: a reference to state law, an emphasis on education to prevent abuse, an offer of counseling and other assistance to those who become dependent, and a firm threat of severe sanctions. If the gray areas surrounding alcohol abuse are largely absent, there remains the difficult tension between firmness in enforcement and concern for student well-being.

Institutions evidently find it difficult to decide whether drug use is a sign of wickedness or sickness. If it is the former, punishment is warranted; if the latter, help and counseling are more appropriate. Colleges characteristically acknowledge that both elements may be present. As an illustration I quote the policy of Illinois Wesleyan, whose no-alcohol policy has already been cited:

> The University has never encouraged or condoned the usage of alcohol and supports the administration of laws regarding the sale and distribution of alcohol and other drugs. It is recognized that the use of any drug can lead to a loss of effectiveness in human life and may result in an individual's dependency on the drug being used. Any misuse of alcohol or drugs should be viewed as a symptom of underlying disorders for which remedies should be sought. In light of this, the faculty and administration of Illinois Wesleyan University intend to provide students an educational program regarding the use, abuse, and consequences of alcohol and other drugs in order that the individual student's choice of

abstaining from or consuming these drugs is a considered one. (Illinois Wesleyan, pp. 49–50)

The intent of the policy is clear, but it is poorly worded. A paragraph that begins by urging abstinence ends, in effect, with a plea to students to use LSD and cocaine only after careful consideration. I am sure this was not the intended meaning.

One difficulty that attends the drafting of drug policies is that of identifying exactly which drugs are intended. Many institutions finesse the issue by referring consistently to "illegal drugs." But this suggests that the institution's concern has no deeper rationale than the requirements of the law. Carleton College draws back even further from judgment on student drug use by setting the boundaries of its concerns far more narrowly than those of the law: "The College affirms the right to take action whenever it has reason to believe that the use, possession, sale, manufacture, or distribution of illegal drugs has an adverse effect upon the life and/or academic performance of students or adversely affects or legally implicates others in the community" (Carleton, p. 18). This is the only reference to drugs in the student handbook, save for a brief mention of education programs available to any student "concerned about areas of alcohol or drug use, abuse, or dependency" (p. 8).

This policy rightly emphasizes the college's primary concern with maintenance of a healthy educational and personal atmosphere on campus, and it is free of moralizing or hypocrisy. But it is surely too permissive: It implies that discreet drug use is of no concern to the college, so long as the user submits assignments on time.

To undertake a catalog of illegal drugs and their effects is a complex and risky task, for involves treading a fine line between two opposed dangers—that of exaggerating the harmful effects of drugs, which may prevent knowledgeable students from taking the policy seriously, and that of providing too neutral a description, which may induce inexperienced students to underestimate the risks of experimentation. One college neatly avoids both dangers thus:

> Calvin College prohibits the possession, use, or distribution of all chemical or biological substances which have the effect of substantially altering the physical, emotional, or mental state of a person, unless such use is prescribed by medical or psychiatric authority for that particular person. To list or even classify such substances would be unnecessarily tedious. The competence of the college may for practical purposes be limited to the campus, but the college's concern extends to the lives of all its students in all places without distinction of age. (Calvin, p. 36)

But in the attempt to be general, Calvin provides the strangest example yet of a policy whose intent is betrayed by its actual wording. The prohibition against all substances that alter the "physical, emotional, or mental state of a person" in effect nullifies the responsibility assigned to students in the policy that immediately precedes it, which charges students with the responsibility to "make responsible choices about whether or not to use alcoholic beverages." Even moderate use of alcohol violates the drug policy just quoted. The prohibition against any substances that substantially affects one's "physical, emotional, or mental state" is worded so inclusively, in fact, that it effectively prohibits drinking coffee. Even eating a meal would appear to be a violation.[25]

Notwithstanding this internal conflict, Calvin's is nearly the only student conduct code, among all those sent to me, that carries the tone of having been written by a real person—a person who is somewhat distant and frequently judgmental, yet keenly aware of the complexities of student life. Other administrators would do well to strive for such a tone, if not to adopt precisely the policies cited.

The ambiguities and conflicting attitudes that surround drinking, and to some degree drug use, suggest that there can finally be no solution to these campus problems simply through the promulgation and enforcement of regulations. Instead, colleges and universities need to concentrate far more on educating students on the hazards of drug and alcohol use and then on providing effective models of responsible behavior, both among students and student organizations and among faculty and staff. "Do as I say, not as I do" is an especially hollow injunction in an area where societal attitudes are confused and inconsistent.

Sexual and Social Mores

We have already surveyed in Chapter 3 the present situation as regards student sexual behavior, employing, albeit with some skepticism, the testimony of the anthropologist in the residence hall. What do institutions have to say about such matters? What is the role of the college or university in regulating the social and sexual life of its students in the last decade of this century?

Among all the student handbooks that I reviewed, not one willingly accepts the mantle of the college's traditional role *in loco parentis*.

None speaks to students in the voice of a concerned parent warning a daughter against the path of looseness, vice, and degradation. Survey responses showed that only six of forty-nine institutions either proscribe or "strongly discourage" sexual relations among unmarried students. Indeed, two-thirds permit students to receive overnight guests of the opposite sex in the residence hall. Surprisingly, it is not always the smaller or more conservative institutions that have such a policy. The institutions that prohibit cohabitation include Yale as well as Saint Olaf, UCLA as well as Dickinson.

The rule, if any, against cohabitation is usually presented without any explicit justification or elaboration, moral or pragmatic. The University of Delaware's policy, repeated twice in the space of a few pages without elaboration in its handbook, has a certain moral undertone: "The University does not condone members of the opposite sex staying overnight in a residence hall" (Delaware, pp. 108, 112). This policy is evidently intended, however, as an application of the general residence-hall policies put forth elsewhere in the handbook, which include these passages:

1. Residence hall regulations are designed to protect individual rights and freedoms. *Students are expected to respect the rights of others and to assert their own rights.* Any time individuals feel their rights are being violated, they are expected to confront, with the assistance of Residence Life staff members when necessary, those individuals who are violating them. . . .

6. The visitation policy provides the opportunity for members of the opposite sex to visit in student rooms. *In exercising visitation privileges, the rights of roommates must not be violated.* Guests must not interfere with the roommate's use of the room. (Delaware, pp. 84–85; italics in original)

What are these rights that he or she is required both to respect and to assert? The handbook nowhere enumerates them or discusses whether upholding one student's rights can ever infringe the rights of others. The goal of residence hall policies is couched entirely in woolly abstractions—"to maximize growth," to create "the most productive" community—that are never translated into terms having a clear meaning.

Fortunately, few students take seriously the university's directive to confront their fellows every time they "feel their rights are being violated"—as if the character of the community hinged solely on their feelings, not on the responsible or irresponsible behavior of others. To live in strict accord with this charge, in the absence of any explicit basis to distinguish my legitimate rights against others' interference from "rights" that I make up for the occasion, would be the very antithesis of the spirit of compromise and cooperation that the university seeks to instill. Even among the minority of institutions that prohibit opposite-sex visitors, none extends its restrictions to same-sex guests. This creates a double standard, it could be argued, by permitting gay and lesbian students a degree of freedom in pursuing romantic relationships that is denied to their heterosexual classmates. In reality this disparity has virtually no effect, for the social sanctions against open avowal of homosexuality on the college campus are severe. Even at Rutgers, a very diverse urban campus, Moffatt observed that a majority of male students and a substantial number of women were intolerant of homosexuality. Several students wrote in their anonymous essays that they did not dare discuss their own homosexuality with fellow students.[26] Other campuses are even less tolerant.

Frequently there are some rules or guidelines regarding "visitation." Delaware's policy, quoted in part above, imposes no University restrictions at all but permits a student option to do so. "All residence halls, apartments, and special interest houses permit visitation on a 24–hour-a-day basis," the handbook states (making it sound as if it would be rude for a visitor to depart before twenty-four hours are up). For coeducational residence halls, that is the end of the matter. But students in the single-sex buildings may choose to establish some limits:

> Students in single-sex halls may call for a vote to restrict the hours or days during which visitation is permitted in their residence hall. If 15 percent of the residents of the building request such a vote, it will be conducted. . . . A simple majority of those who participate in the vote will determine any hour-of-day restrictions. (Delaware, pp. 112–13)

Similar local options are offered elsewhere. The women of Smith are allowed to receive gentleman callers and keep them overnight, but the policy governing the residential "houses" includes this statement:

> The regulations of each house concerning male guests (such as permissible length of stay, bathroom use, procedures to be followed in double rooms and suites, etc.) shall be reviewed by the house members at the beginning of each semester. Establishment of the regulations shall be posted in each house, and a copy should be sent by the house president to the associate dean for student affairs. (Smith, p. 45)

At Wellesley, it is added that "in deciding whether or not a roommate will have a guest, the roommate without the guest will have priority use of the room" (Wellesley, p. 42).

UCLA administrators seem to have had the same end in mind in writing their policy:

> Residents may accommodate overnight guests of only the same sex pending prior arrangements with their roommate or with approval from the Assistant Director/Resident Director. (UCLA, p. 38)

But the actual wording of the policy contains several absurdities. First, there is the reference to guests "of only the same sex." Why hermaphrodites pose a special threat to good order in the UCLA residence halls is not explained. Worse yet, the wording of the policy makes it not just administratively but metaphysically impossible to obey. To offer accommodation "pending prior arrangements," i.e., while awaiting arrangements that have already been made, is logically impossible. The university's philosophy department, long renowned in philosophical logic, should have been asked to proofread.

In an earlier era, restricted visiting hours typically applied only to women's residence halls. The feminist revolution seems to have achieved at least this small victory: So far as I can determine, women's and men's hours at every institution are now precisely the same.

The once-common custom of curfew hours, on the other hand, has disappeared entirely from all forty-nine of the campuses. Residence halls may be locked at a specified hour, but students carry building keys. Westhampton College has instituted an ironic reversal of the long-abandoned social tradition that women should not be seen in society without a male escort: Male visitors to the women's residence halls are required to be "escorted by a female resident of that hall at all times" after the doors are locked at midnight (Westhampton, p. 29). The motivating factor is not social propriety but safety.

Westhampton and its sibling men's college, Richmond College, have precisely the same visiting hours for opposite-sex guests: from 10 A.M. until 2 A.M. daily, extending until 3 A.M. on Friday and Saturday nights. Some other institutions are more restrictive. Saint Anselm, for example, permits "intervisitation"—an archaism that has passed from use elsewhere—only until 12:15 A.M. on weeknights, 1 A.M. on Friday and Saturday, and 6 P.M. on Sunday. Southwestern imposes visiting-hour restrictions only in "freshman halls," not in upperclass residences (Southwestern, p. 32). Unique among the residence-hall codes, Southwestern's handbook describes the difference between a "visitor," whose presence for a brief period is permitted, and a "cohabitant,'' whose presence is not permitted. A visitor crosses over into the latter category when he or she begins ''maintaining clothes or possessions in the room, staying in the room overnight for more than 3 nights, using the amenities of the hall such as the laundry room on a frequent basis'' (Southwestern, p. 32).

The question of visitation policies on any campus is complicated by the virtual impossibility of articulating, let alone enforcing, any campus-wide moral code for social and sexual conduct. Conservatives lament the collapse of a moral consensus that sex belongs only in marriage. Others believe it is not so much our values but our tolerance for hypocrisy that has changed.

Whether it is sin that has become more popular or pretence that has become less so, no dean of students today would presume on the moral support of the campus community for a campaign against premarital sex. Any such effort would elicit hoots of derision not just from students but from faculty and staff colleagues as well. For there exists no consensus on any campus, even the most homogeneous, concerning sexual morality. Every campus includes—among students and in most cases among faculty as well—some traditionalists, some untrammeled hedonists, and many who occupy a middle ground. The numbers who hold to these positions may vary from campus to campus, depending on whether it is located in New York City or rural Iowa and whether students come from one ethnic or religious community or from every corner of society. But even at the most homogeneous of today's college campuses, an attempt to regulate student sexual conduct would quickly provoke philosophical as well as pragmatic opposition.

Equally important, the legal recognition of student rights to privacy blocks any attempt to control essentially private behavior. Recent legal developments have made it clear that, no matter what moral judgments college administrators may hope to instill in students, students' sphere of personal privacy bars intrusive means of enforcement, on campus or off.

The present situation as regards campus discipline is probably an inevitable outcome of changes both on the campus and in the larger society. Unable to call on any moral consensus as a basis for rules regarding sexual relations, institutions choose one of two courses. Most simply impose no limits at all and leave the regulation of social and sexual life to the good counsel of students and their peers. A minority impose some restrictions on the margins, by prohibiting cohabitation or restricting visitation on campus, even though they realize that this may alter the location but will not substantially change the character of students' personal behavior.

There is one exception, among the colleges responding to my request, whose "open house" policy merits quotation at length. Not only does this policy defy the pattern of withdrawal from the control of conduct; it also offers a more explicit and honest rationale than does any other policy.

Open house at Calvin College is intended to serve several purposes. First of all, it provides an opportunity for men and women students to interact with each other by hosting visits in their rooms. Secondly, it provides a setting of increased privacy for those students who use visitation as an extension of a dating situation. While the college recognizes the need for privacy among students who are in the process of developing relationships with members of the opposite sex, it seeks to avoid situations of absolute privacy because of the potential for abuse. For this reason, a regulation of the open house policy is that one's room door remain unlocked and free swinging at all times that guests of the opposite sex are being entertained. The rationale is as follows: The present open door policy provides privacy for students, while at the same time recognizing the temptations which closed door privacy may represent. It seeks to create a setting which encourages responsible and thoughtful relationships between men and women. It also takes realistic account of the fact that some students confuse Christian liberty with sexual license and do not accept the standards of the College on sexual behavior. Calvin College holds to the conviction that premarital intercourse is in conflict with Biblical teaching, and that conduct promoting such intimacy, e.g., nudity, lying in bed together, is unacceptable behavior. (Calvin, residence hall policy, p. 21)

After a summary of the hours during which residence halls may host an open house, a definition of what counts as "open" is added—anticipating student casuistry in interpretation:

The room door is to remain open. To avoid accidental closing, the lock may be turned outward so that the door will remain out of the door frame and will be free swinging. A door blocked by a dresser, bed, or other object is not open. (p. 22)

The uncredited author of this policy must surely be one of the younger members of the student-affairs staff. Only someone whose own student days are fresh in his or her memory would understand the necessity of defining what counts as an open door.

The Calvin policy presumes a shared religious ethos among students and faculty. When I was a student at Calvin twenty years ago, the attitudes of student leaders combined respect for the religious and academic traditions that underlay the restrictions on student conduct, on the one hand, with impatience with the pettiness and hypocrisy that often attended their enforcement, on the other. No doubt this ambivalence remains. All the same, a college that undertakes to explain just what its policy means and why it has been adopted demonstrates more respect for students than does a university that can offer no more than unelaborated and vague platitudes about positive experiences and respect for unstated rights.

Two topics merit a brief note before we leave the topic of social and sexual behavior. The first is the threat of AIDS, mentioned in a few of the student handbooks not as a topic for disciplinary regulation but as an unavoidable element in students' sexual expectations and behavior. There are signs that the prospect of death from a mysterious disease is succeeding, where sermonizing has failed, in reining in the carefree sexual experimentation that prevailed on some campuses a generation ago.

The risk of AIDS is not of direct relevance to our topic, even if in some ways it has taken the place of the puritanical dean of a past era in discouraging sex. Institutions that incorporate a statement regarding AIDS in their student handbooks stress the need for accurate information, the grave health risks that attend any practice through which AIDS can be transmitted, and the institution's commitment to equal treatment of AIDS victims. Because such policies are likely to be adopted at many more campuses in the near future, I include two examples in the supplementary materials—one from Mount Holyoke, the other from Saint Anselm. Both of them add to the forgoing topics a commitment that the college will not require AIDS screening and will preserve complete confidentiality if a student discloses that he or she has AIDS to the college health service.

A second topic demands a longer footnote. If the majority of colleges have withdrawn from any attempt to regulate most aspects of student sexual morality, there remains one specific area in which institutional concern, and measures at control, are greater in extent than ever before: that of sexual harassment. I received copies of sexual harassment policies from a half-dozen campuses, even though I had not specifically asked for them.

Sexual harassment is a problem of campus discipline, not of student conduct, and hence falls outside the scope of this study. Sexual harassment policies seek primarily to prevent and punish inappropriate behavior by faculty and staff members directed either toward junior colleagues or toward students. All the same, because this is a topic within the larger realm of sexual ethics on campus—and because a few survey respondents chided me for omitting it—it is appropriate to take note of a few representative policies.

A brief statement covers the topic in the Williams handbook:

> The term "sexual harassment" covers a broad range of behavior. Even though it is not possible to define the term without ambiguity or to produce a non-controversial list of illustrative cases, the term includes repeated or coercive sexual advances toward another person contrary to his or her wishes. It also includes behavior directed at another person's sexuality with the intent of intimidating, humiliating, or embarrassing the other person.
>
> Sexual harassment, even in its mildest forms, presents unnecessary obstacles to the free and full development of the potential of each individual student. Therefore, it will not be tolerated on the Williams campus. Aggravated cases of sexual harassment are serious offenses which will ordinarily lead to suspension or expulsion of the offender. (Williams, pp. 45–46)

The Williams policy adds that allegations of assault or rape fall into "another sphere altogether," to be dealt with not through formal or informal campus disciplinary procedures but by referral to the police for criminal prosecution.

This statement articulates clearly the basis of the college's concerns over harassment. But because it is couched in such general terms it provides little guidance to someone wondering whether he or she has been the victim of harassment. Furthermore, it makes no reference to the comparative positions of the perpetrator and the victim of harassment. Repeated requests from one's senior thesis adviser to go out on a date would fall into the same category, by this standard, as would similar requests from a classmate. The two instances might be equally annoying, but only the former fits accepted legal and ethical definitions of harassment.

Newly enacted policies at several institutions incorporate the missing distinctions by citing the authority of the perpetrator over the victim—that of chairman over junior colleague or of professor over student, for example—as a defining condition of harassment and by describing several kinds of inappropriate conduct. Columbia's policy begins with a reference to the victim's position of vulnerability, and it adds a word concerning sexual badgering by someone not in a position of authority:

Sexual harassment occurs when someone in a more powerful position attempts to coerce another, less powerful person into unwanted sexual activity, subjects that person to unwanted attention on the basis of sex or sexual preference, or makes that person's learning or working environment intimidating, hostile or offensive through sexual comments, suggestions, or pressures. It can range from coerced sexual relations or physical assault to constant joking or repeated generalized sexist remarks or behavior.

While harassment by "equals" (for example, your class or suitemates) is not considered sexual harassment by strict legal definition of the University's Policy Statement, it, too, is unacceptable within the Columbia community.

The policy goes on to list four specific forms of harassment: coercion into sexual activity by threats of punishment; solicitation of sexual favors through promises of rewards, such as grades or fellowships; inappropriate, offensive behavior such as repeated requests for dates or physical touching, without accompanying offers or threats; and "generalized sexist remarks or behavior" (Columbia, p. 86).

Still another aspect of sexual behavior—one involving interaction among students, not between students and staff—has drawn a great deal of media attention, yet only one of the handbooks sent to me has anything directly to say about it. I refer to the phenomenon of what is variously termed "date rape" or "acquaintance rape," consisting in forced sexual intercourse with a person who has entered willingly into a situation of social companionship but who has not consented to his or her companion's sexual advances.[27] Despite the silence of the published discipline codes, student-affairs administrators are very much aware of the problem, as the narrative comments on the questionnaires show. Most such assaults, they observe, are byproducts of alcohol abuse by one or both parties.

Princeton's harassment policy stands out both in acknowledging this link and in highlighting both similarities and differences between harassment and assault. Its definition of harassment, regrettably, is even more inclusive than is the Williams statement quoted earlier: Princeton prohibits "abusive or harassing behavior, verbal or physical, which demeans, intimidates, threatens or injures another because of his personal characteristics or beliefs," which "include but are not limited to sex, sexual orientation, race, national origin, religion, and handicap" (Princeton, p. 17). Enforced strictly, this would prohibit nearly every joke told on campus.

When the policy comes to specifics, however, it is clear and forceful.

The two major categories of violation of sexual standards are spelled out clearly:

Definition of sexual harassment. Unwelcome sexual advances, requests for sexual favors, and other verbal or physical contact of a sexual nature constitute sexual harassment when:

1. Submission to or rejection of such conduct is made implicitly or explicitly a term or condition of instruction, employment, or participation in other University activity;

2. Submission to or rejection of such conduct by an individual is used as a basis for evaluation in making academic or personnel decisions affecting an individual; or

3. Such verbal or physical conduct has the effect of unreasonably interfering with an individual's work, academic performance, or living conditions by creating an intimidating, hostile, or offensive atmosphere.

Definition of sexual assault. Princeton University defines sexual assault (including but not limited to rape) as committing any of the following acts:

1. Any sexual physical contact that involves the use or threat of force or any other form of coercion or intimidation;

2. Any sexual physical contact with a person who is unable to consent due to incapacity or impairment, mental or physical. "Incapacity" or "impairment" normally includes but is not limited to being asleep or under the influence of alcohol or drugs. (Princeton, p. 18)

Rape, it is added, defined as "sexual assault involving an act of penetration," is considered an "especially serious offense," whether perpetrated by a stranger or by an acquaintance. Any occasion when one person coerces another into sex, however, is a clear violation of the policy against sexual assault.

Growing public awareness of the problems of sexual harassment and date rape, and growing recognition of such problems in the legal system, will doubtless motivate many more campuses to enact policies similar to those just cited. To promulgate such a policy is a relatively easy task. To enforce it, giving the rights both of the victim and of the accused their due, is far more difficult. I will return to the question of enforcement, with particular application to the dilemmas posed by date rape, in later chapters. Meanwhile, this chapter will close with a brief look at one other area that has given rise to much recent debate over student conduct—"hate speech" and racist writing.

Abusive Speech and Writing

In January 1991, Brown University junior Douglas Hann was expelled from the university for violation of its policy against abusive speech and behavior. One evening during the previous semester, his judgment clouded by the effects of the refreshments he had imbibed in celebration of his twenty-first birthday, Mr. Hann had "started shouting antiblack comments involving a common obscenity and the word 'nigger' " while walking through a campus quad, according to an only partially euphemistic account later published in the *New York Times*. When challenged by a student, Mr. Hann had demanded, "Are you a faggot? Are you a Jew?" and continued in a similar vein as a small crowd gathered. When the student whom he thus confronted filed a formal complaint, a campus disciplinary committee found Mr. Hahn guilty of violating several policies, including rules against drunken or disrespectful behavior as well as newly adopted rules against racial, sexual, and ethnic harassment. In response to this incident and to several previous disciplinary infractions involving drinking and disruption, the university imposed the relatively severe sanction of expulsion.[28]

The Brown case quickly became a focus of debate over the legitimacy of institutional regulation of derogatory and abusive speech and writing. The topic had already received national attention on several other campuses. In 1989, for example, a district court in Michigan invalidated the University of Michigan's newly enacted antiharassment policy because its requirements were unacceptably broad and vague. The policy in question prohibited "stigmatizing or victimizing" individuals or groups on basis of race, ethnicity, religion, sex, sexual orientation, creed, national origin, ancestry, age, marital status, handicap or Vietnam-era veteran status. The district court found that enforcement of the policy could violate due process requirements and noted in addition that its application to "verbal conduct" violated students' rights under the First Amendment to the Constitution. Thus, both in its stated requirements and in its actual application, the antiharassment rule was overbroad.[29]

The University of Michigan responded to the ruling by adopting a more narrowly drawn policy against racial and ethnic abuse. A spokesman for the University reported that, where one hundred twenty complaints had been filed under the old policy during the year it was in force, the new policy had been cited in fewer than twenty complaints.[30] At Emory University a code barring sexual and racial denigration adopted in 1988 was cited in only three complaints in two years.[31]

Mindful of the Michigan ruling, the University of Wisconsin adopted a narrower policy that prohibited only slurs and epithets directed against an individual, if based on the individual's race, sex, religion, sexual orientation, disability or ethnic origin. In the fall of 1991, however, a federal district court struck down this code, too, as an infringement of students' First Amendment rights. The Constitution permits regulation of speech only in circumstances that threaten an immediate breach of the peace, the court observed; but the Wisconsin rule includes no such requirement. Furthermore, the court ruled, the prohibition against speech that demeans the listener and creates an intimidating and hostile environment is "unduly vague" because it leaves ambiguous whether it is the actual effect brought about or the speaker's intent that is at issue. In another 1991 case, a Virginia court overturned the suspension of a fraternity at George Mason University for holding an "ugly woman" contest in which a white man dressed in a black face and wore women's clothing. Minority students present in the cafeteria where the skit took place had complained to university officials, who took disciplinary action. But the court found that even such a patently offensive performance "contained more than a kernel of expression" and therefore "demands First Amendment protection."[32]

The topic of hate speech will be the subject of a forthcoming volume in this series. Therefore, although a brief discussion is essential in the present survey of discipline codes, readers who are seeking a full account of the legal and social aspects of such controls should turn to the forthcoming study.

I have opened this quick look at speech codes by referring to recent legal developments because this is the only area of student conduct in which the very authority of the university to impose controls is in dispute in the courts. Disagreement over the propriety of such policies is evident on the campuses and off. Some argue that the attempt to control such behavior represents an unnecessary and ultimately ineffectual attempt to shield students from offensive but harmless behavior. Others, although generally sympathetic to the university's desire to prevent ethnic and racial abuse, nevertheless fear the potentially chilling effect of antibias policies on the free discussion of political and ideological views. The director of the Rhode Island chapter of the American Civil Liberties Union, for example, opposed Brown's policies because he found them "so broad and vague that they provide no guidance whatsoever in attempting to distinguish between speech and conduct."[33]

I received copies of policies governing discrimatory or abusive speech and writing, or a closely related area, from about ten of the institutions responding to the survey. I also received a copy of Yale University's formal statement of why it has no such policy, which states:

We take a chance, as the First Amendment takes a chance, when we commit ourselves to the idea that the results of free expression are to the general benefit in the long run, however unpleasant they may appear at the time. The validity of such a belief cannot be demonstrated conclusively. It is a belief of recent historical development, even within universities, one embodied in American constitutional doctrine but not widely shared outside the academic world, and denied in theory and in practice by much of the world most of the time. . . .
No member of the university with a decent respect for others should use, or encourage others to use, slurs and epithets intended to discredit another's race, ethnic group, religion, or sex. It may sometimes be necessary in a university for civility and mutual respect to be superseded by the need to guarantee free expression. (Yale, pp. 10–11)

The civil libertarian stance defended in this report expresses eloquently the reasons why organizations such as the ACLU have consistently opposed any restrictions on abusive speech on campus.

Yet a growing number of institutions, in response both to incidents of campus bigotry and to faculty and student demands, have instituted policies that proscribe some forms of speech. Civility and mutual respect, these institutions implicitly argue, are not secondary values but are to be ranked alongside freedom of expression.

How can one reconcile the competing demands of freedom in expressing offensive viewpoints and freedom of minorities from abuse and harassment? The president of Brown University, Vartan Gregorian, insists that his university has enacted no limits whatever on freedom of speech but merely bans abusive or demeaning behavior.[34] But this distinction cannot stand close scrutiny. For speech is itself a human action, a form of behavior, as the philosopher J. L. Austin has reminded us.

To speak certain words in the appropriate context—"I pronounce you husband and wife" or "Your sentence is commuted," for example—is to perform an action with far-reaching consequences.[35] Words are actions, whether the action be simple assertion, dissent from another's statement, creation of a marriage, or commutation of a sentence. There are a great many things that can be accomplished using spoken words, and not all of them fall properly within the scope of the protected category of free speech.

If I say to another man, "Your mother is a half-breed whore," and he punches me, it would be disingenuous of me to claim that I was merely making what I judged to be a correct factual statement. Nor could I plausibly charge my assailant with undermining my constitutional rights to free speech. In speaking these words, I act in an offensive way that is calculated to provoke anger.

Because speech can be action, and action like speech can convey threats and insults, it is not possible to prohibit discriminatory acts while giving speech free rein. Among the few institutions that have attempted to formulate rules for campus civility, two alternative paths can be discerned. Some seek to promulgate a broad prohibition against either words or acts that denigrate and debase others on a racial or religious basis. Others frame their prohibitions more narrowly, proscribing only a few specified kinds of abuse.

Among the former, a policy newly adopted by Carleton College in 1990 can serve as a model, and it is reproduced in full in the appended materials. The policy begins by invoking the college's commitment to "the principle of free expression and exploration of ideas in an atmosphere of civility and mutual respect" (Carleton, p. 21). Against this background, the college states, "the presentation of a reasoned or evidenced claim about a societal group that offends members of that group is to be distinguished from a gratuitous denigrating claim about, or addressed to, an individual or group." Only behavior of the latter sort is prohibited, and only if its effect is to "demean, degrade, or victimize in a discriminatory manner."

Carleton's policy is commendable for its forthright statement of the competing values that govern the issue of abusive speech. Yet it places a very large burden of discretion on administrators and committees charged with enforcing the policy and imposing sanctions. Such a policy may have a salutary effect on the campus atmosphere if it is taken seriously and discussed widely. Indeed, the last paragraph of the policy calls for just such a discussion, mandating distribution to all faculty, students, and staff each year. But as a basis for actual sanctions it is so open-ended as to invite the very claims of vagueness and arbitrariness that have caused other policies to be invalidated by the courts.

Worries about such vagueness have motivated a few institutions to take the other alternative: to prohibit only specific sorts of clearly bigoted action, drawing the lines narrowly so as to avoid ambiguity even at the cost of tolerating much of the behavior that causes the greatest offense. A 1990 policy statement adopted by Stanford provides an example. Its intent is "to clarify the point at which protected free expression ends and prohibited discriminatory harassment begins," and its key clauses state:

> Prohibited harassment includes discriminatory intimidation by threats of violence, and also includes personal vilification of students on the basis of their sex, race, color, handicap, religion, sexual orientation, or national and ethnic origin.
> Speech or other expression constitutes harassment by personal vilification if it
> (a) is intended to insult or stigmatize an individual or a small number of individuals on the basis of their sex, race, color, handicap, religion, sexual orientation, or national and ethnic origin; and
> (b) is addressed directly to the individual or individuals whom it insults or stigmatizes; and
> (c) makes use of insulting or "fighting" words or non-verbal symbols.
> In the context of discriminatory harassment by personal vilification, insulting or "fighting" words are those "which by their very utterance inflict injury or tend to incite to an immediate breach of the peace," *and which are commonly understood to convey direct and visceral hatred or contempt for human beings on the basis of their sex, race, color, handicap, religion, sexual orientation, or national and ethnic origin.* (Stanford, pp. 5–6, italics added)

The last explanatory phrase is crucial. An appended rationale for the policy points out that the Supreme Court has exempted "insulting or 'fighting' words" from free-speech protection.[36]

The policy prohibits only "use of gutter epithets and symbols of bigotry: those words, pictures, etc., that are commonly understood as assaultive insults whenever they are seriously directed against members of groups subject to pervasive discrimination" (p. 21). It is not enough that members of the group themselves judge certain words or symbols offensive. They must "also be so understood across society as a whole before they meet the proposed definition." The drafters of the policy acknowledge:

> Making the prohibition so narrow leaves some very hurtful forms of discriminatory verbal abuse unprohibited. Substantively, this restriction is meant to ensure that no *idea* as such is proscribed. There is no view, however racist, sexist, homophobic, or blasphemous it may be in content, which cannot be expressed, so long as those who hold such views do not use the gutter epithets or their equivalent. Procedurally, the point of the restriction is to give clear notice of what the offense is, and to avoid politically charged debates over the meaning of debatable words and symbols in the context of disciplinary proceedings. (Stanford, p. 22)

This policy provides a useful model of a code of conduct that is clear in its requirements, carefully targeted against the most offensive forms of abuse and verbal harassment, and persuasively grounded in a larger statement of individual responsibilities. Furthermore, it provides a counterexample to the worries of civil libertarians that every attempt to control offensive speech will inevitably trample on legitimate rights to free expression of personal and political views. When drawn as narrowly and precisely as in this policy, the prohibition of abusive speech can leave more than enough room for every kind of desirable political debate—and for a great deal that is undesirable as well—while drawing the line at speech that excludes minority groups from the campus, and indeed the human, community.

This policy appears to remedy the deficiencies that have caused the Michigan and Wisconsin codes to be invalidated in the courts. It imposes only the most minimal sorts of restraint on the expression of anyone's political or racial views, so that there would appear to be little serious conflict with First Amendment rights. Moreover, its requirements are stated clearly and unambiguously. Still, given the high priority that the courts have placed on free-speech rights, it is possible that even such a narrowly drawn policy will eventually be ruled unconstitutional. If Stanford's policy should meet the same fate as Michigan's and Wisconsin's, it is hard to imagine what sort of policy could fare better. Universities would then do well to abandon the task of controlling abusive speech and writing through disciplinary rules.

Several institutions that have enacted disciplinary rules against abusive speech report that they are seldom, if ever, actually applied. At Kalamazoo College, for example, an antiharassment policy adopted in 1989 has not been used once, in the first three years that it has been in effect, to discipline a student. Nor have any cases been brought under the rule adopted in 1990 at the University of Arizona. Administrators at Eastern Michigan University told a reporter of one case arising under its policy; at UCLA there have been two.[37] These reports corroborate the results of the survey summarized in Chapter 3: seventy-one percent of responding institutions reported having had no discipline cases involving hate speech in the past year, and only four percent reported more than five such cases.

No doubt part of the reason for the small number of cases can be traced to institutions' fear that their rules, too, will be challenged successfully in court. Then, too, rules such as these may have been intended from the outset not so much as policies for disciplinary enforcement but as symbolic statements. This is a legitimate role for rules of conduct, but failure ever actually to enforce hate-speech rules is likely before long to undermine their credibility.

The last paragraph of Stanford's explanatory statement could serve as a useful introduction to disciplinary policies on any of a number of topics.

> In general, the disciplinary requirements that form the content of the Fundamental Standard are not meant to be a comprehensive account of good citizenship within the Stanford community. They are meant only to set a floor of minimum requirements of respect for the rights of others, requirements that can be reasonably and fairly enforced through the disciplinary process. The Stanford community should expect much more of itself by way of tolerance, diversity, free inquiry and the pursuit of equal educational opportunity than can possibly be guaranteed by any set of disciplinary rules. (p. 22)

These words provide an eloquent conclusion to our review of the specific provisions of student conduct rules at colleges and universities across the country.

It is time now to turn from what is to what might be. In the following chapters I propose several goals that ought to govern student conduct rules, and I sketch several alternative models for achieving these goals.

Notes

1. Thus I am unfortunately unable to cite any of the policies enumerated, for example, in the handsomely printed booklet entitled, "Student Conduct Code: Greivance [*sic*] and Appeals Procedure of the Evergreen State College."

2. A list of the responding institutions can be found in Appendix C, together with the text of the questionnaire and a tabulation of responses.

3. Citations to disciplinary handbooks are made in abbreviated form in parentheses in the text: I cite only the name of the institution, together with an abbreviated title when needed, and a page number. A complete list of the college handbooks cited is included in the bibliography in Appendix D.

4. Perhaps the linguistics department could support this by showing that, contrary to appearances, the term "kitchenette" has nothing to do with kitchens but is derived from some other term entirely—a corruption, say, of a German aphorism, "Kitsch ist nett."

5. "Scandal Over Cheating at M.I.T. Stirs Debate Over Limits of Teamwork," *New York Times*, May 22, 1991, p. A23.

6. Not all respondents who sent me discipline codes included their statements regarding plagiarism and academic honesty, perhaps because the em-

phasis in the questionnaire itself on other matters of student conduct suggested that this was not within the scope of my study.

7. The handbook does precede the plagiarism definition with the statement, "The following is published to provide basic information on the subject. First, there is reproduced a definition of plagiarism which, by furnishing examples, illustrates the improper use of source material" (Duke, p. 62). So the lengthy account is described as "reproduced." But from what sources? From an earlier handbook? From other university documents? From an independent source? No indication is given, and no source is cited anywhere.

8. The handbook is Harold C. Martin, Richard M. Ohmann, and James M. Wheatly, *The Logic and Rhetoric of Exposition*, 3rd ed. (New York: Rinehart and Winston, 1969). Further reading produced still another complication. The Wellesley handbook quotes precisely the same few pages, save for a few evidently original typographical and grammatical errors, but identifies the quote as the work of all three of the authors, citing not the third edition cited by Wesleyan but the first, copyrighted six years earlier. Of the three handbooks, only Wellesley's includes a copyright notice and acknowledges that reprint permission has been granted (Wellesley, pp. 89–91).

9. An apparent exception was *Valentine v. Ind. School Dist.*, 101 Iowa 1100, 183 N.W. 434 (1921), where a court required a high school to grant diplomas to three women students who had been barred from participating in graduation ceremonies. But what offended the Iowa court was precisely the use of academic sanctions to punish non-academic offenses, and the case is therefore not an exception after all.

10. See Aims McGuinness, "The Great Rebellion of 1807," *Princeton Alumni Weekly* 91(14):8–12 (April 17, 1991). The quotation from the broadside is not in the text of the article; I have transcribed it as best I can from an accompanying, barely legible reproduction of its first page.

11. Troy (N.Y.) *Gazette*; quoted in McGuinness 1991, p. 12.

12. *New York Times*, January 26, 1992, p. A54.

13. Thomas Arkle Clark, "College Discipline," in Fulton 1926, pp. 374–80, at 374–75.

14. David Starr Jordan, "College Spirit," in Fulton 1926, pp. 400–409, at 401–2.

15. "Ban on Keg Beer Being Pulled Back But With Limits," *New York Times*, January 26, 1992, p. A35.

16. "New Rules Lead Some Drinkers to Go Off Campus," *New York Times*, February 10, 1991, p. I:41.

17. "Ban on Kegs Opposed by Those of Drinking Age," *New York Times*, April 28, 1991, p. I:41.

18. Smith also adds a puzzling rule that I encountered nowhere else: "No kegs of any type may be above the first floor of Smith houses." Are there no public areas above the first floor, or is the reason for this peculiar rule that the houses' staircases are negotiable only when sober but pose a life-threatening

hazard to the inebriated? Without inspecting the campus I dare not hazard a guess.

19. A footnote explains that this term "refers to so-called 'half-kegs,' " the kind of kegs evidently most widely used at student parties.

20. I have removed from this quotation the setting of several sentences entirely in upper-case letters, which lends a certain air of unnecessary hysteria.

21. Courtney Leatherman, "College Officials Are Split on Alcohol Policies," *Chronicle of Higher Education*, January 31, 1990, pp. A33, A35.

22. "Alcohol on Campus Assailed," *Philadelphia Inquirer*, February 11, 1992, pp. B1, B2.

23. "Stanford Faces Sanction in Drug Dispute," *New York Times*, April 23, 1991, p. A8.

24. "Threatened with Loss of U.S. Funds, Stanford Suspends Instructor in Drug Case," *Chronicle of Higher Education*, May 1, 1991, p. A1.

25. This point was brought to my attention by my thirteen-year-old daughter when I read the policy to her. I know from my experiences as a Calvin alumnus and temporary faculty member that the consumption of several daily cups of coffee is nearly a sacramental obligation in the Dutch American community in which Calvin is rooted, and I doubt that the students and faculty have any notion that they are violating college policy when they consume a substance that demonstrably alters their physical and mental state.

26. The residents of one floor, Moffatt writes, "were so liberal that a gay male had come out among them without much grief, something that both gay and straight students at Rutgers agreed hardly ever happened in the Rutgers dorms" (p. 175 n. 22).

27. The victim of such an offense may be either male or female, although discussion of the issue in the popular media has tended to consider only heterosexual rape.

28. "Student at Brown is Expelled Under a Rule Barring 'Hate Speech,' " *New York Times*, February 12, 1991, p. A17; Anthony DePalma, "Battling Bias, Campuses Face Free Speech Fight," *New York Times*, February 20, 1991, p. B9. Some details of the case are mentioned in Chapter 1, n. 1.

29. *Doe v. University of Michigan*, 721 F. Supp. 852 (E.D.Mich. 1989).

30. DePalma, "Battling Bias."

31. DePalma, "Battling Bias."

32. Anthony DePalma, "U.S. Judge Upholds Speech on Campus," *New York Times*, August 25, 1991, p. A25.

33. DePalma, "Battling Bias."

34. DePalma, "Battling Bias."

35. DePalma, "Battling Bias."

36. J. L. Austin 1962.

37. Fighting words are "those which by their very utterance inflict injury or

tend to incite an immediate breach of the peace," 315 U.S. 568, 572. See Gifis 1984, s.v. "Fighting Words."

38. "Campus Codes that Ban Hate Speech Are Rarely Used to Penalize Students," *Chronicle of Higher Education*, February 12, 1992, p. A36.

Chapter 5

The Goals of Student-Life Policies

In preceding chapters we have reviewed the rules and procedures by which institutions seek to regulate student conduct. In some areas, such as abusive speech, we found these policies to vary widely. Some institutions have adopted lengthy and detailed guidelines, accompanied by extended explanations of their purpose and by the threat of severe sanctions. Others have no stated policy at all, or include in their discipline codes an explanation that the institution has made a deliberate decision not to prohibit certain categories of conduct such as hate speech. Alcohol policies also differ somewhat from campus to campus. All seek to discourage irresponsible drinking, but the rules range from a blanket prohibition of alcohol on campus to rules that prohibit only flagrant excess.

In other areas, different institutions use different means to essentially the same end. Both the spirit and the procedures involved in a student-oriented honor code differ from those of a more conventional academic dishonesty policy, for example. Institutions that have chosen either course tend to have requirements and procedures similar to those of others in the same group. Thus the honor-code model often brings with it greater student involvement in its enforcement, an expectation that students will report violations, and a somewhat more traditional tone. Yet both models seek essentially the same end—so much so that the statement of purpose that prefaces the plagiarism policy at one institution could be slipped into the student handbook of another without creating any noticeable incongruity. On matters of plagiarism, too, campus policies differ in their level of detail and their specific prohibitions, but all are directed to the same end.

115

In still other areas of conduct, most notably that of drug policy, the policies on all campuses are almost entirely interchangeable. Unanimous prohibition is the rule, dictated both by concern for student welfare and by recent federal pressures.

Our review of formally stated policies and the procedures set forth for their enforcement tells us very little, as yet, about the rigor or laxness with which these policies are enforced on each campus. Is the atmosphere on campus loose or strict, permissive or restrictive? What attitude toward the rules do residence hall supervisors and deans communicate through their actions—one of strict regard for rules, or one of tolerance and even admiration toward those who evade them? Do they more nearly emulate a strict but supportive coach, on the one hand, or a permissive and ineffectual substitute teacher, on the other?

To assess the actual functioning of disciplinary rules on a campus is an undertaking fraught with traps for the unwary and the naive. Every party that is in a position to provide information—administrator, faculty member, student, member of the surrounding community—is also susceptible to strong incentives to skew the picture in one way or another. To arrive at any reliable generalization concerning the effectiveness of enforcement and the overall disciplinary atmosphere on fifty campuses would pose extraordinary difficulties both of data gathering and of interpretation.

No doubt on every campus a great many violations of college policy escape detection and punishment. Every campus is likely to have, on a given day, a few unauthorized guests staying overnight, a number of substandard extension cords in use, and a few illegal dimmer switches installed. Nor can even the strictest alcohol policy prevent all excessive drinking at weekend parties. In any case, greater recognition of student rights to privacy has curtailed intrusive measures to enforce rules against cohabitation and drinking in the room, where such rules are still on the books.

Yet the responses to the survey summarized in Chapter 3 indicate that rules of student conduct are not mere bluff or sheer hypocrisy. They are evidently the basis for regular disciplinary action. Ninety-three percent of the campuses disciplined at least one student for plagiarism offenses in 1989–90, and a large majority also disciplined students for drug and alcohol violations. Sixty-one percent punished ten or more students for alcohol violations. The policies in these areas, at least, can be seen by students to be more than mere show.

What Counts as Success?

What we want to know is not how many students were punished for drinking but rather—a much larger question—whether campus rules are, on the whole, effective. Before we can even attempt an answer, we must pose a prior question: "Effective at what task?" We cannot judge success or failure, except in the narrowest way, until we have a clear notion of the ends that these policies are intended to achieve.

The first place we might turn to answer the question of goals is, once again, the student handbook, and in particular to its preamble or summary. Recall, for example, the "Fundamental Standard" according to which Stanford students "are expected to show both within and without the University such respect for order, morality, personal honor, and the rights of others as is demanded of good citizens" (Stanford, p. 4). In a similar vein, the University of North Carolina code of student conduct places on every student the responsibility "to conduct oneself so as not to impair significantly the welfare or the educational opportunities of others in the University community" (University of North Carolina, p. 5).

Such broad statements help set the background for more specific provisions, but they are so inclusive in their language that it is extremely difficult to assess whether an institution and its students have fulfilled them. We need to translate generalities into more specific characteristics of the campus before we can begin to assess success or failure.

Mindful of the extraordinary difficulty of documenting the achievement of goals as lofty as "respect for order, morality, and personal honor," other institutions prefer to formulate the goals of student-conduct policies on a more concrete level. Some of the student handbooks state the goal of the disciplinary system, for example, as ensuring that every complaint receives a fair hearing and that every proven offense leads to an appropriate sanction.

Concrete goals such as these, however, are far too easily, and trivially, satisfied. What is intended, no doubt, is that there should be a thorough and fair system for the enforcement of rules. But the goal of giving every complainant a fair hearing would equally be achieved by a campus atmosphere so anarchic, and a discipline system so hobbled by inefficiency, that no one saw any point in registering a complaint. Moreover, to formulate the goal of campus discipline in these terms speaks only to questions of procedure and not to the overall effect of the discipline system on the campus atmosphere as a whole. Nor does such a procedural goal offer any help in deciding, for example, whether areas of conduct such as cohabitation and abusive speech ought to be included in the scope of student rules.

What should be the goals of institutional regulation of student conduct? We need some set of standards that is more specific than a vague and inspirational statement about mutual responsibility that suggests no observable measures of success or failure. The goals must also be more inclusive than the merely procedural. Ideally they should provide a benchmark against which to judge the entire system of student conduct regulation on a particular campus.

We should not expect to be able to arrive at one set of goals that will fit every campus. Surely one of the lessons to be drawn from the variety of different rules we have reviewed is that student conduct codes must reflect particular circumstances of geography, tradition, and student background. Rules for residence-hall visitation at Columbia in Manhattan must be far more attuned to security considerations than they need be for Carleton in a small Minnesota town or Berea in rural Kentucky. Factors other than geography are of equal importance. Where an honor code has been developed and nurtured over the course of several decades, it exerts a strong influence and may become almost self-enforcing. But where such a code is absent, or has been newly introduced, procedures for dealing with dishonesty require explicit and frequent dissemination.

Even though rules and procedures must reflect local circumstances, the rules may still serve many of the same ends. In this chapter I will argue that such a common ground does exist, and that overall goals can be articulated in a way that is broad enough to transcend different implementations but specific enough to offer a basis for assessing success.

There are three distinct goals, I propose, that a system of campus discipline seeks to achieve. They are related but separable both in analysis and in practice. It is possible to place so much weight on one that others are neglected. Yet they are by no means exclusive, and measures that seek to achieve one of the three can contribute to the attainment of the others as well. I separate them in my exposition, accordingly, but I do not intend to suggest that they need be pursued separately.

To prevent exploitation and harm

The first goal is *to prevent exploitation of and harm to students*. The system of student discipline should protect students so far as is reasonably possible from others who would prey on their vulnerability if given the opportunity. Hence the necessity of policies prohibiting theft, physical violence, sexual assault, verbal harassment and denigration, and the sale of mind-altering drugs. Academic dishonesty is also a form of exploitation. By enacting and enforcing such policies, the college should seek so far as possible to protect students against others' malevolent acts. What moral ground justifies the college's concern with prevention of harm? Simply the obligation of every individual to assist in protecting another from injury, especially in circumstances in which the other is particularly vulnerable to harm that could be averted by one's own actions. This basic obligation to prevent harm to others is recognized by every ethical system, whether it posits the ultimate ground of this precept in a Kantian theory of duty, in an Aristotelian concept of character, or in a morality of consequences.

Those who govern an institution such as a university carry into their official capacity the same duty to protect others that they have as individuals. Their capacity to set policies and practices enlarges the consequences of their acts and hence their responsibility. A carefully framed and scrupulously enforced policy regarding assault may deter dozens of attacks that would have occurred in an atmosphere of laxness and inattention.

The primary concern of such rules of conduct is to prevent harm done by fellow students. The reason is not that students are more likely than outsiders to do harm. Indeed, they are less likely to injure each other than are any random collection of strangers, because their shared status as students contributes to a sense of common purpose. Only students, however, are directly subject to the institutional code. The institution can apply a range of sanctions to students to prevent them from harming others and punish them if they do. Its authority over outsiders is more limited.

Harm of the sort that is already subject to criminal prosecution, such as rape, physical assault, theft, embezzlement, and the like, is not the primary concern of the disciplinary code. All the same, a college can seek to prevent such acts in a variety of ways, many of them having nothing to do with codes of conduct. The prevention of theft and violent crime should be a criterion in building design, campus lighting and landscaping, student transportation options, and the practices of campus security officers. Administrators should also cooperate in every way possible with local police in preventing and punishing violent crimes.

But the problem of violent crime is not unique to the campus, and the means available in the student disciplinary system are not an adequate substitute for legal means of deterrence and punishment. On becoming a student, a young man or woman gains no immunity from criminal law and surrenders none of the protections of the civil community against crime. The institution may augment but should not to seek to replace these protections.

On becoming a student, however, a young person does become especially vulnerable to other sorts of harm that may fall outside—or just at the borders of—the criminal law. The possibility that one's work will be stolen and used dishonestly by others, for example, is an unavoidable byproduct of any academic program. Another example is the phenomenon of "acquaintance rape." Its incidence is by no means limited to the campus. But the close personal relationships and powerful peer pressures that obtain at college, together with the ready availability of alcohol, increase the dangers of such assault. In neither case are legal remedies readily available. Copyright violation can be prosecuted, to be sure, but it would be absurd to deal with every case of cheating on a midterm by lodging legal charges. Criminal penalties for rape are severe, but the nature of acquaintance rape makes it difficult for the victim to press charges and easy for the guilty to escape punishment.

The institution ought therefore to take special measures to prevent both cheating and acquaintance rape, as these are harms that are typically imposed by one student on another and for which there is little likelihood of legal redress. The same can be said concerning the institution's special responsibility to prevent the abuse of alcohol and drugs. Such abuse is common enough off campus as well, but the intense social pressures of the campus need to be balanced by firm campus rules and consistent penalties.

The aim of averting harm is to a certain extent paternalistic, and in this limited sense the old ideal of the institution as standing *in loco parentis* needs to be upheld. The college cannot put itself forward any longer as a censorious moral arbiter, an institutional chaperone holding the young men and women in its charge on the path of virtue. With rare exceptions, institutions do not want to resume this role, and in any case students will not stand for it. But the college's concern is not limited to protecting students against others. It extends also to protection of students against themselves.

The harm done by drug use and excessive drinking is done principally by the individual to himself or herself, not inflicted on another. It is nonetheless serious, and nonetheless a legitimate concern of the university. This is so not merely because it is likely to contribute to other, graver harms—to physical injury, subsequent disability, and sexual assault, for example. The diminished capacity for academic work and for responsible behavior that results from such substance abuse is itself a harm that the institution ought to seek to prevent.[1] An institution places itself in a position very much like that of a parent in saying to students: We seek to protect you from grave harm, even when you would suffer it willingly. To do so is to prevent students from acting in a way that amounts to an assault against themselves and their future prospects.

So much for the prevention of harm. To rest with this first goal alone would be to mistake the function of the entire system of student discipline with that of a campus police force. Colleges and universities also pursue two further goals of comparable importance to the whole institution.

To promote an atmosphere of free discussion

A second goal of student conduct rules is *to promote an atmosphere conducive to free discussion and learning.* The campus is not merely a place where students can go about their business relatively free from fear of assault and exploitation. It is also characterized by the free and open exchange of ideas, arguments, and ideologies, a place where vigorous debate flourishes and ruling orthodoxies are regularly confronted by new evidence and by new interpretations. The campus is dedicated to the ideal of the open mind, the readiness to subject even one's most cherished beliefs and ideals to challenge and possible revision.

The moral ground for this second purpose is distinct from that underlying the first, but it is a principle equally widely cherished: A good society is one that grants its members as broad a range of personal and political freedom as is consistent with the rights and liberties of others. Similar ideals of religious and intellectual freedom motivated the founding of the United States, but they have frequently been compromised by the pressures of social conformity and jingoistic nationalism. The universities have from their inception held themselves up as beacons to the broader vision of freedom. But even on campus there is a constant struggle between the principle of free discourse and the tendency of institutions to adopt and enforce an official ideology.

This point has been made repeatedly and stridently by the cultural critics on the political right, who decry what they judge to be a stultifying atmosphere of intellectual orthodoxy on the nation's campuses in which students are force-fed doctrinaire Marxism and feminism. Because their complaints involve several aspects of the student disciplinary system, from residence-hall visitation to speech codes, a brief digression to examine some of their criticisms is appropriate.

One prominent critic, Dinesh D'Souza, cites several anecdotes concerning dubious accusations of racism and sexism as evidence of a "new hooliganism of the left" that punishes any dissent from "the governing taboos" on race and gender with systematic intimidation and harassment.[2] He quotes approvingly the remarks of Yale dean Donald Kagan:

> There is an imposed conformity of opinion. It takes real courage to oppose the orthodoxies. To tell you the truth, I was a student during the days of Joseph McCarthy, and there is less freedom now than there was then.[3]

The last claim seems absurd on its face, for the alleged intimidation tactics of the so-called "thought police" on campus, such as interrupting classes and guest lectures and filing complaints with the dean, hardly bear comparison with the inquisitorial tactics employed by zealous anti-Communists in the 1950s. Although McCarthyism made Hollywood its special target, destroying the careers of many gifted actors and directors, it did not spare the universities.[4]

An essay by a Colby College government professor, G. Calvin Mackenzie, offers a useful corrective to the charges of ideological dictatorship.

> The critics who coined the term political correctness see it as a set of invidious trends in which fad brushes aside tradition. The problem is that save in exceptional and transitory cases, the picture that critics paint bears little resemblance to life on contemporary college campuses. Some outrages have certainly occurred in the name of political correctness, but if you've been paying attention, you'll note that the same handful of examples are cited over and over again.

The conservative critics, Mackenzie observes, greatly underestimate the capacity of today's students for independent thought and the difficulty of inducing them to adopt a professor's viewpoint on any important issue, because "students generally are a hard sell" whose "skepticism is well honed" and whose "views on most political and social issues are well formed by the time they arrive at college." Moreover, college faculties are anything but homogeneously liberal, representing instead a broad range of intellectual commitments and political ideals.⁵

The vision of the nation's campuses cowering for fear of giving offense to feminists and Marxists is no more than a fantasy. The vast majority of all faculty members at the vast majority of institutions are centrist in their politics and traditional in their modes of teaching and research. A recent survey of more than thirty-five thousand faculty members on nearly four hundred campuses, for example, found that forty percent described themselves as "moderate" in their political views, more than chose either "liberal" (thirty-seven percent) or "conservative" (eighteen percent). Fewer than thirty percent indicated that, on their campuses, many courses include feminist perspectives. Asked to identify what priorities ranked high at their institutions, only twenty-one percent cited "helping students learn to bring about change in American society." A larger proportion, but still fewer than half, chose "increasing the representation of minorities in the faculty and administration." More than half cited "maintaining a campus climate where differences of opinion can be aired openly."⁶

Even if the sweeping claims of conservative critics are ungrounded, they may serve all the same to focus attention on potential threats to free and open discourse on campus. On every campus some factions seek from time to time to silence others. The danger that a reigning orthodoxy will stifle dissent is never wholly absent. Any claim that a particular party line has gained the ascendancy on campus—whether of the left or the right, whether Marxism or libertarianism—should provoke our skepticism. Yet the atmosphere of openness that is essential to the educational mission of colleges and universities is a rare and fragile thing, and vigilance is needed to prevent its erosion.

In totalitarian societies the universities have often functioned as oases of free discourse amid seemingly irresistible political pressures. Sometimes this role has placed them in the forefront of revolutionary change, as in several countries of Eastern and Central Europe in the cataclysmic events of 1989. On other occasions it has provoked retaliation, as when the Israeli military occupation forces closed most of the universities of the West Bank for more than four years in response to the political uprising that began in late 1987.

In American society, the universities have frequently served to remind other institutions of the ideals of freedom and inquiry that underlay the creation of the United States. When the homogenizing tendencies of mass media and television politics tend to obscure all but the safest middle-of-the-road viewpoints, it is often left to members of college and university faculties to articulate a vision of the future that cannot find a network sponsor. At no time in recent history has this function been clearer than during the Persian Gulf War—a war that, to judge from the coverage provided in broadcast media, was more popular, and raised fewer moral problems, than the *Cosby Show*. Among the few who questioned the wisdom of rushing to arms in the fall of 1990, faculty members and students were prominent. Defenders of the air war and the later ground war against Iraq were numerous among both students and faculty, to be sure, but other voices were regularly heard as well. In few places other than the nation's campuses was it possible to find honest and public debate over the wisdom of the war as it was being waged. If the debate at times strained civility, it also demonstrated once again the value of the unique atmosphere of free discussion to which colleges and universities are dedicated.[7]

Recent events involving two faculty members at City College, part of the City University of New York, have further illuminated the difficulty of balancing the ideals of fairness to controversial ideas and openness to all individuals and groups. A member of the philosophy faculty, Michael Levin, came under fire in 1990 for a book review and two published letters to editors in which he claimed that the results of standardized intelligence tests provide convincing evidence of racial differences in intelligence.[8] At the same time, his City College colleague, Black Studies chair Leonard Jeffries, was widely criticized for making claims in his classes about the cold and calculating rationality of the northern European races and for public speeches alleging Jewish domination of Hollywood and Jewish responsibility for the slave trade.[9]

Neither man's theories have drawn significant support from colleagues. Levin's position was roundly condemned by his departmental colleagues in a subsequent letter to the editor, and Jeffries' eccentric views have been repudiated by both sociologists and historians. Whether either man's defense of views that are both unpopular and offensive to many ought to be protected as exercises of their right to free speech is a thorny issue. The City College administration believed it had found a way to allay student protests against Levin's racial views by offering his students an opportunity to transfer to sections taught by other instructors. But a federal court ruled that even this minimal discipline, as well as the school's investigation of Levin's fitness to teach on the basis of his racial views, violated the principles of free speech and due process.[10] The court ruled that Levin's "academic freedom has been infringed by administrative interference with his expression of ideas and his class assignments," and that he was "improperly deprived of his Fourteenth Amendment life and liberty interests."[11] The handling of these contrasting cases illustrates the difficulty of the university's dual task. It must ensure a fair hearing for every serious position, modeling for society an ideal of openness and reasoned disagreement. At the same time it is also committed to the principle that no one should be judged on the basis of race or ethnicity.

The aim of preserving freedom mandates broad discretion for students in planning debates, inviting speakers, publishing their opinions in campus newspapers, and the like. Some student codes of conduct emphasize this by including a formal "Bill of Rights" setting out the extent of student freedoms.

The same goal of ensuring an atmosphere of free discourse also justifies institutions' concern with abusive and degrading speech and writing. When policies prohibiting racial and sexual abuse are carelessly written, they cast a pall over discussion of controversial issues and deter open expression of unpopular views. Such policies need to target precisely those rare sorts of abusive speech that have the effect of ruling other members out of the community of discourse by reducing them to less than human status. If their target is thus carefully restricted, the policies themselves contribute to an atmosphere conducive to learning and insight, for they bar the door only to those who by their very choice of words would exclude others on the basis of race, sex, or homosexuality.

The concern for an atmosphere conducive to free discourse and learning is also an important part of the reason why institutions ought to make and enforce rules for student conduct in on-campus housing. Clear rules concerning drinking and cohabitation in residence halls, when fairly and consistently enforced, contribute to an ethos in which students' social and academic lives are closely and effectively intermingled. The absence of such rules, on the other hand—or even laxness in their enforcement—renders residence halls essentially useless for purposes of study, at least in the evening hours, and thus it effectively removes academic work from the center of student social life.

Just what sorts of regulations may be needed depends not only on the character and traditions of the particular institution but also on the architecture of the residence halls. It is not necessary to appeal to either paternalism or moralism to warrant regulation of student life in the residence halls. Such control is necessary to prevent social and academic pursuits from being entirely divorced from each other. It may be necessary, in effect, to invoke old means to a new end. The student deans of a previous generation forbade drinking and cohabitation in the dormitory in their role *in loco parentis.* Such rules have been dropped on most campuses, and their effect is much diminished on the rest. It may be necessary today to impose some of the same restrictions not for moral reasons but because without them the residence halls have become exactly what they are supposed not to be—mere "dormitories," in which serious students can sleep, fitfully, but cannot "reside" as students. To permit this to happen is not merely to withdraw from the moralistic ambitions of an earlier era but to compromise the mission of the university to provide an atmosphere where study and learning flourish.

To nurture a sense of community

A third goal of student conduct regulation is *to nurture a sense of mutual responsibility and moral community in students.* This third aim is both more inclusive and more controversial than the first two. Some would reject it as extending beyond the proper role of a modern university, which ought to stick to education and not pry into the private affairs of students. But to neglect this third purpose, I believe, would be an abdication of one of the critical responsibilities of the college and university in American society.

The formation of character was once upheld as a central purpose, if not the central purpose, of higher education. Thomas Jefferson spoke of the "aristocracy of talent and virtue" that higher education ought to provide to the new United States.[12] In the nineteenth century, President Francis Wayland of Brown University claimed that "The most important end to be secured in the education of the young is moral character."[13] This tradition is honored rhetorically in the preamble to many a college catalog, where the language of character, citizenship, and moral community is laid on with a trowel. Yet today few colleges, and even fewer universities, take their own lofty rhetoric seriously in planning their programs and carrying out their affairs.

The typical college of the eighteenth and nineteenth century made the behavior of students its business and sought to inculcate both moral and religious orthodoxy. The typical college of our own century proclaims its lofty goal of building responsible citizens and nurturing the sense of moral and social accountability only in the first few pages of the catalog, while its actions carry another message entirely. The message of its actual conduct—the reality behind the superficial layer of borrowed rhetoric—might be summarized thus: "We hire excellent scholars for our faculty, maintain a good library, and fill the flower beds for parents' weekend; and we sincerely hope that the students will turn out all right." In the closing sections of this chapter I consider what a more ambitious goal of community might imply.

Derek Bok on Moral Character

Among those who have called on the universities to reclaim the earlier tradition of moral formation, one of the most eloquent is Derek Bok. He reviewed the history of this theme in a series of lectures published in 1990, as he was completing his presidency at Harvard, under the title *The Universities and the Future of America*. "Elaborate codes of conduct were the natural outgrowth of a larger effort to stress the importance of self-control and self-discipline in developing character," Bok observes, adding that in the 1860s the code of student conduct rules for Harvard students was forty pages long.[14] Harvard's president once assigned a grade to every undergraduate, with assistance from the college tutors, on a scale of merit that combined academic achievement with personal behavior.

Noah Porter, Yale's president in the 1870s and 1880s, observed in his inaugural address, "The most efficient of all moral influences in a college are those which proceed from the personal characters of the instructors."[15] During his tenure as president of Princeton, early in this century, Woodrow Wilson was reported to have said that, if the choice were between a scholar and a gentleman for a faculty appointment, he would choose the gentleman without hesitation.[16] At many colleges, from their founding until the beginning of the twentieth century, all seniors were required to take a "capstone" course on moral philosophy, taught in many cases by the president. A visitor once saw posted on the door of Yale president Porter this notice: "At 11:30 on Tuesday Professor Porter will reconcile science and religion."[17]

Such quaint stories are familiar to anyone who has studied the history of American higher education. What is surprising in Bok's account is his call to recover that tradition. American universities underwent radical change, he observes, both because of the importation of new models of scholarship and learning from Europe in the early twentieth century and because of rapid expansion in their size and complexity. The goal of civic education "stood little chance against the rising tide of discipline-based majors and vocationally oriented undergraduate programs."

Bok proposes that the modern university take up once again the task of moral guidance, not only in students' lives but in society. Granted, the moral support for this mission in times past—most crucially, a shared religious and theological commitment—is not present in the modern university, and they cannot now be recreated. Instead, Bok suggests, the universities must build on the underlying values of a diverse and democratic society and seek to instill such values in students. The lack of consensus on many moral issues is not an obstacle to moral education but, on the contrary, itself offers an opportunity for learning.

> Although moral issues sometimes lack convincing answers, that is not necessarily the case. Besides, universities should be the last institutions to discourage a belief in the value of reasoned argument and carefully considered evidence in analyzing even the hardest human problems. And universities should be among the first to affirm the importance of basic norms such as honesty, promise-keeping, free expression, and helping others, for these are not only principles essential to civilized society; they are values on which all learning and discovery ultimately depend. There is nothing odd or inappropriate, therefore, for a university to use them as the foundation for a determined program to help students develop a strong set of moral standards.[18]

Bok argues further that rules for student conduct, standards for the conduct of the institution's own affairs, and hiring policies ought to reflect these basic values.

While Bok's reaffirmation of the moral role of the university deserves support, his proposals are more problematic in application than he acknowledges in these lectures. In the first place, the cardinal virtues that he invokes—"honesty, promise-keeping, free expression, and helping others"—are a mixed lot, mingling qualities of personal character with social duties. Some are directly amenable to institutional regulation and influence, while others must be instilled in students primarily through example and encouragement, not rules and policies.

Bok's prescription for restoring moral education to the university is considerably less persuasive than is his diagnosis. Some of his suggestions are worthwhile in themselves but represent only minor additions to the enterprise of the university as it stands. He recommends development of courses in applied ethics, for example, both in liberal-

arts undergraduate programs and in the context of professional education, and urges that trustees and foundations give greater attention to
moral factors in their decisions regarding the governance and support
of universities. Such changes are desirable, without doubt, but they
will have minimal impact on the experience of most undergraduates.
Thus, eloquent as is his call to fill the ethical gap in education, Bok
fails to bridge the large gulf between the far-reaching goals he articulates and the specific changes he suggests.

Implications of Community

Rather than judge the university's fulfillment of its responsibility by
its success in instilling honesty and benevolence, I suggest that the
third goal of student life policies is better framed in terms of the
character of the campus community that such policies create. Whether
graduating seniors are paragons of moral virtue or cynical opportunists
is a matter largely beyond the control of the institution and its faculty.
Moral character has already been largely shaped before students reach
college, and even during the college years other factors—family, peer
judgments, the mass media, and personal reflection—are likely to
exercise a more profound influence than will any acts or policies of the
institution. The goal of producing moral and sensitive citizens is
simply not realistically attainable, whatever the preface to the catalog
may boast.

All the same, the university can and should seek to create a campus
atmosphere characterized by respect, openness, and mutual recognition of both rights and responsibilities. Students learn quickly, as much
from unspoken signals as from speeches and handbooks, what sort of
behavior is expected on campus. An instructor who tolerates rampant
cheating on the first exam cannot expect better behavior on the rest,
for students will not take his warnings seriously. An institution that
takes no steps to prevent and punish alcohol abuse tells its students
that, whatever the stated rules may be, they are enrolled in a party
school.

Conversely, when cribbing and excessive drinking meet firm and
consistent discipline, students know that they will be held responsible
for their actions and for their academic work. Moreover, the behavior
of administrators and faculty members can communicate far more than
can any set of rules.

When students regularly find their instructors engaging in spirited and open-minded argument with students over moral and social issues, they learn that the institution expects more of students and faculty than the mere transmission of knowledge. When a controversy regarding the campus policies and governance is resolved through close cooperation among students, staff, and faculty, the institution contributes profoundly to the moral education of students—not by informing them of the right answers to moral questions but by modeling the right way to voice and, if possible, to reconcile viewpoints that are initially in sharp conflict.

The dominant political ideology of Western society sees moral choices as fundamentally individual decisions. This ideology has been vital in establishing a broad range of personal and political liberties, and yet it is grossly inadequate as an account of our moral life and action. We make our choices in community, in a social context. Morality is found above all in our stance toward each other. This is the reason that a cooperative response to the challenges that confront a campus community is so vitally important—because the community itself is the context in which morality arises, is articulated, and is put into practice.

Consider a hypothetical example. Suppose a crisis erupts when members of a fraternity taunt and harass gay students, provoking protests by the gay and lesbian student organization and counterprotests by other fraternities. What should be done? Should the students responsible for the original incident of harassment be punished, or is this a situation where students should work out their own differences without interference from the institution?

To let such behavior pass without comment is unsatisfactory, for it suggests that the university approves, or at least finds it unnecessary explicitly to disapprove, of the harassment of gays. But disciplinary action alone, punishing the individuals without addressing what may have led to their behavior, is inadequate as a response.

If the campus community is working as it ought, the result of such a crisis might well be a process of deliberation through which the gay students gain a broader audience for their concerns, the fraternity members have a chance to correct their own problems and look for constructive ways of preventing similar behavior in the future, and everyone on campus learns something about what it is like to find oneself the subject of abuse because of others' insecurities and fears. Moreover, this can be a process in which students, staff, and faculty all participate, each seeking to balance the competing goals of freedom of expression, freedom in personal choices, and mutual understanding among diverse communities. Through such a process students do not simply learn to respect differences and stop shouting insults; they learn what it means to be a member of a moral community.[19]

I am not suggesting that every instance of harassment merits such a full-court response. Context is crucial. An isolated incident on a campus where gay students feel generally accepted might be no cause for alarm or for any public response. At the other extreme, a pattern of repeated and vicious attacks demands a firm disciplinary response, not an extended dialogue between offenders and victims. In the circumstances that fall between these extremes, however, what is initially just an unpleasant incident can be the catalyst for a vivid demonstration of the meaning of moral community on campus.

The community of learning, both intellectual and moral, that exists on campus is unique in American society, and it is threatened from within and from without. The suspicions of legislatures and anxious parents, the economic and political agendas of private and public donors, and the carping of reactionary critics are no more dangerous than the tendencies of faculty and students themselves to retreat into individualism, careerism, and political apathy.

The creation and preservation of such a community is a worthwhile third goal, in addition to the prevention of harm and the promotion of an atmosphere of free discussion. What strategies and policies can help to create such an atmosphere is the question to which I turn in the remaining two chapters.

Notes

1. A consistent policy against levels of substance abuse leading to impairment of abilities would require a categorical ban on the use of tobacco, whose addictive power is at least as strong as that of illegal drugs and whose catastrophic consequences for health are better documented and more certain than those of the leading "recreational" drugs. The reasons that motivate institutions to enforce policies against drug use while tolerating smoking have to do with longstanding social custom, and with the immediacy of the impairment that results from alcohol and drug abuse, rather than any accurate assessment of the relative risks.

2. Dinesh D'Souza, "In the Name of Academic Freedom, Colleges Should Back Professors Against Students' Demand for 'Correct' Views," *Chronicle of Higher Education*, April 24, 1991, pp. B1, B3. The quoted phrases are attributed by the author to Eugene Genovese.

3. D'Souza, p. B3.

4. See for example the account in Navasky (1980), p. 335, of the loyalty oaths required of faculty members at many state universities.

5. G. Calvin Mackenzie, "Fallacies of PC," *Chronicle of Higher Education*, September 4, 1991, pp. B1–B2.

6. Carolyn Mooney, "Professors Feel Conflict Between Roles cin Teaching and Research, Say Students Are Badly Prepared," *Chronicle of Higher Education*, May 8, 1991, pp. A15–A17, reporting on University of California at Los Angeles Higher Education Research Institute, "The American College Teacher: National Norms for the 1989–90 H. E. R. I. Faculty Survey."

7. Robin Wilson, "Anti-war Protests Flare at Some Colleges and Universities but Many Students Approve of Decision to Attack Iraq," *Chronicle of Higher Education*, January 23, 1991, pp. A29, A30; "War's End Leaves Supporters and Opponents on Campuses Deeply Divided," *Chronicle of Higher Education*, March 13, 1991, pp. A31, A34; and numerous articles in the intervening weeks.

8. The most widely circulated of these was a letter published in the *Proceedings and Addresses of the American Philosophical Association*, 63(5):62–3 (January 1990), of which I am editor. Levin's letter provoked an outpouring of responses, nearly all of them highly critical of Levin's racial views and of his claim that they are supported by evidence: 63(7):51–65 (June 1990). The publication of his letter has repeatedly been cited as "a letter published in a philosophy journal," implying that Levin's philosophical colleagues had reviewed his submission and judged it philosophically worthy of publication, when this was explicitly not the case.

9. Denise Magner, "Politicians Press Officials at the City College of New York to Punish Black-Studies Chairman for Remarks on Jews," *Chronicle of Higher Education*, September 4, 1991, p. A19.

10. "CUNY Barred from Punishing White Professor," *New York Times*, Sept. 5, 1991, p. B2.

11. *Levin V. Harleston* 770 F. Supp. 895, 925 (S.D.N.Y. 1991), affirmed in pertinent part, 966 F.2d 85 (2d Cir. 1992).

12. *The Complete Jefferson*, edited by Saul Padover (Freeport, N. Y.: Books for Libraries Press, 1943), p. 1098; quoted in Bok 1990, p. 63.

13. Quoted in Bok 1990, p. 63.

14. Bok 1990, p. 64.

15. Quoted in Bok 1990, p. 65.

16. Bok 1990, p. 65.

17. Rudolph 1962, p. 347.

18. Bok 1990, p. 100.

19. This is, more or less, what occurred when in the spring of 1990 a University of Delaware fraternity decided to address problems of homophobia and harassment by inviting representatives of the gay and lesbian student organization to spend an evening explaining their concerns and their purposes to the fraternity members. The session was not provoked, to the best of my knowledge, by any specific act of harassment, but members of both groups reported that it led to a substantial reduction in subsequent tensions.

Chapter 6

Supervision of Student Behavior: An Analytic Framework and Three Models

I have argued in the preceding chapter that the goals of the institutional policies concerning student conduct should be broad in scope, encompassing not merely the prevention of harm and exploitation and the preservation of an atmosphere of free discussion but also the fostering of a moral community in which individuals recognize mutual responsibilities that are more extensive than respect for others' rights. What kind of institutional rules and procedures can achieve these goals? It is to that question that I turn in the remainder of this study.

My aim is not to specify in detail what the student conduct code of any campus should contain. That would be an impossible task, given the necessity of adaptation to local history and circumstances. Rather, I hope to clarify the major alternative approaches that institutions can adopt with respect to specific kinds of misconduct and to make a case for one of them, an approach that avoids the moralistic and often hypocritical codes of a previous generation and yet contributes not only to civility but to moral education as well.

Before sketching these alternative approaches, let me suggest a simple analytical framework that can clarify the similarities and distinctions between policies in the various areas that have been surveyed. The framework permits us to correlate these areas of behavior with the distinct purposes of student-life supervision that were put forward in the preceding chapter.

Applications of the Goals of Student Rules

The three goals enumerated in the previous chapter constitute a summary of the legitimate purposes of student conduct regulation. The apparatus of such regulation accordingly can be described under one or more of three corresponding descriptions. We should be able to classify a particular rule, policy, or procedure as serving:

1. To prevent or punish exploitation and harm inflicted or suffered by students; or
2. To prevent or punish behavior that undermines the academic values of free discussion and learning; or
3. To foster a sense of moral community and mutual responsibility.

A specific policy may serve more than one of these purposes, or it may serve different purposes in different contexts. The first of these is more centrally the concern of the off-campus legal system than of campus codes, but there are many institutional rules that seek this end as well. The third—the only one of the three whose legitimacy some would question—is in my judgment no less important as the others, but it is achieved at least as much through informal means as through the disciplinary system.

We can now classify each of the major areas of student conduct as to the relevance of one or more of these three purposes. Rules about refrigerator size, extension cords, holiday decorations, and ironing boards are motivated by purposes such as fire prevention and mainte-nance of a safe environment, which fall into the first category above—if they even deserve a place in the discussion of student conduct. They concern students essentially as tenants of institutional property, and in that light they are more closely analogous to safety rules in the physics laboratory than to alcohol and drug policies. We can continue to set them aside, therefore, as having little relevance to our concerns.

Matters of plagiarism and academic honesty fall under both the first and the second categories. Cheating on graded work harms other students, and it is also a direct affront to the values of the entire enterprise of learning. The institution's responsibility goes beyond simply preventing and punishing cheating, however. The procedures and policies governing academic honesty ought also to help students come to understand what it means to be individually responsible for one's work while collaborating closely with others. A good set of policies regarding plagiarism, and a good program for dissemination and enforcement, contribute to the campus community and to students' sense of their place in it.

Alcohol abuse is both illegal and dangerous. In seeking to prevent illegal use of alcohol—drinking by minors, for example—the university is applying to its students the requirements of the law, and its policies also serve the first purpose of preventing harm. The harm in question encompasses both harm to the drinker caused by irresponsible consumption and the harm that results to others in consequence. But the third purpose is involved as well, for a good program to combat alcohol abuse makes education of students one of its principal aims. Because alcohol is widely used and abused in American society, students need to learn to distinguish, in their own behavior and in others', between responsible drinking and excess. To learn that difference, and to stand ready to intervene when friends and family members cross the line, is vital for every member of a community whose members accept responsibilities toward each other.

The control of drug use raises similar issues of harm to self, consequent harm to others, and education regarding risks of abuse. The risks of harm to others are far smaller than in the case of alcohol, yet the law recognizes no threshold below which drug use is permissible. The institution thus finds itself forced to adopt a certain degree of hypocrisy, or at least disingenuousness. Powerful drugs such as heroin, cocaine, and their derivatives can cause severe physical harm with repeated use, to be sure, but occasional use of ''soft'' drugs such as marijuana and tranquilizers appears, on the evidence available, to be substantially less dangerous than are drinking and smoking tobacco. Yet the institution's obligation to uphold the law, newly reinforced by the federal regulations mentioned in Chapter 4, requires it to prohibit all use of illegal drugs, while moderate drinking, and any degree of addiction to tobacco, are tolerated. This inconsistency is not unique to the university, of course, but simply reflects divided and inconsistent attitudes in society at large.

This is not to say that the enforcement of drug laws is a legal duty with no deeper warrant. Real risk of lasting harm is involved. In the case of ''hard'' drugs, and in instances of psychological or physical dependence on any drugs, the college's principal concern is prevention of harm to the student. In addition to this paternalistic concern, it also seeks to educate students regarding the nature and consequences of drug use, in order to guide their future behavior and to equip them to recognize problem signs in others. Drug policies thus serve purposes 1 and 3.

Whether the sexual mores of students are of any concern at all to the college, absent the use of force, is a disputed point. Some campuses restrict student behavior only by prohibiting cohabitation in the residence halls. Others omit even this minimal constraint. To the extent that institutions do seek to influence student sexual behavior, their policies and practices fall under purpose 3. Rules and procedures concerning sexual coercion, however, fall under 1 as well as 3. Rape of any kind, whether by strangers or by acquaintances, is a serious legal offense as well as a grave harm to the victim. Measures to build awareness of the problem in the community are a part, but not the whole, of an appropriate response.

The prevention of abusive and derogatory speech and writing, finally, fits all three categories. In some circumstances to subject other students to racist abuse is in itself to cause them serious harm, particularly if oral or written defamation is associated with or triggers physical attack. More often, the college's concern is with the atmosphere of openness and freedom that is central to education—a concern that cuts in both directions, for it motivates the prohibition of the most serious forms of abuse while at the same time mandating caution in imposing any limits at all on expression. Just as important as issues of free expression and open inquiry are the effects of racist and sexist attacks on the moral community that exists among students, faculty, and administrators.

Critics charge that antiharassment policies seek to prevent anyone from being made uncomfortable by others' words. That goal is both undesirable and unattainable, for to find one's deeply held views challenged by others is an essential part of education. A college ought not to attempt to prohibit students from giving offense to others. But this does not entail that it ought not to prohibit any student or group from using language that effectively rules others out of the community of discourse and brands them as unworthy of respect or consideration. It is the latter goal that motivates policies and practices in this area.

We can sum up these distinctions in Table 6–1. This analytic framework illustrates the overlapping purposes of behavioral regulation in all of the areas that we have discussed. There is no single purpose that in itself grounds rules in every area. But the three purposes we have cited—each of them firmly rooted in basic moral ideals—provide a sufficient and persuasive grounding for the college's concern with aspects of student life that lie outside the narrowly academic sphere. To identify them facilitates a recognition that different areas of student conduct pose distinct but related problems of campus life.

Table 6–1: Purposes of Specific Areas of Discipline

Policy area	1. To prevent harm	2. To uphold freedom	3. To foster community
Plagiarism	■	■	■
Alcohol abuse	■		■
Drug use	■		■
Sexual mores			■
Rape	■		■
Abusive speech	■	■	■

Their articulation also helps answer questions that may arise concerning other areas of student conduct that either now are, or may become, the subject of rules of conduct. In the first place, we have already observed that the numerous regulations concerning refrigerators and extension cords are not, strictly speaking, regulations of student conduct at all, for their concern is simply with reasonable control over the conditions under which students live as tenants in university-owned housing. The same policies are commonly applied to temporary summer tenants in the residence halls, whether high school students or banking executives, even though the other rules of student conduct would be irrelevant to them. None of the three goals identified is at stake. Hence, despite the fervently moral tone of some of the extension-cord policies, these are not truly issues of student conduct.

Identifying the three goals also helps in assessing proposals to expand supervision of student life. Suppose, for example, that a faculty member puts forward a proposal to bring back some sort of dress code on campus—not a single common uniform but a set of rules defining a reasonable compromise between comfort and formality. He is tired of seeing beach attire and perforated jeans in his classes, he says, and wants to restore a sense of dignity to the classroom. Moreover, he is convinced that students will eventually, if not immediately, support the rules. Would this be a reasonable exercise of the institution's concern with student behavior?

Clearly there is no serious harm to students or others at stake. A dress code diminishes rather than expands freedom, however, and that is a good reason to hesitate. The only possible argument in its favor is that it would have a strongly beneficial effect on the character of the campus community. Such an argument seems on its face implausible. But there might be some circumstances in which it would be persuasive—an urban public university, for example, where students from poor families are ridiculed by affluent students because they cannot afford to adopt trendy and expensive modes of attire.

Possibly a dress code would bring a needed element of equality to a campus such as this. In such circumstances its adoption should be considered seriously. In any other circumstances it would be inappropriate—not because students would resent it, not because there is any inherent constitutional right to dress as one pleases, but simply because none of the legitimate purposes of student conduct regulation would be served by the enactment of a dress code.[1]

The classificatory scheme proposed above helps to identify the reasons for student conduct regulation and to assess proposals for new rules. It does not in itself answer the crucial question of whether a college or university ought to seek to control student behavior in any of these areas. The benefits identified above must be weighed against the attendant costs. To adopt a rule prohibiting an undesirable form of conduct is likely to diminish the frequency of such conduct. But there are costs of several kinds: those of receiving and adjudicating complaints of its violation, of inflicting penalties, and of dealing with appeals. There may also be a less tangible cost in the form of increased mistrust between staff and students.

If a rule is not enforced—because detection is difficult, or simply because administrators do not make a serious attempt at enforcement—the institution will not only gain no diminution in the offending behavior but will subtly undermine the effectiveness of its other policies. If a rule is enforced strictly but its legitimacy is not accepted by students, the end result may be to poison the campus atmosphere with ill will and resentment that outweigh the improvement, if there is any, in student conduct. All of these factors must be weighed in deciding whether to enact, or to maintain, institutional regulation over a particular area of student conduct.

Three Places to Stand: *In Loco Avi,* etc.

With respect to any particular category of undesirable student behavior, there are essentially three stances that an institution may adopt. I will conclude this chapter by outlining these three models very briefly. In the concluding chapter I will employ them to classify the strategies that institutions have adopted, or might adopt, in the major areas of student conduct.

In the first place, an institution may decide that the undesirable behavior warrants strict regulation. It may accordingly impose and enforce relatively strict standards. It may assume the controlling and directive stance that was pervasive in an earlier era, setting the limits of student discretion within narrow bounds. We may call this the *restrictive stance.*

A substantial number of colleges and a few universities adopt this stance with respect to a broad range of student conduct, even matters of personal judgment such as sexual ethics and alcohol use. Characteristic of these institutions is that they consciously define themselves as having a distinctive character—a character that arises in many instances from a sponsoring church, in others from a strong local tradition. Students who attend such an institution have made a choice to join a specific sort of moral community, and they know that in doing so they place themselves under greater restrictions than at most other institutions.

The same strategy is adopted by nearly every institution in at least some areas, moreover. Plagiarism is one example, whether it is treated as a disciplinary violation or by means of an honor code. Rules against sexual assault and harassment, where they exist, are similarly strict, as are rules proscribing drug use.

In these areas, even universities and colleges that have explicitly renounced their former status *in loco parentis* still act in the way that was mandated by that model. Their concerns are not simply paternalistic and maternalistic, however. The extent of the rules of conduct has been relaxed substantially at most institutions. Few still impose curfew hours or require chaperones at social functions. We might accordingly characterize the restrictive stance as operating not precisely *in loco parentis* but rather *in loco avi,* "in the place of grandparents."[2] The institution stands for an identifiable set of values. Even if it allows more slack than a nervous parent, it makes its expectations for student behavior known. This is the first of the three possible stances.

A majority of institutions today appear to have adopted a quite different posture, however, with respect to visiting hours, alcohol use, and sexual mores—indeed, to all areas of student behavior that do not involve specifically academic offense or illegal acts. However objectionable student behavior in these areas may be, these institutions believe, both the legal status of students and the lack of any clear moral authority of the institution militate against any attempt at control. The institutions have therefore responded by abandoning any attempt to direct student behavior. We might characterize this as the *permissive stance*, or, to maintain the classical tone, the philosophy of *non sum mater tua* ("I'm not your mother").

Such institutions have elected not to attempt to set behavioral rules except as they are mandated by law and by minimal standards of civility. Their handbooks emphasize students' responsibility to make their own moral decisions and the institution's inability to make decisions for them. Supervision of on-campus housing is minimal and specifically avoids any attempt to tell students what they ought or ought not to do in the privacy of their rooms. Alcohol policies are oriented toward helping students who become dependent or who drink themselves into unconsciousness at parties, not on controlling the drinking of the majority of students who avoid these excesses.

The problems of abusive speech and writing elicit from such institutions a reaffirmation of the value of political freedom and the importance of respect for others, not policies prohibiting such behavior. In the area of sexual conduct, the institutions provide students with information, with contraceptives or instructions on how to obtain them, and with means of ending unwanted pregnancies. The only moral counsel that is officially offered is the admonition to be sure that one's sexual activities result from personal decisions and not from social pressures.

This is the stance to which most public and many private institutions adhere with respect to sexual mores. Whether institutions also take a permissive stance with respect to alcohol is debatable—to answer the question would require looking closely not just at student handbooks but at the records of disposition of discipline cases as well. In any case, my purpose here is simply to mark this out as a clear alternative to the restrictive stance. It is not, however, the only alternative.

There is a third possible stance that is neither restrictive nor permissive. We might call it the *in loco avunculi* ("in the place of the uncle") philosophy, or more concisely the *directive stance*. An institution that adopts this approach seeks neither to control behavior directly nor to leave it wholly to student discretion, but rather to influence behavior by means other than disciplinary rules and sanctions. It may employ a variety of means to shape student conduct, from the incorporation of units on alcohol or drug use into freshmen composition courses to the promulgation of high expectations of faculty and staff behavior.

Such an approach is most appropriate in precisely the same areas in which permissiveness would otherwise rule—the areas of substance abuse, personal responsibility, and sexual mores. It is also an important element in an effective honor code, although in this case sanctions typically add a restrictive element. In whatever ways may be appropriate, an institution that adopts the directive stance communicates two guiding principles: First, that the institution is not neutral with respect to the conduct in question; second, that it relies on example and persuasion, not on specific rules and their enforcement, as the means of preventing undesired conduct.

None of these models is likely to be found in pure form, or in application to every area of student conduct, on any campus. All the same, they exemplify three distinct disciplinary philosophies each of which has adherents on contemporary campuses. I will use these differing approaches to explore possible future directions for the control of student behavior.

In the closing chapter of this study, I begin by noting some essential presuppositions of any program to shape student conduct, and I then sketch several alternative models of good discipline in a campus context. In doing so I hope to demonstrate that the third model—the institution standing *in loco avunculi*, not *in loco parentis* or even *in loco avi*—offers the most appropriate place for the college to take its stand today.

Notes

1. This is essentially the reasoning followed by the courts in invalidating dress and grooming codes in secondary schools, as was noted in Chapter 2.

2. Literally, this means "in place of the grandfather." I am indebted to Mary Whitlock Blundell, a classicist and philosopher at the University of Washington, whom I met through the exchange of messages on Internet, for help in correcting the vestigial Latin that remains with me from one term's study.

Chapter 7

Models of Good Discipline

On any campus, we have noted, the rules for student conduct ought to reflect local traditions, any particularly vexing institutional problems that may exist, and the changing expectations and capabilities of students. All the same, it may be a useful exercise to put aside for the moment any worries about local problems or customs in order to imagine how we might try to control student misconduct if no such hindrances intervened. What would the student discipline code be like in an ideal situation—a Utopia University, if you will?

The answer depends on how nearly perfect—and thus how implausible—we make our ideal. Shall we stipulate that the ideal campus contains only students who are never destructive, always cooperative, and scrupulously respectful of the rights of others? Such students would need few rules to guide their behavior, and the disciplinary procedures put in place to deal with violation would scarcely ever be put into use.

This would be an exercise in sheer fantasy. The stock of such benevolent individuals is extremely limited, and despite the best efforts of the admissions office and the philosophy department, no campus will ever be fully populated with them. All the same, it may be prudent to overestimate rather than underestimate the numbers of such paragons of virtue—to expect too much rather than too little of students, that is to say—in establishing a basic strategy for dealing with student misconduct. To place a large measure of responsibility on students for self-regulation is likely to bring about a higher level of compliance and cooperation than would otherwise be obtained. High expectations are often self-fulfilling, as is evident in the relative success of student-controlled honor-code systems in limiting academic dishonesty. To expect little, on the other hand—to build a system of

143

rigid control on the presumption that students will exploit every opening—is likely to elicit even less responsibility than the code presumes.

At the end of this chapter I will return to the theme of Utopia U, and I will sketch a more realistic ideal that could serve as a useful model. Before I do so, however, several related topics need to be addressed. We need to examine more explicitly, for example, just what a good program of student behavioral regulation seeks to accomplish and what ends it pursues. To do so will enable us to link the various areas of student conduct that were examined in Chapters 3 and 4 to the three approaches—restrictive, permissive, and directive—that were put forward in Chapter 6.

The maxim of classical conservatism in government seems to apply in this context: The discipline system is best, we might say, that disciplines least. On the whole, the more successful a code of student conduct is in achieving its aims, the less it is needed and the less frequently its procedures are called into use. A system of rules that adequately protects the rights of all and also enjoys broad student support may become almost invisible in its influence on student conduct.

If violations of rules are frequent and flagrant, on the other hand, it is not just the discipline code that is failing to work as it should. Changing the code of conduct and its enforcement may fail to address deeper problems of mistrust and alienation, of which disciplinary problems such as excessive and open drinking, racial harassment, and rampant cheating are merely the most visible symptoms. When students disregard the official rules of conduct habitually and openly, they thereby undermine not only the credibility of the system of student conduct regulation but the credibility of the entire institution in its students' eyes.

The question of how to control student conduct is therefore one with far-reaching implications for the entire educational enterprise on campus. Unfortunately, even as such problems have grown more acute and more complex, the sense of responsibility felt by faculty for the realm of student life has steadily diminished. For this trend we can identify at least two causes. The first is simply the exceptionally competitive academic marketplace of the 1970s and 1980s, which has compelled younger faculty members to concentrate on preparing research for publication to keep their jobs and have a chance at tenure. Teaching has often taken second place, and other campus affairs have come in a distant third. Academic competition has also discouraged junior faculty from criticizing longstanding policies for fear of provoking controversy and opposition.

There are exceptions to this pattern. Some untenured faculty speak their minds bravely, and some conceive of their vocation broadly in spite of publication pressures. Every institution professes to value teaching and engagement in the campus community alongside published research, and a few have adopted policies that make this value visible. All the same, the pressures felt by junior faculty have diminished faculty involvement in both the formulation and the implementation of student conduct policies. And when junior faculty do join the senior faculty, habits once formed are likely to persist.

A second reason for diminishing involvement by faculty has been the growing size and complexity of university administration in the period after World War II, which has contributed both to fragmentation and specialization among administrators and to a general sense of greater distance between faculty and administration. This development is especially visible, and has especially troubling consequences, in the area of student affairs.

When faculty felt a personal responsibility for both shaping and enforcing student conduct rules, they sought to ensure that disciplinary rules and procedures were in keeping with the institution's academic program and its overall aims. Today such matters are too often left wholly in the hands of the student-affairs office and the residence-hall staff. Relatively few senior academic administrators besides deans of students, and even fewer faculty members, now take an active interest in discipline except when particular problems affect them personally. Thus the ironic and unintended result of higher standards and expectations for student-affairs personnel has been the erosion of any sense of shared responsibility for matters of student conduct.

I hope by means of the present study both to demonstrate and to foster broader faculty interest in student life issues—to demonstrate my own interest, as a faculty member with no direct responsibility for student affairs, and to foster it in colleagues who share my concerns even if they do not wholly endorse my conclusions.

The Moral Basis for Student Conduct Codes

The concerns of this study can be summarized in broad terms in a few questions: To what extent should an institution seek to control behavior that is destructive, foolish, or irresponsible? What is it about some categories of misbehavior that makes them suitable objects for disciplinary control, in contrast to other areas in which institutional enforcement is inappropriate?

We can begin to answer these questions—and have already done so—by considering various examples. Drug use and alcohol abuse are obviously appropriate areas for regulation. Spreading unsubstantiated rumors about a classmate's character is wrong, but it is not the sort of behavior that should be brought before a college judiciary. Can the difference be made more explicit? Are there features that characterize the categories of behavior that are appropriate for disciplinary control?

In the clearest cases, I suggest, three distinct conditions hold and together provide a moral basis for the institution's effort at control. They are:

1. *The prohibited conduct is unacceptable on campus.*
2. *The prohibited conduct can be effectively prevented or deterred.*
3. *Reliable and fair measures of enforcement are available to the institution.*

The necessity of the first condition is obvious. To prohibit conduct is to state clearly to everyone in the campus community that this conduct is incompatible with the institution's basic purposes, violates the rights of others, or is for some other reason impermissible. Including this condition in effect excludes a great many of the specific rules of residence-hall life, such as the rules about extension cords, refrigerators, and lofts that take up page after page in many handbooks. These are not really matters of student discipline but have rather to do with safety and order in the residence halls.

The second assumption—that the behavior can be controlled through regulation—is equally crucial. If it is false, then any regulations that may be adopted will be merely empty words. The absence of this condition, I believe, rules out some areas that institutions now attempt to control. Any rule categorically prohibiting students from smoking or from engaging in premarital sex will inevitably fail to achieve its end, because this second condition is lacking—and because the physiological and social factors that work to undermine obedience, in both cases, are extraordinarily powerful.

These social and physical factors are not causally determinative, to be sure. Some students do quit smoking. Many resist the pressure to become involved in sex. Still, it is unrealistic to expect that an institutional discipline code can effectively dictate such decisions.

A prohibition against smoking in campus buildings, or against sexual intercourse in the residence halls, would be very difficult to enforce, but in principle it could be made effective. A categorical prohibition that applies to students at all times and places, however, is unenforceable. Most other areas of student conduct are far more amenable to institutional influence.

The third presupposition is a further specification of the second: Misbehavior is appropriate for disciplinary prohibition when it is not only amenable to influence by sanctions but possible for the institution to detect and prevent, through either the threat or the actual imposition of sanctions. There are some kinds of behavior such that enforcement of institutional rules, whatever its effect on behavior, necessitates intolerably intrusive measures. In these circumstances, even highly undesirable and readily influenced behavior must be reluctantly tolerated.

This may well be the the the case, for example, in the case of acquaintance rape, a topic to which I will return below. The occurrence of forced intercourse among students is deplorable, and it evidently occurs with alarming frequency. According to one study, one-fourth of all college women are the victims of a sexual assault or an attempted assault during their college years, although only a tenth of them report it to authorities.[1]

We shall look more closely at the issues that surround acquaintance rape shortly, but I wish here simply to call attention to the special difficulty represented by the third of the assumptions enumerated above. There is seldom any reason for college authorities to become involved in adjudication of charges of violent sexual assault by a stranger, because such charges demand both the stiffer penalties and the greater procedural protections afforded by the legal system. If a college makes no attempt to punish such behavior, it is not thereby condoning it but rather is acknowledging that external authorities are far better able to deal with it. Rape by an acquaintance, however, is much less likely to be reported to the police than is assault by a stranger, both because of the attendant embarrassment and because, rightly or wrongly, victims fear that their charges will not stick without independent evidence. Hence the pressure on colleges to make acquaintance rape a major concern in their disciplinary rules and procedures. To fail to do so, it is said, is to show indifference to the victims' suffering.

But to yield to these pressures might be a grave mistake. Without doubt the occurrence of acquaintance rape could be reduced if a college undertook to investigate all charges that came to its attention and to punish those found guilty. But to establish adequate procedures to adjudicate between the conflicting accounts of the accused and the alleged victim, very often without the testimony of any other witnesses, is extraordinarily difficult. Each time a case is brought, there is a very real risk either that a rapist will be exonerated or that an innocent student will be convicted falsely. As charges of sexual assault come into the discipline system in greater numbers, the difficulties of providing a thorough and even-handed response to each become all the greater.[2]

These reasons mandate great caution in attempting to formulate and enforce a rule against acquaintance rape through the campus judicial system, unless the third condition can be satisfied and adequate protections for both victim and accused can be put into place. But even if this condition fails, it does not follow that the institution should tolerate acquaintance rape or say nothing on the topic. It follows only that a strictly disciplinary response is inappropriate. The institution's stance, in other words, should then be neither restrictive nor permissive, but directive.

Disciplinary control over behavior—the restrictive stance—is appropriate only when all three conditions enumerated above are fulfilled: that the proscribed behavior is unacceptable; that it can be deterred or prevented; and that appropriate means of enforcement are available to the institution. We can now ask more systematically under what conditions, and with reference to what specific behaviors, these judgments are warranted.

We noted in the previous chapter that there are three distinct stances that an institution may adopt toward disapproved behavior. It may decide, in reference to a specific sort of behavior, to be *restrictive*; it may choose to be *permissive*; or it may choose to be *directive*. It may prohibit the behavior; it may establish no rules and permit the behavior; or it may undertake to reduce the incidence of the undesired behavior in less direct ways.

These three stances correlate with the three conditions that characterize behavior appropriate for discipline, in the following way. First, as was just noted, it is appropriate to be restrictive only when all three of the conditions identified above hold. When neither the second nor the third condition obtains, however, then—no matter how undesirable the behavior—a permissive stance is the only appropriate one. If the first two conditions are satisfied but the third is not, however, then a directive stance is appropriate. These correlations can be summarized in Table 7–1. Note: Cells marked [Yes] indicate that, although the stance indicated may be appropriate, it is unlikely to be used as more forceful means are also available.

We can observe this correlation in each of the areas of student conduct that we have reviewed. *Plagiarism*, in the first place, is an evident affront to the basic educational and intellectual values of the institution. Its occurrence is very much dependent on how rigorously it is pursued and punished. Detection and enforcement, even though always imperfect, can be quite effective. Therefore the restrictive stance is appropriate. Every one of the institutions surveyed has indeed adopted such a stance, whether in the form of a code of rules administratively enforced or in the form of an honor code.

On the *use of drugs* the same conditions hold, with some qualifications. To enforce an antidrug policy rigorously might require many intrusive measures, from room searches to mandatory urine tests for all students. These would involve considerable costs both in staff time and in student resentment. Even more important, such intrusive measures would infringe students' legal right to privacy. The first assumption, that the behavior at issue is unacceptable, is also open to debate. Some would argue that moderate use of "soft" drugs should be no concern of the institutions, because it poses no serious threat to safety and good order, or at any rate none more serious than that posed by moderate use of alcohol.

The support for both the first and the third judgments, therefore, is at least potentially a matter of dispute. All the same, we have noted that every campus has adopted a restrictive policy toward drug use and that enforcement is generally strict. It seems likely that the

Table 7–1: Conditions for the Three Disciplinary Approaches

	Appropriateness of policy stance		
Which conditions hold?	Restrictive	Directive	Permissive
1, 2, and 3	Yes	[Yes]	[Yes]
1 and 2 only	No	Yes	[Yes]
1 only	No	No	Yes

strongly restrictive stance has at least as much to do with external pressures—from parents and from the federal government—as with objective assessments of the situation on campus. Without such pressures, the response to drugs on campus might well consist of a combination of restrictive policies regarding some drugs and directive measures to deal with substances that do less harm.

In the area of *alcohol use*, the major difficulty is that of distinguishing moderate use by students of legal age, permitted by law and (with few exceptions) by the institution, from excessive drinking and drinking by minors, which are clearly undesirable but very difficult either to detect or to deter. Not long ago, at most campuses except those closely tied to a sponsoring church, the predominant stance in practice was permissiveness, with discipline an option only in the most flagrant cases of drunken misconduct. Today institutions are increasingly acknowledging that drunkenness and underage drinking can be, and ought to be, prevented through a combination of education, selective encouragement, and punishment for misconduct. As institutions come to accept the truth of the second and third conditions, in other words, they may be moving from a permissive toward a restrictive stance.

In the area of *sexual behavior*, even the first condition is highly controversial. Many would argue that behavior engaged in by students with mutual consent is no concern of the college's and that the only morally permissible stance for the institution is to keep its nose out of student sexual morality. Indeed, only the more conservative church-related colleges, in the sample we examined, have anything at all to say about student sexual conduct in their handbooks. Among the rest, a substantial number impose certain minimal constraints by restricting opposite-sex visitors in the residence halls. But such policies merely control the location, not the character, of student behavior.

Thus, with very few exceptions, institutions have adopted a permissive stance toward student sexual behavior. This stance is under challenge, however, in the area of *sexual assault* and *acquaintance rape*. At several institutions, female students have charged that student-life administrators were lax in failing to prevent repeated occurrences of acquaintance rape by the same male students. In some instances legal charges of negligence have been lodged against the college. In response, campuses are considering whether to adopt a more restrictive stance and to seek to adjudicate such charges when they are made.

The same movement—from permissiveness to restrictiveness—can also be observed in the case of *abusive speech*, which became a topic of heated debate on campus only in the late 1980s. Until recently, when racist or antihomosexual speech led to assault, it was prosecuted strictly; but when it remained verbal, it was tolerated. Today many institutions are seeking ways of preventing and punishing verbal attacks targeting nonwhite or homosexual students.

There is troubling evidence that incidents of such abuse are becoming more frequent. The reduction of their incidence would be a real improvement in the campus atmosphere. The attempt to do so through restrictive measures, however, is likely to fail because the third condition above is not satisfied. It remains an open question whether any measures to detect and punish abusive speech can be sufficiently attentive to student rights to fair treatment and free speech.

Among the issues that we have quickly reviewed, two resist easy categorization and pose particular problems of enforcement: that of hate speech and that of sexual mores. In the next few pages I will look more closely at why these two issues pose special difficulties and suggest ways in which they might be resolved. This discussion will lead us in turn to look more closely at the measures of behavioral influence that are available to institutions apart from the explicit enactment and enforcement of rules. Such measures, I will suggest in the last section, would be an important part of an ideal system of student behavioral supervision.

Two Hard Cases: Hate Speech and Sex

I begin with the issues of abusive speech. The Stanford rationale statement that was quoted in Chapter 4 builds a persuasive case against any but the most narrowly drawn regulations. The expression of offensive political and moral views is doubly protected on campus—by the constitutional rights that students hold as citizens, and by the unique nature of the university as guardian of intellectual liberty. These freedoms are under threat from many quarters and need continual defense.

Stanford's policy, we noted in Chapter 4, specifically prohibits the use of a small number of "insulting or 'fighting words,' " enumerated in the policy, that have the effect of assaulting certain groups and ruling them out of the community of discourse. If any policy against abusive speech is justified, this one is, for it specifically exempts from its strictures any responsible presentation of a political or moral opinion, however extreme in its racism or sexism, that is framed in words suitable for common discourse.

But when the prohibition is so narrowly framed it is unlikely ever to be called into use. Most apologists for racist politics are savvy enough to avoid offensive terms in public. Changing a few words and phrases in even the most patently offensive speech or article is sufficient to bring it into compliance with such a policy. Indeed, we noted in Chapter 4 that several campuses where hate-speech rules have been enacted have not brought charges against a single student in the first few years that they have been in effect. A policy that has so minimal an effect on the misconduct it aims to control seems scarcely worth the trouble of writing and promulgating.

It would be more honest, and probably also more effective, to acknowledge that the potential infringement of a hate-speech rule on student rights rules out disciplinary enforcement and to take up instead other institutional measures. The appropriate stance, in other words, is not restrictive but directive.

A university can communicate in many ways its condemnation of racism, sexism, and other kinds of discrimination. University faculty and administrators can serve as models of tolerance and respect for all groups, particularly for those who face special difficulties on their campus, whether these be gays, lesbians, Hispanics, Catholics, agnostics, or any other identifiable group. Faculty and administrators can lend visible and willing assistance to groups that are formed to combat racial and sexual abuse. In the content of commencement speeches and syllabi, in the topics of upper-level seminars, in the books featured in the bookstore, and in countless other ways, they can create a climate that unites free exchange among strongly opposed viewpoints with a systematic emphasis on equality, expanded opportunity for all, and mutual respect.

A hint of the potential effectiveness of such measures can be found in a recent experiment conducted by a member of the psychology faculty at Smith. The interviewer stopped students on campus and asked for their judgment on the seriousness of certain racist acts that had been committed on campus. Their responses varied but tended to follow the lead of others who were being interviewed at the same time. In the presence of others who discounted the incidents as trivial, students tended to agree. If they heard others express serious concern, however, they expressed similar concern.[3]

That peer pressure influences adolescents, of course, is hardly news.

Still, the experiment provides an intriguing illustration of the way in which moral judgments are shaped by social context. Through directive measures such as have been described, an institution can accomplish as much or more than it could through a restrictive policy of punishing racist speech. The institution can thus convey to students, and to outsiders as well, this message: Racism and exclusion have no place on this campus. Those of you who dissent are free to say so, in public or in private; but you should be in no doubt that in so doing you are attacking the ideals to which the entire community is dedicated.

Turning now to the second of the problem areas, very much the same thing could be said concerning *sexual behavior* on campus. The restrictive stance has already been abandoned by nearly all institutions. Rather than retreat to a permissive stance, institutions could seek to encourage responsible personal behavior and prevent harmful conduct through directive means.

To be sure, not every institution has abandoned the restrictive stance. A few colleges still claim the moral authority to state and enforce a restrictive code of conduct, at least on campus. If that stance is clearly understood by all, and if students willingly accept the restrictions placed on them, the college may achieve an unusual degree of moral consensus concerning issues of personal behavior.

The consensus is likely to be continually under challenge. Students and faculty will find some of these restrictions necessary, others excessive yet not intolerable, still others needlessly enfettering. Judgments will differ from person to person and from time to time. The campus will regularly have to make difficult and controversial decisions concerning which regulations should be retained, which scrapped, and which tightened. These decisions, difficult as they are, offer a practical laboratory in which the commitment of faculty, administrators and students to the guiding ideals of the institution can be more clearly articulated and put into application. When the process of revision is open and provides a voice for all who are affected, the result of such changes will be not just a better discipline code but a stronger community.

Institutions that live up to this ideal are rare in American higher education. They are becoming rarer each year as a result of both internal and external forces. Most colleges with historical religious ties now seek to define themselves more broadly and inclusively. At many Protestant colleges, confessional and ethnic homogeneity has given way to greater diversity. The role of sponsoring religious orders in

Catholic institutions is also much diminished. It is possible to maintain a strong sense of institutional identity and moral community through such changes. Yet a more diverse body of students and faculty is likely to demand more tolerance in behavioral standards as well.

Many outside such communities regard them as backward holdovers from an earlier era whose institutionalized moralizing runs counter to the purposes of education. But to make such a judgment is itself to take a narrow and blinkered view of the enterprise of education. At the time of their founding, the colleges of the new United States conceived of their responsibility as encompassing the character no less than the intellect of their students. Today most universities and many colleges have retreated from that self-understanding, whose traces survive only in the opening pages of the college catalog.

But why should a campus community not count certain ideals of character and morality among the elements in the institution's identity? Such a commitment needs to be made clear to students and faculty before they join the community, and it must be continually reaffirmed in words and actions if it is to remain meaningful. Hypocrisy and intolerance will rule if an institution's purported ideals are invoked only to punish its critics. Yet it is possible to uphold a demanding moral code consistently and without hypocrisy. If a campus community shares the moral belief that premarital sex has no legitimate part in the life of its members, then the rules for behavior in residence halls ought to reflect that judgment. Those who regard that view as hopelessly out of date simply ought to seek admission or employment elsewhere. Some students and faculty members thrive in an atmosphere of general agreement on political and moral matters, even when they are among the dissenters. Others need the challenge of forming their moral views in a context where there is no such guiding ideal.

For most institutions a restrictive stance on such matters of personal behavior is not a possibility, for reasons both principled and pragmatic. On most campuses it is impossible to arrive at any consensus on matters such as student sexual conduct, save to agree that no agreement is possible. A substantial number of faculty members, administrators, and students on most campuses subscribe to the moral dogma that there are no categorical moral rules in the realm of sexual ethics. They recommend that the college withdraw from any attempt to control behavior, because it has no basis on which to condemn any behavior to which all parties consent. Others may reject such moral agnosticism and yet believe it impossible to draw any clear line between ethical and exploitative behavior. In the face of such divergence of judgment, there can be no consensus on what kinds of behavior the institution ought to prohibit.

The practical obstacles to a rigid code of personal conduct are equally great. To undertake to detect and punish abusive and exploitative sexual behavior would require intrusive measures of surveillance. Even close and continual supervision in the residence halls may simply move the prohibited behavior off campus.

There is only one area in which there is widespread sentiment for restoration of a traditional code of moral conduct on campus: that of acquaintance rape. But the same obstacles that make it impossible for most campuses to proscribe fornication apply with equal force to rules against forced intercourse. Indeed, the situation is in some ways even more problematic. To prohibit premarital sex is to prohibit an act whose nature is clearly definable, even if its occurrence may often be hidden from any but the participants. To ban date rape is to prohibit behavior whose character is nearly always disputed by those immediately involved. In rare instances in which witnesses can lend their testimony, they may be no more able to render an objective judgment on whether participation was consensual than is either of the participants. For just this reason, as has been noted above, it is extraordinarily difficult for an institution to create procedures that can effectively detect and punish the offense.

The most egregious cases of rape typically are not adjudicated by colleges at all, precisely because of the graveness of the offense, but are turned over to the legal system. Cases of acquaintance rape fall within the college's jurisdiction when there is insufficient evidence to make legal prosecution feasible. This only compounds the difficulties of weighing and evaluating conflicting testimony.

In several specific instances that have come to my attention, women students have come forward with allegations of acquaintance rape and have been invited to present their charges either before a special ad hoc committee or before a disciplinary board. The accused has been given a chance to answer the charges, and there was a semblance of fairness about the procedure. But the fairness was only superficial, because there was no impartial or reliable means of testing the veracity of each party. Without the elaborate procedural safeguards that protect those accused in the courts—in a community where confidentiality is difficult to maintain—neither party can guard effectively against manipulation of the process by the other.

Against a false accusation of theft or plagiarism, a student can gather exonerating evidence. Against false charges of acquaintance rape, the only defense is likely to be the student's own uncorroborated testimony. If judicial boards, wary of this risk, seek to avoid false convictions by demanding too high a standard of evidence, real offenses will go unpunished—and the impression will be created that the college condones rape.

If I have dwelt at length on the issues of sexual behavior, that is precisely because campuses have devoted so little attention to these matters until recently, when the controversial issue of acquaintance rape has arisen. In effect, campuses face the same dilemma in regard to sexual conduct as in regard to abusive speech. In both instances they are confronted by behavior that is deeply out of harmony with the institution's goals and ideals, yet is inappropriate for formal disciplinary control. In neither case ought the institution to stand back and withhold judgment on the propriety of the behavior. Yet to enact rules against these categories of misbehavior is to risk trampling on students' rights to due process and freedom of expression.

There are many other kinds of sexual behavior besides rape that are out of place in a community dedicated to the well-being of its members. The use of others merely as interchangeable and disposable means to sexual gratification is an example. Sexual contact that puts another unwittingly at risk of contracting AIDS is another. To the extent that such acts can be prevented by institutional actions they should be. But enacting rules against such acts would be pointless. Their detection and enforcement, too, would pose insuperable practical and legal problems.

Some rules against hate speech may be so narrowly drawn, we have noted, that infringement on free speech is very unlikely. It may also be possible for an institution to devise procedures to hear allegations of acquaintance rape that would ensure due process and fairness to all. In either case, however, a policy of prohibition is likely to entail severe difficulties of enforcement, disproportionate to any diminution of the problem that the policy is intended to resolve.

What is needed in both cases is a directive rather than a restrictive approach, by which the institution can communicate both to its members and to the world outside the inappropriateness of the behavior in question. It can thus guide students away from such abuses without legislating against them.

Three Steps Toward Moral Community

How can an institution achieve this? How is it possible to convey institutional disapprobation without the formal structure of rules and sanctions? We can distinguish three steps that might be taken.

As a necessary first step, an institution's principal administrators should acknowledge the importance of the values that are under threat and the seriousness of the offenses that threaten them. If administrators belittle the signs of a serious problem on campus, their hypocrisy is immediately evident both on campus and from the outside. But if the dean and president give an honest account of the problem and also state clearly and forcefully why the behavior in question is out of place on campus, they have already contributed significantly to a solution. Such a statement of the institution's concern may not be enough to affect the behavior of the worst offenders, but it puts other students on notice that what may have appeared to them harmless fun is nothing of the sort.

Second, administrators and members of the faculty should engage students actively and creatively in an effort to resolve the problem. Behavior of either of the kinds mentioned—sexual abuse or racial harassment—primarily victimizes students. The views of victims and potential victims should therefore be solicited first of all. But the involvement of other students is vital. The offending behavior is likely to be caused by social pressures and peer expectations that are far more evident to students than to administrators.

Third, in cases in which the promulgation of rules and enforcement of sanctions is ill-advised and ineffective, institutions should seek instead to shape behavior by identifying positive models in the campus community. What this means in practice, above all, is a policy of systematic encouragement to on-campus groups whose members model responsible behavior, while official support is denied to other groups that repeatedly contribute to the problems in question.

The rhetoric of the catalog notwithstanding, there is really no single campus community in any but the smallest and most homogeneous college. This is the reason, we have already noted, that we cannot invoke a single set of shared moral and religious values as the basis for a code of personal conduct. Instead, many distinct communities coexist on campus, overlapping to a considerable extent in their purposes and membership. These include athletic teams, fraternities, student volunteer groups, debating societies, newspaper staffs, and many more.

Students' fundamental moral commitments are largely in place before they matriculate. Yet their moral and political views are affected by their experiences on campus. And it is the smaller communities in which students participate that most decisively affect their personal codes of morals and of behavior. When a former Young Republican becomes infatuated with socialism, a religious skeptic moves toward a more traditional religious stance, or a rigidly moralistic student changes her view on premarital sex or homosexuality, more often than not the change begins in one or another of these subcommunities. In these groups a student has the opportunity both to talk about her commitments and their grounding, and to interact with others whose behavior and values are different from hers. In effect, the smaller communities in which students carry on their lives on campus provide a setting for experimenting with personal values and personal identity. The values that are ranked most highly by the leading members of the community, in words and action, are likely to prove contagious.

The result can be destructive as well as constructive. Fraternities on many campuses provide a dispiriting example. If they once served to inspire students to high ideals of mutual respect and ethical concern, today they often stand for a life dedicated to sex and booze, punctuated by occasional publicity stunts to raise money for crippled children. The newspapers regularly carry reports of gang rapes, hazing injuries, and students nearly killed by alcohol poisoning at fraternity parties. Such horrors are not typical of all fraternities, and yet their recurrence on campus after campus provides evidence that the fraternity culture is one where irresponsible behavior is more often admired than scorned. Even so, most fraternities continue to enjoy the active cooperation and administrative assistance of the institutions to which they are attached.

Religious organizations such as the Newman Center, the Hillel Foundation, Lutheran or Episcopal campus ministry, and Campus Crusade for Christ are likely to uphold explicit moral as well as theological views. Their meetings and activities, too, shape students' sense of moral responsibility, of what is acceptable behavior. Ironically, such groups are frequently denied assistance of any kind by university administrators. State institutions' exaggerated fear of unconstitutional entanglement with religion, and private institutions' desire to distance themselves from the evangelistic fervor of some of these groups, both work in effect to convey to the members of such groups that their membership in religious groups is somehow at odds with their status as students.

But in fact these groups make an indispensable contribution to the formation of moral maturity in students. A state-funded institution cannot endorse or directly contribute to the aims for which religious groups are organized. Yet the influence of such groups on students' moral perspectives is profound. Surely any institution, public or private, ought to encourage students to participate actively in those groups that, on the whole, model responsible decision making in personal, political, and institutional contexts.

One of the persistent themes of recent work in moral philosophy is the indispensable role of community in shaping our moral universe. Writers whose views of the substance of morality are strongly opposed—Alasdair MacIntyre, Richard Bernstein, and Martha Nussbaum, for example, defending very different readings of the history and current state of ethical inquiry[4]—are united in their insistence that moral conviction and moral action can be instilled only in the company of others. We learn to be moral by modeling ourselves on others whose judgment and integrity we respect. Even when we reject or surpass our models, we do so in a social context.

In this light, to rely on ever more strenuous enforcement of disciplinary rules and codes is an inherently ill-suited tactic, if one's goal is to assist students to become mature and responsible moral agents. Institutions ought rather to devote their efforts to systematic encouragement of the smaller communities contained on campus in which moral reflection and thoughtful choice flourish. These may include religious, political, and service organizations of many kinds. The encouragement offered to them may take a variety of forms, formal and informal.

Rather than attempt to describe in detail matters that must of necessity vary greatly from campus to campus, I shall suggest the kind of disciplinary policy I have in mind by returning to the question with which we began this chapter: What might an ideal campus disciplinary system be like? How might a campus meet the goals of student conduct that we have identified: to prevent harm, maintain order, and build community? I will offer the beginnings of an answer to that question, and at the same time an ending to this study, in the following sketch.

A Visit to Nolocus College

The institution I describe is imaginary, and perhaps impossible as well. Its similarity to existing institutions, however, is fully intentional. In offering this fictional account I draw on many of the features that characterize the actual institutions that have been discussed in the preceding chapters.

The pattern I sketch here, based on no concrete institution's particular social and historical situation, is for that reason unsuited as it stands for adoption by anyone. It is my hope, all the same, that some of its features will suggest appropriate adaptations for other institutions that occupy actual acreage in the real world.

Nolocus College is an institution of moderate size, located in a middle-sized city not far from the middle of the country. Nolocus (hereafter, NC) began as a school for missionaries and ministers in a large Protestant denomination. None of its present faculty or administration is certain just what denomination it was—some say Presbyterian, others Methodist—but they are sure they could find the information in the library. Today the church influence is discernible only in the central location of the building that once housed daily chapel services. It now houses the copy center and a cafeteria.

The NC student handbook deals with many of the same topics, and contains many of the same elements, as those of most other colleges. It opens with a hortatory statement from the president concerning the unique traditions of the college, its character as a place where students are both nurtured and challenged, and the like.

Immediately after this statement is another brief essay, this one written by last year's student government president. She echoes some of the same themes, but she writes more frankly about the difficulties of campus life and the tensions between freedom and order that the rules of conduct address. She also outlines the ways in which students assist in both revising and enforcing the code of conduct.

The same pattern is repeated in the sections that follow, each of which deals with a particular area of student conduct: plagiarism and academic honesty; use of alcohol, drugs, and tobacco products; and residence-hall life. Opening each section is a brief statement by a college administrator—the academic dean, the dean of students, and the residence-hall director, respectively. These are paired with statements by last year's valedictorian, by the student chair of the alcohol education committee, and by the student head of the residence-hall council. Each outlines the basic purposes underlying the regulations that follow, highlighting any recent revisions and any particularly difficult problems of enforcement that may have occurred in recent years.

The policies that follow consist in each case of a statement of purpose, an enumeration of required and proscribed actions, a summary of the procedures by which violations are charged and adjudicated, and a summary of the scale of sanctions for violation. A concluding paragraph in each section identifies what body adopted the policy as it now stands and what procedures should be followed by a member of the campus community who wishes to suggest its revision.

One of the remarkable things about NC's handbook—one that distinguishes it from all the handbooks I reviewed—is that everything in it except the contents page and the index is specifically attributed to some individual or a committee. Nothing appears anonymously or without attribution. There are no policies at NC that have materialized out of thin air or the reigning spirit. All have been adopted by identifiable bodies, and the preface to each is written by a named individual.

In a preface to the handbook, the dean of students avows overall editorial responsibility. The book as a whole, however, speaks in diverse voices. Both student and staff authors occasionally offer pointed criticisms of the way in which particular policies have been enforced recently, while suggesting ways of avoiding such problems in the future.

After the specific codes there is an account of the composition and procedures of the various disciplinary and appeal boards on campus. Each has student representation. Those dealing with academic matters have a faculty majority, while those entrusted with residence-hall regulations have a student majority.

So far the handbook's contents and organization are similar to those of many other institutions. The remainder of the book—the second half—is more unusual. In it we find a series of essays by administrators, faculty, and staff outlining what each takes to be the defining values of the campus and their implications for a variety of areas of controversy. One essay deals primarily with the issue of abusive speech and writing, arguing that it ought not to occur on campus even though it is not formally proscribed. Two are addressed to the experience of gay and lesbian students, taking somewhat opposed viewpoints. The first, by a faculty member, deplores past acts of exclusion and prejudice and calls on all members of the community to affirm and celebrate diverse modes of sexual and personal identity. The second, by a student, also condemns acts of discrimination but argues that it is naive of gay and lesbian students to expect full acceptance in a community most of whose members are unsure of their own sexuality and afraid of confronting others who make choices fundamentally different from their own. Gay and lesbian students who want to live openly and to feel that they fit in, she argues, should transfer out of NC. In a relatively conservative community like this one, they are entitled to equal treatment but not to affirmation.

And so on for several more essays. The past chair of the women's concerns committee has contributed an essay on the seriousness of the problem of acquaintance rape. Some of her claims are disputed by a member of the sociology faculty, who urges women to take responsibility for their own choices and not to fall into the trap of blaming others when they make bad choices. A particular incident in the local community two years ago, when several students acknowledged their part in vandalizing the Planned Parenthood office and then found themselves the target of rocks thrown through their windows, is recounted by the college chaplain as an illustration of the danger that disagreement may spark violence.

These essays change each year. A few are added, and a few subtracted, to reflect new problems and new circumstances. The handbook itself is published each year in mid-summer and sent immediately to all entering freshmen. Its contents, particularly the essays in the last half, are the basis for a series of four seminars held in the fall term in which ten freshmen, ten seniors, and two faculty members gather for an evening to talk about the character of the campus community. These meetings serve some of the purposes of traditional freshman orientation—some time is devoted to mechanics of course registration, choice of major, and extracurricular options. But they also convey to the entering students a sense that the college expects more of its students than mere compliance with the stated rules.

Neither the departmental structure nor the curriculum at NC is our concern, and I will not take the trouble to describe either in detail. The structure of the curriculum is conventional, except for an unusually large number of options for independent student work, not just for advanced majors but for first- and second-year students as well. Several student-faculty teams are engaged in long-term research projects, in the humanities as well as the sciences, which form a part of the students' individualized concentrations. The college has a large and distinguished philosophy department, of course, housed in a handsome suite of offices adjacent to the library.

One element in the college's hiring practices is especially worthy of note. The college seeks new faculty in the usual way, through advertisement in the disciplinary job newsletters, but from prospective faculty members it requests a dossier that attests not just to teaching and scholarship but also to personal character. In addition to the *curriculum vitae* each applicant is asked to solicit personal as well as academic letters of recommendation. The form letter sent to referees asks the writer's assessment of the candidate's scholarship, teaching, and personal qualities, stressing the close collaboration that is expected at NC among faculty, administrators, and students.

The judicial system at Nolocus is typical of those that we surveyed earlier. Academic rules are enforced by an honor-code system, and other disciplinary matters come before a student board aided by faculty advisers. Procedures for appeal, spelled out in detail in the handbook, are occasionally invoked.

The rules that this system undertakes to enforce are stricter in some areas, more permissive in others, than those on other campuses. Rules governing residence-hall life, in particular, are relatively restrictive. Use of alcoholic beverages is limited to the private rooms of students over twenty-one, overnight visitors are prohibited, and loud stereos are barred except during specified hours. At the same time, there are opportunities on campus to escape these restrictions. In the dining halls are several lounge areas where students congregate and where most parties take place.

The rules at Nolocus strive above all to maintain appropriate campus areas as residences and areas for study. They leave to students' discretion how they will conduct their lives off campus, and even in the less regulated areas on campus. The rules are more permissive than most with respect to hate speech, which leads to disciplinary action only if it is accompanied by actual acts of violence or abuse, and with respect to political and religious gatherings. Even though it is a state institution, Nolocus encourages use of campus facilities of all kinds—meeting rooms, party areas, film screening rooms—by religious groups in which students take part. Residence-hall supervisors and student affairs staff frequently help student groups plan outings and activities, whether it is the Sociology Club or the Hillel Foundation that is the sponsor.

To suppose that student misbehavior poses no problems at Nolocus College would be to leave the bounds of what can reasonably be imagined and enter the realm of fantasy. NC students are young men and women, not angels. When rule infractions occur, the campus community responds in a way that allows students as much self-government and self-regulation as is consistent with maintenance of an effective environment for learning. Students and faculty sit together on the judicial committees, and when possible they impose sanctions that have a constructive effect. Students found guilty of drug or alcohol offenses may be required to take several overnight shifts on the crisis hotline, for example. Plagiarists may be sentenced to spend twenty hours helping the library staff catch up with cataloging.

What especially distinguishes Nolocus College is something that at first seems to have nothing at all to do with the disciplinary system. It is the constant presence of faculty and staff, mingling with students at every formal and informal event. Faculty members are regularly present at meetings of student political discussion groups and religious fellowships. The president and the deans participate in evening panel discussions on local or national issues. There is a sense that, though students and faculty have their separate functions and responsibilities, all participate in numerous small communities and in a loose, larger community of communities. In this context, faculty and administrators are continually aware of student concerns, of developing problems in a particular residence hall, and of the character of the campus as students experience it.

What characterizes our imaginary ideal, in other words, is an interlocking set of moral communities. There is no central authority who stands *in loco parentis* over student behavior. Instead there is a vigorous and continuous process of dialogue among students, faculty, and administrators over a host of issues—disposition of discipline cases, possible adoption of a hate-speech code, whether porn films may be screened on campus, whether the student newspaper should accept advertisements from a white-supremacist group—that in itself both reflects and creates an atmosphere of mutual responsibility.

Conclusions

Morality on campus today is not, and cannot be, articulated by one voice on behalf of the institution. Rather, it is formed and shaped in dialogue. We cannot restore the ethical dimension that has largely vanished from the campus demands by reimposing the paternalistic rules of an earlier generation. Students will no longer heed a code of conduct handed out like the pronouncements of a distant parent. They insist that their views, their modes of life, and their rights to privacy and self-determination be respected.

Respect for the autonomy of students does not entail surrender to a wholly individualistic conception of morality, however. The ideal of the independent individual accountable to no laws save those he imposes on himself—an ideal drawn from philosophical liberalism that underlies much of modern politics and psychology—distorts our moral experience and misrepresents our ethical selves.

We are moral beings because we are beings who live in community and who shape our ideals in dialogue. The fictitious Nolocus College has a student discipline system that reflects this understanding both structurally and procedurally, by drawing all segments of the community into close but flexible relationships of discussion and cooperative action. The structure of most universities and colleges, in contrast, nurtures the fiction that the members of a campus community live their lives in independence and isolation from each other.

To rely so extensively on collaboration and dialogue is to risk failure, if the members of the community fall short of what is expected of them. It is also to take a risk that the very structures of dialogue and common purpose may be used to exclude dissenters and disarm their criticisms. Close-knit communities, on campus as elsewhere, can be intolerant and resistant to change.

These potential problems demand vigilance, as well as explicit measures to protect dissent. But they do not require a retreat from the fundamental goal of shaping, without dictating, the moral atmosphere. The purpose of the college is not simply to keep the community together, after all. The goal is rather to achieve a sense of common purpose even while encouraging dissent and debate. That this goal is difficult to achieve is no reason to abandon it.

In these more philosophical reflections we have moved a long way from our starting point in the assessment of discipline codes as they now exist on campus. The ideal that I have sketched, in this last section, is only a suggestion of the kind of campus environment that might move colleges nearer to their ultimate goals. A commitment to creating moral communities through dialogue and collaboration could be expressed in many other ways to fit particular circumstances. Such a commitment, in whatever form it may take shape, is essential to the restoration of a moral atmosphere on campus.

The moral vacuum that now obtains on many campuses, the absence of any clear motivation or direction for student conduct or for the institution as a whole, has corrosive effects on faculty and students alike. Faculty are encouraged to see their responsibility as limited to research and lecturing; students are given help with the intellectual aspects of self-definition but not with the equally essential moral and personal aspects.

This vacuum can be dispelled, and a constructive moral atmosphere restored, if faculty and administrators alike will dedicate themselves to the task, not by restoring the institutional parent to a position of control but by rebuilding the campus community as a model of moral dialogue. To do so promises not only to address many problems of student behavior more effectively than do other methods of control—from hate speech to alcohol abuse to plagiarism—but also to strengthen the shared sense among colleagues and coworkers of being engaged in a vital common task.

Those of us who are faculty members and administrators can no longer take it as our task to tell students what they ought to do. Instead, we need to explore how best to demonstrate to students what it is like to commit oneself to learning and teaching in community. When we have found effective ways to do that, we will have brought to the campus an atmosphere of moral accountability and mutual respect that can rightly demand our engagement and allegiance.

The words of Justice Douglas, in his dissenting opinion in *Healy v. James*, were specifically directed to questions of free speech and expression on campus, but the terms in which he frames his remarks are of much broader application.

Students as well as faculty are entitled to credentials in their search for truth. If we are to become an integrated, adult society, rather than a stubborn status quo opposed to change, students and faculty should have communal interests in which each age learns from the other. Without ferment of one kind or another, a college or university (like a federal agency or other human institution) becomes a useless appendage to a society which traditionally has reflected the spirit of rebellion.[5]

Students and faculty do indeed have communal interests—that is to say, literally, that they have interests not merely as individuals but as a community. To form a genuine community, by fostering and encouraging the numerous smaller communities in which students and faculty find their place and form their identify, is the ultimate goal of the entire system of student conduct regulation and discipline. I hope that this study will help concerned faculty, administrators, and students to articulate that goal more clearly and, having done so, to work for its achievement.

Notes

1. This figure from a 1987 study by Mary Koss is cited by Ronald Lieber in an Op-Ed article, "Call the Police, Not the Dean," *New York Times*, Sept. 11, 1991, p. A27. It should be added that subsequent discussions in the *Chronicle of Higher Education* have challenged the accuracy of this estimate, which suggests that sexual assault is many times more frequent on campus than off.

2. Michele N-K Collison, "Increase in Reports of Sexual Assaults Strains Campus Disciplinary Systems," *Chronicle of Higher Education*, May 15, 1991, pp. A29, A30.

3. The experiment, which was conducted by Fletcher Blanchard, is briefly described in the *Chronicle of Higher Education*, July 24, 1991, p. A25.

4. See MacIntyre 1981, 1988; Nussbaum 1986, Nussbaum 1990; Bernstein 1986.

5. Douglas, J., dissenting opinion in *Healy v. James*, 92 S.Ct. 2338 (1972), at 2354.

Supplementary Materials

Appendix A

Legal Decisions Affecting Student Discipline

The People v. Wheaton College
(Illinois Supreme Court, 1866)

Mr. Justice LAWRENCE delivered the opinion of the Court:

E. Hartley Pratt, a student in Wheaton college, joined a secret society known as the Good Templars, in violation of the college rules. For this the faculty "suspended him from the privileges of the institution until he should express a purpose to conform to its rules." His father thereupon applied for a mandamus to compel the college to re-instate him as a student. The mandamus was refused, and the relator has brought the case here.

Wheaton college is an incorporated institution, resting upon private endowments, and deriving no aid whatever from the State or from taxation. Its charter gives to the trustees and faculty the power "to adopt and enforce such rules as may be deemed expedient for the government of the institution," a power which they would have possessed without such express grant, because incident to the very object of their incorporation, and indispensable to the successful management of the college. Among the rules they have deemed it expedient to adopt, is one forbidding the students to become members of secret societies. We perceive nothing unreasonable in the rule itself, since all persons familiar with college life know that the tendency of secret societies is to withdraw students from the control of the faculty, and impair to some extent the discipline of the institution. Such may not always be their effect, but such is their general tendency. But whether the rule be judicious or not, it violates neither good morals nor the law of the land, and is therefore clearly within the power of the college authorities to make and enforce. A discretionary power has been given them to regulate the discipline of their college in such manner as they deem proper, and so long as their rules violate neither divine nor human law, we have no more authority to interfere than we have to control the domestic discipline of a father in his family. It is urged that the Good Templars are a society established for the promotion of temperance, and incorporated by the legislature, and that any citizen has a right to join it. We do not doubt the beneficent objects of the society, and we admit that any citizen has a right to join it if the society consents. But this right is not of so high and solemn a character that it cannot be surrendered, and the son of the relator did voluntarily surrender it when he became a student of Wheaton college, for he knew, or must be taken to have known, that by the rules of the institution which he was voluntarily entering, he would be precluded from joining any secret society. When it is said that a person has a legal *right* to do certain things, all that the phrase means is, that the law does not forbid these things to be done. It does not mean that the law guarantees the right to do them at all possible times and under all possible circumstances. A person in his capacity as a citizen may have the right to do many things which a student of Wheaton college cannot do without incurring the penalty of college laws. A person as a citizen has a legal right to marry, or to walk the streets at midnight, or to board at a public hotel, and yet it would be absurd to say that a college cannot forbid its students to do any of these things. So a citizen, as such, can attend church on Sunday or not, as he may think proper, but it could hardly be contended that a college would not have the right to make attendance upon religious services a condition of remaining within its walls. The son of the relator has an undoubted legal right to join either Wheaton college or the Good Templars, and they have both an undoubted right to expel him if he refuses to abide by such regulations as they establish, not inconsistent with law or good morals.

Judgment affirmed

Healy v. James
(United States Supreme Court, 1972)

Mr. Justice POWELL delivered the opinion of the Court.

This case, arising out of a denial by a state college of official recognition to a group of students who desired to form a local chapter of Students for a Democratic Society (SDS), presents this Court with questions requiring the application of well-established First Amendment principles. While the factual background of this particular case raises these constitutional issues in a manner not heretofore passed on by the Court, and only infrequently presented to lower federal courts, our decision today is governed by existing precedent.

As the case involves delicate issues concerning the academic community, we approach our task with special caution, recognizing the mutual interest of students, faculty members, and administrators in an environment free from disruptive interference with the educational process. We also are mindful of the equally significant interest in the widest latitude for free expression and debate consonant with the maintenance of order. Where these interests appear to compete, the First Amendment, made binding on the States by the Fourteenth Amendment, strikes the required balance. . . .

II

[1] At the outset we note that state colleges and universities are not enclaves immune from the sweep of the First Amendment. "It can hardly be argued that either students or teachers shed their constitutional rights to freedom of speech or expression at the schoolhouse gate." Tinker v. Des Moines Independent Community School District, 393 U.S. 503, 506, 89 S.Ct. 733, 736, 21 L.Ed.2d 731 (1969). Of course, as Mr. Justice Fortas made clear in *Tinker,* First Amendment rights must always be applied "in light of the special characteristics of the . . . environment" in the particular case. And, where state-operated educational institutions are involved, this Court has long recognized "the need for affirming the comprehensive authority of the States and of school officials, consistent with fundamental constitutional safeguards, to prescribe and control conduct in the schools." Yet, the precedents of this Court leave no room for the view that, because of the acknowledged need for order, First Amendment protections should apply with less force on college campuses than in the community at large. Quite to the contrary, "[t]he vigilant protection

of constitutional freedoms is nowhere more vital than in the community of American schools." Shelton v. Tucker, 364 U.S. 479, 487, 81 S.Ct. 247, 251, 5 L.Ed.2d 231 (1960). The college classroom with its surrounding environs is peculiarly the " 'marketplace of ideas,' " and we break no new constitutional ground in reaffirming this Nation's dedication to safeguarding academic freedom. . . .

[2,3]   Among the rights protected by the First Amendment is the right of individuals to associate to further their personal beliefs. While the freedom of association is not explicitly set out in the Amendment, it has long been held to be implicit in the freedoms of speech, assembly, and petition. . . . There can be no doubt that denial of official recognition, without justification, to college organizations burdens or abridges that associational right. The primary impediment to free association flowing from nonrecognition is the denial of use of campus facilities for meetings and other appropriate purposes. The practical effect of nonrecognition was demonstrated in this case when, several days after the President's decision was announced, petitioners were not allowed to hold a meeting in the campus coffee shop because they were not an approved group.

[4]   Petitioners' associational interests also were circumscribed by the denial of the use of campus bulletin boards and the school newspaper. If an organization is to remain a viable entity in a campus community in which new students enter on a regular basis, it must possess the means of communicating with these students. Moreover, the organization's ability to participate in the intellectual give and take of campus debate, and to pursue its stated purposes, is limited by denial of access to the customary media for communicating with the administration, faculty members, and other students. Such impediments cannot be viewed as insubstantial.

[17–20]   . . . The critical line for First Amendment purposes must be drawn between advocacy, which is entitled to full protection, and action, which is not. Petitioners may, if they so choose, preach the propriety of amending or even doing away with any or all campus regulations. They may not, however, undertake to flout these rules. Mr. Justice Blackmun, at the time he was a circuit judge on the Eighth Circuit, stated:

"We . . . hold that a college has the inherent power to promulgate rules and regulations; that it has the inherent power properly to discipline; that it has power appropriately to protect itself and its property; that it may expect that its students adhere to generally accepted standards of conduct." Esteban v. Central Missouri State College, 415 F.2d 1077, 1089

(CA8 1969), cert. denied, 398 U.S. 965, 90 S.Ct. 2169, 26 L.Ed.2d 548 (1970).

Just as in the community at large, reasonable regulations with respect to the time, the place, and the manner in which student groups conduct their speech-related activities must be respected. A college administration may impose a requirement, such as may have been imposed in this case, that a group seeking official recognition affirm in advance its willingness to adhere to reasonable campus law. Such a requirement does not impose an impermissible condition on the students' associational rights. Their freedom to speak out, to assemble, or to petition for changes in school rules is in no sense infringed. It merely constitutes an agreement to conform with reasonable standards respecting conduct. This is a minimal requirement, in the interest of the entire academic community, of any group seeking the privilege of official recognition.

[21] Petitioners have not challenged in this litigation the procedural or substantive aspects of the College's requirements governing applications for official recognition. Although the record is unclear on this point, CCSC may have, among its requirements for recognition, a rule that prospective groups affirm that they intend to comply with reasonable campus regulations. Upon remand it should first be determined whether the College recognition procedures contemplate any such requirement. If so, it should then be ascertained whether petitioners intend to comply. Since we do not have the terms of a specific prior affirmation rule before us, we are not called on to decide whether any particular formulation would or would not prove constitutionally acceptable. Assuming the existence of a valid rule, however, we do conclude that the benefits of participation in the internal life of the college community may be denied to any group that reserves the right to violate any valid campus rules with which it disagrees.

IV

We think the above discussion establishes the appropriate framework for consideration of petitioners' request for campus recognition. Because respondents failed to accord due recognition to First Amendment principles, the judgments below approving respondents' denial of recognition must be reversed. Since we cannot conclude from this record that petitioners were willing to abide by reasonable campus rules and regulations, we order the case remanded for reconsideration. We note, in so holding, that the wide latitude accorded by the Constitution to the freedoms of expression and association is not without its costs in terms of the risk to the maintenance of civility and an ordered society. Indeed, this latitude often has resulted, on the campus and elsewhere, in the infringement of the rights of others. Though we deplore the tendency of some to abuse the very constitutional privileges they invoke, and although the infringement of rights of others certainly should not be tolerated, we reaffirm this Court's dedication to the principles of the Bill of Rights upon which our vigorous and free society is founded.

Reversed and remanded.

Mr. Justice DOUGLAS.

While I join the opinion of the Court, I add a few words.

As Dr. Birenbaum says, the status quo of the college or university is the governing body (trustees or overseers), administrative officers, who include caretakers, and the police, and the faculty. Those groups have well-defined or vaguely inferred values to perpetuate. The customary technique has been to conceive of the minds of students as receptacles for the information which the faculty have garnered over the years. Education is commonly thought of as the process of filling the receptacles with what the faculty in its wisdom deems fit and proper.

Many, inside and out of faculty circles, realize that one of the main problems of faculty members is their own re-education or re-orientation. Some have narrow specialties that are hardly relevant to modern times. History has passed others by, leaving them interesting relics of a bygone day. More often than not they represent those who withered under the pressures of McCarthyism or other forces of conformity and represent but a timid replica of those who once brought distinction to the ideal of academic freedom.

The confrontation between them and the oncoming students has often been upsetting. The problem is not one of choosing sides. Students—who, by reason of the Twenty-sixth Amendment, become eligible to vote when 18 years of age—are adults who are members of the college or university community. Their interests and concerns are often quite different from those of the faculty. They often have values, views, and ideologies that are at war with the ones which the college has traditionally espoused or indoctrinated. When they ask for change, they, the students, speak in the tradition of Jefferson and Madison and the First Amendment.

The First Amendment does not authorize violence. But it does authorize advocacy, group activities, and espousal of change. The present case is minuscule in the events of the 60's and 70's. But the fact that it has to come here for ultimate resolution indicates the sickness of our academic world, measured by First Amendment standards. Students as well as faculty are entitled to credentials in their search for truth. If we are to become an integrated, adult society, rather than a stubborn status quo opposed to change, students and faculties should have communal interests in which each age learns from the other. Without ferment of one kind or another, a college or university (like a federal agency or other human institution) becomes a useless appendage to a society which traditionally has reflected the spirit of rebellion.

Bradshaw v. Rawlings
(United States District Court, Third Circuit, 1979)

OPINION OF THE COURT
ALDISERT, Circuit Judge.

The major question for decision in this diversity case tried under Pennsylvania law is whether a college may be subject to tort liability for injuries sustained by one of its students involved in an automobile accident when the driver of the car was a fellow student who had become intoxicated at a class picnic. Another question relates to the liability of the distributor who furnished beer for the picnic which led to the intoxication of the driver. Still another question concerns the tort liability of the municipality where the plaintiff's injuries occurred.

The district court permitted the question of negligence to go to the jury against the college, the beer distributor and the municipality. From an adverse verdict of $1,108,067 each of the defendants has appealed, advancing separate arguments for reversal. The plaintiff has filed a conditional cross-appeal. . . .

A.

[1,2] The college's argument strikes at the heart of tort law because a negligence claim must fail if based on circumstances for which the law imposes no duty of care on the defendant. "Negligence in the air, so to speak, will not do."[1] As Professor Prosser has emphasized, the statement that there is or is not a duty begs the essential question, which is whether the plaintiff's interests are entitled to legal protection against the defendant's conduct. " '[D]uty' is not sacrosanct in itself, but only an expression of the sum total of those considerations of policy which lead the law to say that a particular plaintiff is entitled to protection."[2] Thus, we may perceive duty simply as an obligation to which the law will give recognition in order to require one person to conform to a particular standard of conduct with respect to another person.

These abstract descriptions of duty cannot be helpful, however, unless they are directly related to the competing individual, public, and social interests implicated in any case. An interest is a social fact, factor, or phenomenon existing independently of the law which is reflected by a claim, demand, or desire that people seek to satisfy and that has been recognized as socially valid by authoritative decision makers in society.[3] Certainly, the plaintiff in this case possessed an

176

important interest in remaining free from bodily injury, and thus the law protects his right to recover compensation from those who negligently cause him injury. The college, on the other hand, has an interest in the nature of its relationship with its adult students, as well as an interest in avoiding responsibilities that it is incapable of performing.

B.

[3] Our beginning point is a recognition that the modern American college is not an insurer of the safety of its students. Whatever may have been its responsibility in an earlier era, the authoritarian role of today's college administrations has been notably diluted in recent decades. Trustees, administrators, and faculties have been required to yield to the expanding rights and privileges of their students. By constitutional amendment,[4] written and unwritten law, and through the evolution of new customs, rights formerly possessed by college administrations have been transferred to students. College students today are no longer minors; they are now regarded as adults in almost every phase of community life. For example except for purposes of purchasing alcoholic beverages, eighteen year old persons are considered adults by the Commonwealth of Pennsylvania. They may vote,[5] marry,[6] make a will,[7] qualify as a personal representative,[8] serve as a guardian of the estate of a minor,[9] wager at racetracks,[10] register as a public accountant,[11] practice veterinary medicine,[12] qualify as a practical nurse,[13] drive trucks, ambulances and other official fire vehicles,[14] perform general fire-fighting duties,[15] and qualify as a private detective.[16] Pennsylvania has set eighteen as the age at which criminal acts are no longer treated as those of a juvenile,[17] and eighteen year old students may waive their testimonial privilege protecting confidential statements to school personnel.[18] Moreover, a person may join the Pennsylvania militia at an even younger age than eighteen[19] and may hunt without adult supervision at age sixteen.[20] As a result of these and other similar developments in our society, eighteen year old students are now identified with an expansive bundle of individual and social interests and possess discrete rights not held by college students from decades past. There was a time when college administrators and faculties assumed a role in *loco parentis*. Students were committed to their charge because the students were considered minors. A special relationship was created between college and student that imposed a duty on the college to exercise control over student conduct and, reciprocally, gave the students certain rights of protection by the

college. The campus revolutions of the late sixties and early seventies were a direct attack by the students on rigid controls by the colleges and were an all-pervasive affirmative demand for more student rights. In general, the students succeeded, peaceably and otherwise, in acquiring a new status at colleges throughout the country. These movements, taking place almost simultaneously with legislation and case law lowering the age of majority, produced fundamental changes in our society. A dramatic reapportionment of responsibilities and social interests of general security took place. Regulation by the college of student life on and off campus has become limited. Adult students now demand and receive expanded rights of privacy in their college life including, for example, liberal, if not unlimited, partial visiting hours. College administrators no longer control the broad arena of general morals. At one time, exercising their rights and duties *in loco parentis,* colleges were able to impose strict regulations. But today students vigorously claim the right to define and regulate their own lives. Especially have they demanded and received satisfaction of their interest in self-assertion in both physical and mental activities, and have vindicated what may be called the interest in freedom of the individual will. In 1972 Justice Douglas summarized the change:

> Students—who, by reason of the Twenty-sixth Amendment, become eligible to vote when 18 years of age—are adults who are members of the college or university community. Their interests and concerns are often quite different from those of the faculty. They often have values, views, and ideologies that are at war with the ones which the college has traditionally espoused or indoctrinated.

Healy v. James, 408 U.S. 169, 197, 92 S.Ct. 2338, 2354, 33 L.Ed.2d 266 (1972) (Douglas, J., concurring).

Thus, for purposes of examining fundamental relationships that underlie tort liability, the competing interests of the student and of the institution of higher learning are much different today than they were in the past. At the risk of oversimplification, the change has occurred because society considers the modern college student an adult, not a child of tender years. It could be argued, although we need not decide here, that an educational institution possesses a different pattern of rights and responsibilities and retains more of the traditional custodial responsibilities when its students are all minors, as in an elementary school, or mostly minors, as in a high school. Under such circumstances, after weighing relevant competing interests, Pennsylvania might possibly impose on the institution certain duties of protection, for the breach of which a legal remedy would be available. But here, because the circumstances show that the students have reached the age of majority and are capable of protecting their own self interests, we believe that the rule would be different. We conclude, therefore, that in order to ascertain whether a specific duty of care extended from Delaware Valley College to its injured student, we must first identify and assess the competing individual and social interests associated with the parties.

III.

A.

[4] In the process of identifying the competing interests implicated in the student-college relationship, we note that the record in this case is not overly generous in identifying the interests possessed by the student, although it was Bradshaw's burden to prove the existence of a duty owed him by the college in order to establish a breach thereof. Bradshaw has concentrated on the school regulation imposing sanctions on the use of alcohol by students. The regulation states: "Possession or consumption of alcohol or malt beverages on the property of the College or at any College sponsored or related affair off campus will result in disciplinary action. The same rule will apply to every student regardless of age." App. at 726a–727a. We are not impressed that this regulation, in and of itself, is sufficient to place the college in a custodial relationship with its students for purposes of imposing a duty of protection in this case. We assume that the average student arrives on campus at the age of seventeen or eighteen, and that most students are under twenty-one during the better part of their college careers. A college regulation that essentially tracks a state law and prohibits conduct that to students under twenty-one is already prohibited by state law does not, in our view, indicate that the college voluntarily assumed a custodial relationship with its students so as to make operative the provision of § 320 of the Restatement (Second) of Torts.

Thus, we predict that the Pennsylvania courts would not hold that by promulgating this regulation the college had voluntarily taken custody of Bradshaw so as to deprive him of his normal power of self-protection or to subject him to association with persons likely to cause him harm. Absent proof of such a relationship, we do not believe that a prima facie case of custodial duty was established in order to submit the case to the jury on this theory.

Notes

1. F. Pollock, Law of Torts 468 (13th ed. 1929).
2. W. Prosser, Law of Torts 33 (3d ed. 1964).
3. *See, e.g.*, Pound, *A Survey of Social Interests*, 57 Harv.L.Rev. 1 (1943), Llewellyn, *A Realistic Jurisprudence—The Next Step*, 30 Column.L.Rev. 431, 441–47 (1930).
4. Section one of the twenty-sixth amendment to the United States Constitution provides: "The right of citizens of the United States, who are eighteen years of age or older, to vote shall not be denied or abridged by the United States or by any State on account of age."
5. 25 P.S. § 2811.
6. 48 P.S. §§ 1–5.
7. 20 Pa.C.S. § 2501.
8. 20 Pa.C.S. § 3156.
9. 20 Pa.C.S. § 5112.
10. 15 P.S. § 2621.
11. 63 P.S. § 9.8g.
12. 63 P.S. § 485.9.
13. 63 P.S. § 655.
14. 43 P.S. § 48.3.
15. *Id.*
16. 22 Pa.C.S. § 46.
17. 42 Pa.C.S. §§ 6302, 6303–08.
18. 42 Pa.C.S. § 5945.
19. 51 Pa.C.S. § 301 (seventeen years, six months).
20. 34 P.S. § 1311.316.

Beach v. University of Utah
(Utah Supreme Court, 1986)

ZIMMERMAN, Justice:

Plaintiff Danna Beach appeals from a summary judgment dismissing her claim against the University of Utah, the President of the University, the University Institutional Council, various officials of the College of Science, and a biology professor (collectively referred to as "the University") seeking damages for personal injuries sustained when she fell from a cliff at night during a field trip sponsored by the University. . . .

Beach filed a suit seeking damages from Cuellar, the University, and numerous University officials. The University moved for summary judgment alleging that it owed Beach no special duty of care. For purposes of the summary judgment, the court assumed *arguendo* that the University had a duty to exercise reasonable care to protect and supervise Beach, but concluded that there was no breach of that duty. The trial court therefore granted the University's motion and dismissed Beach's action.

On appeal, Beach asserts that a special relationship existed between the parties which gave rise to an affirmative duty on Cuellar's part to supervise and protect her. She claims that summary judgment was inappropriate because the facts were in dispute concerning whether that duty had been breached.

One essential element of a negligence action is a duty of reasonable care owed to the plaintiff by defendant. *Hughes v. Housley,* 599 P.2d 1250, 1253 (Utah 1979); *Williams v. Melby,* 699 P.2d 723, 726 (Utah 1985). Absent a showing of a duty, Beach cannot recover.

Here, Beach contends that Cuellar and the University breached their affirmative duty to supervise and protect her. Ordinarily, a party does not have an affirmative duty to care for another. Absent unusual circumstances which justify imposing such an affirmative responsibility, "one has no duty to look after the safety of another who has become voluntarily intoxicated and thus limited his ability to protect himself." *Benally v. Robinson,* 14 Utah 2d 6, 9, 376 P.2d 388, 390 (1962). The law imposes upon one party an affirmative duty to act only when certain special relationships exist between the parties. These relationships generally arise when one assumes responsibility for another's safety or deprives another of his or her normal opportunities for self-protection. Restatement (Second) of Torts § 314(A) 1964. The

181

essence of a special relationship is dependence by one party upon the other or mutual dependence between the parties.

To avoid summary judgment, Beach was obligated to prove that she had a special relationship with the University which obligated the University to supervise and protect her and that the duty was breached, causing her injuries. The question, then, is whether the facts in the record establish some basis for imposing an affirmative duty upon the University to protect Beach from her own intoxication and disorientation on the night in question.

At oral argument, counsel for Beach conceded that the mere relationship of student to teacher was not enough to give rise to such a duty. In fact, Beach's counsel conceded that Cuellar had no duty to walk each student to his or her tent or sleeping bag on the night of the accident, a measure that presumably would have prevented the accident. Therefore, to prevail on the special duty issue, Beach must distinguish her circumstances from those of the other students on the field trip.

The primary thrust of Beach's claim before this Court, as demonstrated by her counsel's concessions at oral argument, is that based upon the incident during the earlier field trip to Lake Powell, Cuellar knew or should have known of her propensity to become disoriented after drinking. Because of this knowledge, Beach maintains that the University had a special duty to supervise her on the evening in question. We do not agree that any special duty arose by reason of Cuellar's knowledge.

The Lake Powell incident, which Beach relies upon heavily, is not determinative of whether a special relationship arose. Beach testified that at Lake Powell, she became dizzy when she reached the bushes after leaving the rest of the company. Therefore, there was nothing about her demeanor during the time she was within Cuellar's sight that would have alerted Cuellar or other participants in the field trip to the fact that she had a tendency to become dizzy or disoriented when she consumed alcohol. Equally important, Beach told Cuellar after that incident that what had occurred was not normal behavior for her.

At the time of the final field trip, Beach had attended other field trips and had had no further incidents. She evidenced the judgment and skills of any normal twenty-year-old college student. There was nothing to suggest that she was not in good physical condition; in fact, on the final trip she joined several other students in rappelling from rocks located just above the area where she was later injured. Cuellar testified that on the night of the accident, he did not know that Beach in particular had been drinking. Indeed, Beach testified that when she left the van for her tent, her behavior was normal and would not have suggested to any observer that she was intoxicated or disoriented.

Under these circumstances, we conclude as a matter of law that Beach's situation was not distinguishable from that of the other students on the trip; therefore, no special relationship arose between the University and Beach. Nothing Cuellar knew would have led him to conclude that if he did not walk Beach to her tent and see that she was down for the night, she might wander off and be injured. Because no special relationship existed, the University had no affirmative obligation to protect or supervise her and no duty was breached. . . .

. . . We also must consider the nature of the institution. Elementary and high schools certainly can be characterized as a mixture of custodial and educational institutions, largely because those who attend them are juveniles. However, colleges and universities are educational institutions, not custodial. *Accord Baldwin v. Zoradi,* 123 Cal.App.3d at 281–82, 176 Cal.Rptr. at 813. Their purpose is to educate in a manner which will assist the graduate to perform well in the civic, community, family, and professional positions he or she may undertake in the future. It would be unrealistic to impose upon an institution of higher education the additional role of custodian over its adult students and to charge it with responsibility for preventing students from illegally consuming alcohol and, should they do so, with responsibility for assuring their safety and the safety of others. *Accord Bradshaw v. Rawlings,* 612 F.2d at 138; *Baldwin v. Zoradi,* 123 Cal.App.3d at 290–91, 176 Cal.Rptr. at 818. Fulfilling this charge would require the institution to babysit each student, a task beyond the resources of any school. But more importantly, such measures would be inconsistent with the nature of the relationship between the student and the institution, for it would produce a repressive and inhospitable environment, largely inconsistent with the objectives of a modern college education.

Mullins v. Pine Manor
(Massachusetts Supreme Court, 1983)

LIACOS, Justice.

The plaintiff, a female student at Pine Manor College (college), was raped on campus by an unidentified assailant who was never apprehended. She commenced this action against the college and its vice president for operations, William P. Person, to recover damages for injuries suffered. The case was tried before a jury in the Superior Court. The jury returned verdicts against the college and Person in the amount of $175,000. Pursuant to G.L. c. 231, § 85K, the trial judge reduced the amount of the judgment against the college to $20,000. The college and Person appeal from the denial of their motions for directed verdicts and for judgments notwithstanding the verdicts. We granted their applications for direct appellate review. We affirm the judgments.

There was evidence of the following facts. Pine Manor College is a four year college for women located in the Chestnut Hill section of Brookline. In 1977, approximately 400 students attended the school. The campus is surrounded on all sides by a six foot high chain link fence, except for an area on either side of the main entrance to the campus where the fence stands four feet tall. The college's dormitories are clustered together in three villages. Each village is comprised of a commons building and a number of separate dormitory buildings. The buildings are arranged to form a square. To gain access to a dormitory, a student must enter an enclosed courtyard through either the commons building or one of three exterior gates. Between 5 p.m. and 7 a.m., these gates and the door to the commons building are locked. Students enter their dormitory through locked doors which open directly into the courtyard. Each student had one key which unlocked the doors to her commons building, her dormitory building, and her individual room.

After 8 p.m., all visitors were admitted by a security guard at the main entrance to the campus. The guard would direct them to the appropriate commons building. At the entrance to the commons building, visitors would be stopped by a student on duty and would be registered. The student hostess would be notified and was required to come to the commons building to act as the visitor's escort. No visitors were permitted anywhere on campus unescorted after 1 a.m. on weekends.

At the time of the rape, the college had two guards on duty after midnight. One guard was stationed in an observation post at the main entrance. The second guard was assigned to patrol the campus. He was responsible for making rounds to the villages every fifteen to thirty minutes to check the doors and gates to see that they were locked. The college had no formal system of supervising the guards. Rather, the director of security at the college would make random checks on their work.

Mullins was a first year student and, as required by the college, she lived on campus. Her dormitory housed thirty women. Under college regulations, male visitors were permitted to stay overnight. Mullins was assigned to a single room at the end of a corridor. Another student resided in a room located adjacent to hers. The doors to these two rooms were at a right angle to each other.

On December 11, 1977, Mullins returned to her dormitory at approximately 3 a.m. with two friends. It was a bitter cold night. They entered the village through one of the exterior gates to the courtyard. It was unlocked. They opened the door to their dormitory and proceeded to their rooms. After changing into her night clothes, Mullins, leaving the door to her room open, went to talk with a friend who resided in the room next door. They talked for a few minutes, apparently near the open door to the friend's room. Mullins returned to her room, locked her door, and went to sleep. Between 4 a.m. and 4:30 a.m., she was awakened by an intruder. He asked her where her car was located, and she responded that she did not have a car. The intruder then threatened her and placed a pillow case over her head. He led her out of the building and across the courtyard. They left the courtyard by proceeding under the chains of one of the exterior gates which was not secured tightly. They walked down a bicycle path toward the refectory, the college's dining hall. After marching about in front of the refectory, they entered the refectory through an unlocked door and spent several minutes inside. They proceeded out of the refectory and marched around in front. They then went back inside, and the assailant raped her. The entire incident lasted sixty to ninety minutes, and they were outside on the campus for at least twenty minutes.

Pine Manor is located in an area with relatively few reports of violent crime. In the years prior to this attack, there had been no incidents of violent crime on the campus. The record discloses, however, that one year before the attack a burglary had occurred in one of the dormitory buildings. Additionally, the evening before the rape, a young man scaled the outer fence around the campus and walked into the commons building of Mullins's village, which was the first building he saw. The door to the building was open. The college is also located a short distance from bus and subway lines which lead directly to Boston.

Additional facts, including the testimony of expert witnesses, will be discussed as they become relevant.

1. *Duty to protect against criminal acts.* The defendants argue that they owe no duty to protect students against the criminal acts of third parties. They rely on the general proposition that there is no duty to protect others from the criminal or wrongful activities of third persons. See Restatement (Second) of Torts § 314 (1965). Cf. W. Prosser, Torts § 33, at 173–174 (4th ed. 1971) (actor may usually assume others will obey criminal law). But see Restatement (Second) of Torts §§ 302B, 314A & 448 (1965). We conclude that this rule has little application to the circumstances of this case.

The duty of due care owed the plaintiff by the defendants in the present case can be grounded on either of two well established principles of law. First, we have said that a duty finds its "source in existing social values and customs." *Schofield v. Merrill*, 386 Mass. 244, 247, 435 N.E.2d 339 (1982). See *Pridgren v. Boston Hous. Auth.*, 364 Mass. 696, 711, 308 N.E.2d 467 (1974); *Mounsey v. Ellard*, 363 Mass. 693, 706–708, 297 N.E.2d 43 (1973). We think it can be said with confidence that colleges of ordinary prudence customarily exercise care to protect the well-being of their resident students, including seeking to protect them against the criminal acts of third parties. An expert witness hired by the defendant testified that he had visited eighteen area colleges, and, not surprisingly, all took steps to provide an adequate level of security on their campus. He testified also that standards had been established for determining what precautions should be taken. Thus, the college community itself has recognized its obligation to protect resident students from the criminal acts of third parties. This recognition indicates that the imposition of a duty of care is firmly embedded in a community consensus.

The consensus stems from the nature of the situation. The concentration of young people, especially young women, on a college campus, creates favorable opportunities for criminal behavior. The threat of criminal acts of third parties to resident students is self-evident, and the college is the party which is in the position to take those steps which are necessary to ensure the safety of its students. No student has the ability to design and implement a security system, hire and supervise security guards, provide security at the entrance of dormitories, install proper locks, and establish a system of announcement for authorized visitors. Resident students typically live in a particular room for a mere nine months and, as a consequence, lack the incentive and capacity to take corrective measures. College regulations may also bar the installation of additional locks or chains. Some students may not have been exposed previously to living in a residence hall or in a metropolitan area and may not be fully conscious of the dangers that are present. Thus, the college must take the responsibility on itself if anything is to be done at all. Cf. *Young v. Garwacki,* 380 Mass. 162, 168, 402 N.E.2d 1045 (1980).

[1-3] Of course, changes in college life, reflected in the general decline of the theory that a college stands in loco parentis to its students, arguably cut against this view. The fact that a college need not police the morals of its resident students, however, does not entitle it to abandon any effort to ensure their physical safety. Parents, students, and the general community still have a reasonable expectation, fostered in part by colleges themselves, that reasonable care will be exercised to protect resident students from foreseeable harm.

Dixon v. Alabama State Board of Education

(United States Court of Appeals Fifth Circuit, 1961)

RIVES, Circuit Judge.

The question presented by the pleadings and evidence, and decisive of this appeal, is whether due process requires notice and some opportunity for hearing before students at a tax-supported college are expelled for misconduct. We answer that question in the affirmative. . . .

The evidence clearly shows that the question for decision does not concern the sufficiency of the notice or the adequacy of the hearing, but is whether the students had a right to any notice or hearing whatever before being expelled. The district court wrote at some length on that question, as appears from its opinion. Dixon v. Alabama State Board of Education, supra, 186 F.Supp. at pages 950–952. After careful study and consideration, we find ourselves unable to agree with the conclusion of the district court that no notice or opportunity for any kind of hearing was required before these students were expelled. . . .

Turning then to the nature of the governmental power to expel the plaintiffs, it must be conceded, as was held by the district court, that that power is not unlimited and cannot be arbitrarily exercised. Admittedly, there must be some reasonable and constitutional ground for expulsion or the courts would have a duty to require reinstatement. The possibility of arbitrary action is not excluded by the existence of reasonable regulations. There may be arbitrary application of the rule to the facts of a particular case. Indeed, that result is well nigh inevitable when the Board hears only one side of the issue. In the disciplining of college students there are no considerations of immediate danger to the public, or of peril to the national security, which should prevent the Board from exercising at least the fundamental principles of fairness by giving the accused students notice of the charges and an opportunity to be heard in their own defense. Indeed, the example set by the Board in failing so to do, if not corrected by the courts, can well break the spirits of the expelled students and of others familiar with the injustice, and do inestimable harm to their education.

. . . We are confident that precedent as well as a most fundamental constitutional principle support our holding that due process requires notice and some opportunity for hearing before a student at a tax-supported college is expelled for misconduct.

For the guidance of the parties in the event of further proceedings, we state our views on the nature of the notice and hearing required by due process prior to expulsion from a state college or university. They should, we think, comply with the following standards. The notice should contain a statement of the specific charges and grounds which, if proven, would justify expulsion under the regulations of the Board of Education. The nature of the hearing should vary depending upon the circumstances of the particular case. The case before us requires something more than an informal interview with an administrative authority of the college. By its nature, a charge of misconduct, as opposed to a failure to meet the scholastic standards of the college, depends upon a collection of the facts concerning the charged misconduct, easily colored by the point of view of the witnesses. In such circumstances, a hearing which gives the Board or the administrative authorities of the college an opportunity to hear both sides in considerable detail is best suited to protect the rights of all involved. This is not to imply that a full-dress judicial hearing, with the right to cross-examine witnesses, is required. Such a hearing, with the attending publicity and disturbance of college activities, might be detrimental to the college's educational atmosphere and impractical to carry out. Nevertheless, the rudiments of an adversary proceeding may be preserved without encroaching upon the interests of the college. In the instant case, the student should be given the names of the witnesses against him and an oral or written report on the facts to which each witness testifies. He should also be given the opportunity to present to the Board, or at least to an administrative official of the college, his own defense against the charges and to produce either oral testimony or written affidavits of witnesses in his behalf. If the hearing is not before the Board directly, the results and findings of the hearing should be presented in a report open to the student's inspection. If these rudimentary elements of fair play are followed in a case of misconduct of this particular type, we feel that the requirements of due process of law will have been fulfilled.

The judgment of the district court is reversed and the cause is remanded for further proceedings consistent with this opinion.

Reversed and remanded.

Goss v. Lopez
(United States Supreme Court, 1975)

Mr. Justice WHITE delivered the opinion of the Court.

This appeal by various administrators of the Columbus, Ohio, Public School System (CPSS) challenges the judgment of a three-judge federal court, declaring that appellees—various high school students in the CPSS—were denied due process of law contrary to the command of the Fourteenth Amendment in that they were temporarily suspended from their high schools without a hearing either prior to suspension or within a reasonable time thereafter, and enjoining the administrators to remove all references to such suspensions from the students' records. . . .

We do not believe that school authorities must be totally free from notice and hearing requirements if their schools are to operate with acceptable efficiency. Students facing temporary suspension have interests qualifying for protection of the Due Process Clause, and due process requires, in connection with a suspension of 10 days or less, that the student be given oral or written notice of the charges against him and, if he denies them, an explanation of the evidence the authorities have and an opportunity to present his side of the story. The Clause requires at least these rudimentary precautions against unfair or mistaken findings of misconduct and arbitrary exclusion from school.

There need be no delay between the time "notice" is given and the time of the hearing. In the great majority of cases the disciplinarian may informally discuss the alleged misconduct with the student minutes after it has occurred. We hold only that, in being given an opportunity to explain his version of the facts at this discussion, the student first be told what he is accused of doing and what the basis of the accusation is. Lower courts which have addressed the question of the *nature* of the procedures required in short suspension cases have reached the same conclusion. Tate v. Board of Education, 453 F.2d 975, 979 (CA8 1972); Vail v. Board of Education, 354 F.Supp. 592, 603 (NII 1973). Since the hearing may occur almost immediately following the misconduct, it follows that as a general rule notice and hearing should precede removal of the student from school. We agree with the District Court, however, that there are recurring situations in which prior notice and hearing cannot be insisted upon. Students whose presence poses a continuing danger to persons or property or an

190

ongoing threat of disrupting the academic process may be immediately removed from school. In such cases, the necessary notice and rudimentary hearing should follow as soon as practicable, as the District Court indicated.

In holding as we do, we do not believe that we have imposed procedures on school disciplinarians which are inappropriate in a classroom setting. Instead we have imposed requirements which are, if anything, less than a fair-minded school principal would impose upon himself in order to avoid unfair suspensions. Indeed, according to the testimony of the principal of Marion-Franklin High School, that school had an informal procedure, remarkably similar to that which we now require, applicable to suspensions generally but which was not followed in this case. Similarly, according to the most recent memorandum applicable to the entire CPSS, school principals in the CPSS are now required by local rule to provide at least as much as the constitutional minimum which we have described.

We stop short of construing the Due Process Clause to require, countrywide, that hearings in connection with short suspensions must afford the student the opportunity to secure counsel, to confront and cross-examine witnesses supporting the charge, or to call his own witnesses to verify his version of the incident. Brief disciplinary suspensions are almost countless. To impose in each such case even truncated trial-type procedures might well overwhelm administrative facilities in many places and, by diverting resources, cost more than it would save in educational effectiveness. Moreover, further formalizing the suspension process and escalating its formality and adversary nature may not only make it too costly as a regular disciplinary tool but also destroy its effectiveness as part of the teaching process.

On the other hand, requiring effective notice and informal hearing permitting the student to give his version of the events will provide a meaningful hedge against erroneous action. At least the disciplinarian will be alerted to the existence of disputes about facts and arguments about cause and effect. He may then determine himself to summon the accuser, permit cross-examination, and allow the student to present his own witnesses. In more difficult cases, he may permit counsel. In any event, his discretion will be more informed and we think the risk of error substantially reduced.

Requiring that there be at least an informal give-and-take between student and disciplinarian, preferably prior to the suspension, will add little to the factfinding function where the disciplinarian himself has witnessed the conduct forming the basis for the charge. But things are not always as they seem to be, and the student will at least have the opportunity to characterize his conduct and put it in what he deems the proper context. We should also make it clear that we have addressed ourselves solely to the short suspension, not exceeding 10 days. Longer suspensions or expulsions for the remainder of the school term, or permanently, may require more formal procedures. Nor do we put aside the possibility that in unusual situations, although involving only a short suspension, something more than the rudimentary procedures will be required.

UMV Post v. Board of Regents of U. of Wis.

(United States District Court, Eastern District of Wisconsin, 1991)

WARREN, Senior District Judge.

On March 29, 1990, the UWM Post, Inc. and others ("plaintiffs") filed this action seeking that this Court enter a declaratory judgment that Wis. Admin. Code § UWS 17.–06(2) (the "UW Rule") on its face violates: (1) plaintiffs' right of free speech guaranteed by the First Amendment to the United States Constitution and by Article I, Section 3 of the Wisconsin Constitution and (2) plaintiffs' right to due process and equal protection of the laws guaranteed by the Fourteenth Amendment and by Article I, Section 1 of the Wisconsin Constitution. In addition, plaintiffs request that this Court: (1) enter a permanent injunction prohibiting the Board of Regents of the University of Wisconsin System (the "Board of Regents" or the "Board") and its agents and employees from enforcing the UW Rule; (2) order the Board of Regents to vacate the disciplinary action taken against plaintiff John Doe under the UW Rule and expunge from his files all records related to that action and (3) award plaintiffs their reasonable attorneys' fees and costs pursuant to 42 U.S.C. § 1988.

Now before Court are the parties' cross motions for summary judgment.

I. Background
A. Development of the UW Rule

In May of 1988, the Board of Regents adopted "Design for Diversity," a plan to increase minority representation, multi-cultural understanding and greater diversity throughout the University of Wisconsin System's 26 campuses. Design for Diversity responded to concerns over an increase in incidents of discriminatory harassment. For example, several highly publicized incidents involving fraternities occurred at the University of Wisconsin—Madison. In May of 1987, a fraternity erected a large caricature of a black Fiji Islander at a party theme. Later that year, there was a fight with racial overtones between members of two fraternities. In October of 1988, a fraternity held a "slave auction" at which pledges in black face performed skits parroting black entertainers. *See* the *Capitol Times*, Nov. 17, 1988, p. 25.

Design for Diversity directed each of the UW System's institutions to prepare nondiscriminatory conduct policies. In addition, pursuant to the plan, the Board of Regents approved its "Policy and Guidelines on Racist and Discriminatory Conduct," which stated the Board's general policy against discrimination and provided guidance to the individual campuses in developing their own non-discrimination policies. Finally, the Board established a working group to draft amendments to the student conduct code, Chapter UWS 17, to implement its policy system-wide. With the help of UW–Madison Law School Professors Gordon Baldwin, Richard Delgado and Ted Finman, the group developed a proposed rule based, in part, on a policy being developed simultaneolusly at the UW–Madison. The professors agreed that the proposed rule would likely withstand attack on First Amendment grounds if it included a requirement that the speaker intended to make the educational environment hostile for the individual being addressed.

At its April 7, 1989 meeting, the Board of Regents discussed issuing the proposed rule on an emergency basis in light of the increasing number of incidents of racial and discriminatory harassment. By a 8 to 7 vote, the Board decided not to promulgate the rule on an emergency basis. Instead, the Board advanced the proposal through the regular administrative rule-making procedure. On June 8, 1989, the Board held a public hearing to provide an opportunity for interested persons to comment on the proposed rule. On June 9, 1989, the Board adopted the UW Rule by 12 to 5 vote. . . .

Thus, in order to be regulated under the UW Rule, a comment, epithet or other expressive behavior must:

(1) Be racist or discriminatory;
(2) Be directed at an individual;
(3) Demean the race, sex, religion, color, creed, disability, sexual orientation, national origin, ancestry or age of the individual addressed; and
(4) Create an intimidating, hostile or demeaning environment for education, university-related work, or other university-authorized activity. . . .

Although the First Amendment generally protects speech from content-based regulation, it does not protect all speech. The Supreme Court has removed certain narrowly limited categories of speech from First Amendment protection. These categories of speech are considered to be of such slight social value that any benefit that may be derived from them is clearly outweighed by their costs to order and morality. *Chaplinsky v. New Hampshire,* 315 U.S. 568, 572, 62 S.Ct. 766, 769, 86 L.Ed. 1031 (1942). The categories include fighting words, obscenity and, to a limited extent, libel. *Collin v. Smith,* 578 F.2d 1197, 1202 (7th Cir. 1978) *cert. denied,* 439 U.S. 916, 99 S.Ct. 291, 58 L.Ed.2d 264 (1978).

The Board of Regents argues that the UW Rules falls within the category of fighting words. In the alternative, the Board asserts that the balancing test set forth in *Chaplinsky* leaves the speech regulated by the UW Rule unprotected by the First Amendment. The Board also argues that the Court should find the UW Rule constitutional because its prohibition of discriminatory speech parallels Title VII law. Finally, the Board asserts that, even if the Court finds the rule, as written, unconstitutional, it may apply a narrowing construction which limits the rule's reach to unprotected speech. . . .

Since the elements of the UW Rule do not require that the regulated speech, by its very utterance, tend to incite violent reactions, the rule goes beyond the present scope of the fighting words doctrine. . . .

Since the UW Rule regulates speech based upon its content, it is not proper for this Court to apply a balancing test to determine the constitutionality of the rule. Moreover, this Court finds that, even under the balancing test proposed by the Board of Regents, the rule is unconstitutional. . . .

Because the UW Rule fails under both the fighting words doctrine and the UW System's proposed balancing test, this Court must find the rule overbroad and therefore in violation of the First Amendment. . . .

B. Vagueness

A statute is unconstitutionally vague when "men of common intelligence must necessarily guess at its meaning." *Broadrick v. Oklahoma,* 413 U.S. 601, 607, 93 S.Ct. 2908, 2913, 37 L.Ed.2d 830 (1973). A statute must give adequate warning of the conduct which is to be prohibited and must set out explicit standards for those who apply it. These concerns apply with particular force where the challenged statute affects First Amendment rights. *Village of Hoffmann Estates v. The Flipside, Hoffmann Estates, Inc.,* 455 U.S. 489, 499, 102 S.Ct. 1186, 1193, 71 L.Ed.2d 362 (1982). Nonetheless, the chilling effect caused by an overly broad statute must be real and substantial and a narrowing construction must be unavailable before a court will set it aside. *See Young v. American Mini Theaters,* 427 U.S. 50, 60, 96 S.Ct. 2440, 2447, 49 L.Ed.2d 310 (1976).

In our case, plaintiffs argue that the UW Rule is unconstitutionally vague for two reasons: (1) the phrase "discriminatory comments, epithets or other expressive behavior" and the term "demean" are unduly vague and (2) the rule does not make clear whether the prohibited speech must actually create a hostile educational environment or whether speaker must merely intend to create such an environment. Upon review, it appears that the phrase and term referred to by plaintiff are not unduly vague. However, the rule is ambiguous since it fails to make clear whether the speaker must actually create a hostile educational environment or if he must merely intend to do so. . . .

(2) Ambiguity

The Court concurs with plaintiffs that the UW Rule is unduly vague because it is ambiguous as to whether the regulated speech must actually demean the listener and create an intimidating, hostile or demeaning environment for education or whether the speaker must merely intend to demean the listener and create such an environment.

The problems of bigotry and discrimination sought to be addressed here are real and truly corrosive of the educational environment. But freedom of speech is almost absolute in our land and the only restriction the fighting words doctrine can abide is that based on the fear of violent reaction. Content-based prohibitions such as that in the UW Rule, however well intended, simply cannot survive the screening which our Constitution demands.

Appendix B

Student Conduct Codes

Discipline Procedures (Calvin College)

Every student at Calvin has not only student rights but also student responsibilities. Failure to meet these responsibilities sometimes results in formal discipline. The guiding principle of discipline at Calvin College is based on the assumption that discipline may be equated with guidance towards Christian academic goals. The goal of all discipline should be to give appropriate direction and government to one's behavior. Discipline consists of encouraging desirable behavior and inhibiting undesirable behavior. The college not only expects students to conduct themselves both on and off campus in accord with their statements of religious commitment as they have indicated in the application form, but the college may also discipline or may expel any student who in its judgment displays conduct or attitudes unworthy of the standards of the college.

Disciplinary procedures initiated in the residence halls and specifically involving an infraction of residence halls regulations are handled in the following way: the student who is charged with an alleged misconduct has the option of a hearing either by the residence hall judiciary or by the Resident Director. The Resident Director may refuse to hear the case, and the matter would then be handled by the student's hall judiciary. Any student wishing to appeal a decision must do so in writing to the Vice-President for Student Affairs and ask for reconsideration by the Student Conduct Committee.

Students guilty of infractions of all-campus regulations such as use of illegal drugs, possession or consumption of alcohol, and the like, are dealt with in the following way: the student is given a disciplinary statement in which the alleged misconduct is clearly spelled out. The student is advised of these rights:

1. The student may choose a hearing by either the All-Campus Discipline Committee or the Dean of Men/Women. The Dean of Men/ Women may choose not to hear the case.
2. If a student chooses the All-Campus Discipline Committee, the student may ask a fellow student or a faculty member to advise or represent him/her at the hearing.
3. The student may be present throughout all presentation of testimony and evidence at the hearing.

The student's case must be heard within seven days of the student's receipt of the discipline statement. The student may request a seven-day postponement of the hearing, and the Vice-President for Student Affairs shall determine whether the request is for good cause.

After a decision has been rendered either by the All-Campus Discipline Committee or by the Dean of Men/Women, the student has the right to appeal the decision to the Student Conduct Committee, which serves as a Board of Appeals. Such an appeal must be submitted in writing within fourteen days of the imposition of the sanction. The student may request a seven-day postponement of the hearing, and the judgment of the Chair of the Student Conduct Committee shall determine whether the request is for good cause. The committee may reverse or modify the decision of the All-Campus Discipline Committee or the appropriate dean. The President of the college or his designee shall be responsible for the final disposition of all discipline cases.

A complete and detailed conduct code has been adopted by the faculty, the student senate, and the board of trustees. The general categories of prohibited behavior include, but are not limited to, the following: dishonesty; violence; disruption; stealing; policy violation; alcohol standards violations; sexual misconduct; illegal and/or unprescribed drug possession and use; profane or obscene language; unauthorized entry; disobedience of official college bodies.

The list of sanctions below may be imposed on students when they are judged guilty of violating the provisions of this code. These are merely formal categories of discipline. The judicial bodies are free to modify or qualify these sanctions in accord with the individual circumstances.

1. Admonition
2. Warning
3. Personal probation
4. Disciplinary probation
5. Suspension
6. Expulsion
7. Restitution
8. Fines

Any student wishing to review the Student Conduct Code in detail may pick up a copy at the Student Affairs Office or the Student Senate Office.

Residential Life Disciplinary Procedures (University of California, Los Angeles)

Philosophy of Discipline

The basic philosophy of discipline at the University of California, Los Angeles is one of education. As such, it focuses on the growth and development of the individual student by encouraging self-discipline and by fostering a respect for the rights and privileges of others.

Regardless of the means by which discipline is processed, the ends remain the same: to redirect the behavior of the student into acceptable patterns and to protect the rights of all students within the residential community. The unique advantage of a student disciplinary board lies in the ability of its members to influence the attitudes and subsequent behavior of other students through a formally constituted judicial mechanism. Without question, peer influence, exercised through the disciplinary process, can often be more effective in redirecting the behavior patterns of students than any other method of discipline within the institution.

Typical college students are of an age when they are making the final transition from adolescence to adulthood. They are striving for independence, hoping to prove to themselves and to others their capacity for directing their own lives. In the past, they have often been told what to do and how to do it by various adult authority figures. The college experience provides students with a kind of freedom from restraint which can, on occasion, create difficulties. Most students learn that all societies place certain restraints upon their members and that residence hall living is hardly atypical. In fact, it might be argued that residence halls require a higher degree of social control than other residential settings.

The question becomes how to choose the best means to maintain conduct appropriate for a residential experience that exists to serve the academic purposes of the institution. Theoretically, it could be argued that student government cannot be genuinely effective unless students are able and willing to assert formal control over other students. The disciplinary system presents an opportunity for students to communicate to fellow students the attitudes which seem most conducive to creating a positive environment within the residential community.

It should be understood that there is a fundamental difference between the nature of student discipline and that of criminal law. Regardless of the type of proceeding used (Disciplinary Board, Assistant Directors, Hearing Officers, Associate Director, Director), the disciplining of students within a University community must be consistent with the educational mission of the institution. For this reason, the procedures employed and the types of sanctions used on campus differ from those used in the criminal process. Although students' rights to due process and fairness must be carefully observed, the rules of criminal law are neither required nor necessary to achieve the educational goal of University discipline.

Finally, there is no substitute for fairness, objectivity, and good judgment. Well-earned respect will always transcend performance geared to gaining popularity. The success of a student board is contingent upon the conviction of its members to achieve a suitable living environment while affording individual students maximum personal freedom within institutional guidelines.

Procedures

Disciplinary sanctions may be applied to students who violate On Campus Housing and University rules and regulations. These sanctions may be applied to a student only after the student has been found "in violation" of an On Campus Housing and/or University rule or regulation. A student is considered innocent of a violation until guilt has been established in accordance with specific procedures. These disciplinary procedures must be implemented according to guidelines established by the Regents of the University of California. These procedural guidelines require "due process," that is, a fair, objective and timely hearing of facts related to the incident of misconduct. The accused student has certain "rights", such as notification of the charge, information about the incident, the right to prepare a defense, the right to be represented, the right to cross-examine witnesses, and the right to appeal decisions.

This summary description of disciplinary procedures indicates that the process of applying discipline is very specific and complex. Procedural errors or inequities may result in the dismissal of a case. Therefore, it is important that staff be extremely careful to follow proper procedures. Further, it is important that Staff and students have a clear understanding of their responsibilities in the process.

Resident Assistants typically report incidents on "Incident Report" forms or "Duty RA Report" forms. Encourage residents to report incidents, investigate reported incidents, and appear as witnesses at hearings. In writing an incident report a Resident Assistant should be descriptive, detailed, precise, and as objective as possible. The more information provided, the better. Also, Resident Assistants may be asked to provide information about student violators by Assistant Directors or Resident Directors when they consider what sanction to impose.

Cases proceeding to hearing are usually scheduled before the Disciplinary Board. A Disciplinary Board is a student "peer" review system. There are 14 Disciplinary Board members, two from each hall and suite. They are trained to conduct hearings to determine the facts of a case and to report their findings at the conclusion of a case. The Disciplinary Board provides students with another leadership opportunity in the Residence Halls. A Hearing Officer may substitute if the Disciplinary Board is unable to meet.

How Complaints Are Filed: Complaints concerning violation of On Campus Housing rules or regulations should be filed with the Assistant Director ("AD") or Resident Director ("RD") on an Incident Report form.

Notice to Students: When a complaint is filed, the AD or RD shall notify the student in writing of the following:

1. The nature of the conduct in question, including a brief statement of the factual basis of the charges, the time, date, and place it is alleged to have occurred, and the On Campus Housing rules or regulations allegedly violated.

2. That the *Residential Life Disciplinary Procedures* will be followed, and that the student should refer to his or her copy of these procedures; and

3. That the matter will be referred to a Residential Life disciplinary hearing;

4. That if the student wishes, the matter can be resolved by the AD or RD in an Initial Interview prior to a hearing;

5. That the student may contact the AD, RD or Hearing Coordinator

to examine the Incident Report form and any other relevant documents;

6. That within two (2) business days the student should schedule an appointment with the AD or RD who sent the notice;

7. That the matter may also be referred to the Dean of Student's Office, in the case of alleged violation of University policy or Campus rules and regulations. The factual determination of the case rendered by the Dean of Student's Office would be binding in the UCLA Residential Life Disciplinary Procedures.

Cheating, Plagiarism, and Documentation (Yale University)

Academic dishonesty is a serious offense against the academic community; at Yale, as at most other universities, such dishonesty ordinarily results in suspension, i.e., required temporary withdrawal. (The normal duration of such suspension at Yale is two terms; shorter or longer penalties of suspension, or even permanent expulsion, are possible, depending on the gravity of the offense and the offender's previous disciplinary record.) Thus it is important for every student to understand the standards of academic honesty assumed in a university and the consequent need to avoid dishonesty by acknowledging intellectual indebtedness. The provisions in the *Undergraduate Regulations* against cheating must be understood to include all forms of misrepresentation in academic work, including:

a. The submission of the same paper in more than one course without the explicit authorization of the appropriate instructors;

b. Cheating on tests, examinations, problem sets, or any other exercise;

c. Any form of plagiarism, especially failure in an essay to acknowledge ideas or language taken from others, and the submission of work prepared by another person;

d. Submission of a scientific research report that misrepresents in any way the work actually done.

A. Multiple Submission

You may not submit the same paper, or substantially the same paper, in more than one course. This applies whether or not the courses are being simultaneously taken. You may not submit in a course you are presently taking a paper you wrote last term or last year, nor may you submit a single paper for two courses you are taking in the same term. In the latter case, if you think you have sound intellectual reasons for combining your work in two related courses, you must obtain the permission of both instructors before doing so. Similarly, to revise and extend a paper from an earlier course may well be academically appropriate; but before doing so you must seek explicit permission from your present instructor, who obviously cannot grant it without inspecting and approving your plans for adequate further work.

B. Cheating on Examinations

One form of cheating is either to copy answers from a nearby student, or to refer surreptitiously to notes or books. Though cheating of this kind may escape direct observation at the time, it can be detected by coincidences of languages or argumentation, either with textbooks or with another student's examination, that emerge in the course of grading. Verbatim memorization of long stretches of text is a highly implausible excuse for such coincidences, and would be improper in any case, since you are expected in an examination to put ideas in your own words in order to show that you understand them.

Another form of cheating is to change one's answers on a returned examination and then request regrading. Students who submit examinations for regrading are warned that instructors in whose courses tests are permitted to be returned for a possible revision of a grade have usually taken steps to prevent changes from going undetected. It is your responsibility to make sure that you submit the examination exactly as it was; any alteration is culpable. The assertion that changes are merely "notes to yourself" will not be believed.

For take-home examinations, and for examinations for which the questions are distributed in advance, instructors should make the rules clear, and students should obey them to the letter. If you are in any doubt as to the meaning of the instructions governing such exercises, you should seek explicit clarification from your instructor. The ordinary expectation is that you will prepare your answers by yourself; collaboration with others is acceptable only to the degree precisely and specifically described by the instructor. In any case, the answer you finally submit must represent your own understanding of the issues. If you think that it has been significantly influenced by consulting books or other people, you should say so, just as you would in a paper.

Problem sets in economics and mathematics, language-laboratory exercises and other kinds of homework exercises, when submitted for a grade, though they may be discussed with others or worked on in common, must never be simply copied. Nor may someone else sign in for you at the language laboratory. The apparent slightness of an exercise is irrelevant: cheating is still cheating, on a quiz or homework as well as on a midterm test or on a final examination. Nor should you feel freer to cheat or plagiarize because a course is peripheral to your chief interests. Cheating is also still equally cheating, plagiarism still equally plagiarism, for example, in a course you are taking on the Credit/Fail option in order to fulfill a distributional requirement. Any dishonesty in any student's work is a serious invasion of the academic standards of a university.

C. Plagiarism

Plagiarism is the use of someone else's work, words, or ideas as if they were your own. Thus most forms of cheating on examinations are plagiarism; but in ordinary academic parlance the word applies to papers rather than to examinations. Whereas all students know pretty well what they may or may not do on examinations, many are less sure concerning papers, and so it is conceivable that an honest student might plagiarize out of mere ignorance. It is therefore up to you to learn the standard practices of documentation. The Dartmouth College pamphlet *Sources, Their Use and Acknowledgement* has been given to you, and you are expected to have familiarized yourself carefully with its contents. Above all you should realize that failure to acknowledge specific indebtedness to others is not simply a writing error but a form of theft—possibly unpremeditated, but not probably, and culpable in any case, since it is your responsibility to know and to indicate what is yours and what is not yours. The absence of a clear intent to deceive may mitigate an offense, but is certainly not likely to absolve it altogether. Read *Sources* carefully and thoroughly. Yale College distributes it as a supplement to the *Undergraduate Regulations,* and you are as responsible for knowledge of its contents as you are for knowledge of the provisions of the *Undergraduate Regulations.*
Some further points:

a. Take clear notes in which you keep your own thoughts distinct from those you derive from your reading, so that you do not inadvertently submit the words or ideas of others as your own.

b. Remember that you should acknowledge unpublished as well as published sources. This includes the work of other students and ideas that you may have derived from lectures and conversations.

c. Do not suppose that because your instructor is an expert in the field, he or she needs little or no documentation in your work. An essay must stand on its own and not as a form of conversation with the instructor. In preparing a paper, it will help you to assume a larger audience than your instructor; imagine everyone in your class, for example, reading your paper; this will give you a surer sense of what to document and what to take as common knowledge.

d. Mark and identify all quotations; give the source of translations; regularly acknowledge specific ideas; and give the source of facts not commonly known. If you are in doubt as to what may be "commonly known," that is a signal that you should document it, even at the risk of appearing overcautious or simplistic.

Submission of an entire paper prepared by someone else is an especially egregious form of plagiarism, and is grounds for the imposition of a particularly serious penalty, even for expulsion from the University.

Academic Regulations (Princeton University)

General Requirements for the Acknowledgment of Sources in Academic Work

The academic departments of the University have varying requirements for the acknowledgment of sources, but certain fundamental principles apply to all levels of work. In order to prevent any misunderstanding, students are expected to study and comply with the following basic requirements.

Quotations. Any quotations, however small, must be placed in quotation marks or clearly indented beyond the regular margin. Any quotation must be accompanied (either within the text or in a footnote) by a precise indication of the source—identifying the author, title, place and date of publication (where relevant), and page numbers. Any sentence or phrase which is not the original work of the student must be acknowledged.

Paraphrasing. Any material which is paraphrased or summarized must also be specifically acknowledged in a footnote or in the text. A thorough rewording or rearrangement of an author's text does not relieve one of this responsibility. Occasionally, students maintain that they have read a source long before they wrote their papers and have unwittingly duplicated some of its phrases or ideas. This is not a valid excuse. The student is responsible for taking adequate notes so that debts of phrasing may be acknowledged where they are due.

Ideas and Facts. Any ideas or facts which are borrowed should be specifically acknowledged in a footnote or in the text, even if the idea or fact has been further elaborated by the student. Some ideas, facts, formulas, and other kinds of information which are widely known and considered to be in the "public domain" of common knowledge do not always require citation. The criteria for common knowledge vary among disciplines; students in doubt should consult a member of the faculty.

Occasionally, a student in preparing an essay has consulted an essay or body of notes on a similar subject by another student. If the student has done so, he or she must state the fact and indicate clearly the nature and extent of his or her obligation. The name and class of the

208

author of an essay or notes which are consulted should be given, and the student should be prepared to show the work consulted to the instructor, if requested to do so.

Footnotes and Bibliography. All the sources which have been consulted in the preparation of an essay or report should be listed in a bibliography, unless specific guidelines (from the academic department or instructor) request that only works cited be so included. However, the mere listing of a source in a bibliography shall *not* be considered a "proper acknowledgment" for specific use of that source within the essay or report.

Laboratory Work, Problem Sets, Computer Programs and Homework. The organization of laboratory and computational courses varies throughout the University. In many courses, students work in pairs or in larger groups. In those cases where individual reports are submitted based on work involving collaboration, proper acknowledgment of the extent of the collaboration must appear in the report. In those cases where there are two or more signatories to a submitted report, each student's signature is taken to mean that the student has contributed fairly to the work involved and understands and endorses the content of the report. If for any reason, a set of observations or calculations has been invalidated or left incomplete, and permission has been granted by the instructor to obtain the data from other sources, the sources must be specifically acknowledged in the report.

Multiple Submission. Under certain conditions, the student may be permitted to rewrite an earlier work or to satisfy two academic requirements by producing a single piece of work, more extensive than that which would satisfy either requirement on its own. In such cases, however, the student must secure, *in writing,* prior permission from each instructor involved. If the student has revised an earlier essay, the earlier essay must be submitted with the final version. If a single extended essay has been written for more than one course, the fact must be clearly indicated at the beginning of the essay.

Oral Reports. Students required to submit written notes for oral reports must clearly acknowledge any work that is not original, in accordance with the requirements stated above.

Standard Forms of Reference. For standard forms of quotations, footnotes, and bibliographies, the student may consult one of the following: James Thorpe, *Literary Scholarship* (Boston, Houghton Mifflin, 1964). Chapter III, pp. 63–88; *The MLA Handbook* (Modern Language Association of America, 2nd ed., New York, 1984); *A*

Manual of Style, 13th ed. (Chicago, University of Chicago Press, 1982); or a style sheet provided by a department of the University.

Student Acknowledgment of Original Work

At the end of an essay, laboratory report, or any other requirement, the undergraduate must write the following sentence and sign his or her name: *"This paper represents my own work in accordance with University regulations."*

Definitions of Academic Violations under the Jurisdiction of the Faculty-Student Committee on Discipline

With regard to essays, laboratory reports, or any other written work submitted to fulfill an official academic requirement, the following are considered academic infractions or, as the committee may determine, academic fraud:

Plagiarism. The use of any outside source without proper acknowledgment. "Outside source" means any work, published or unpublished, by any person other than the student.

Multiple Submission. The failure to obtain prior written permission of the relevant instructors to submit any work that has been submitted in identical or similar form in fulfillment of any other academic requirement at any institution.

False Citation. The attribution to, or citation of, a source from which the material in question was not, in fact, obtained.

False Data. The submission of data that have been deliberately altered or contrived by the student or with the student's knowledge.

In determining whether academic fraud has occurred, the committee will take into account whether the student should reasonably have understood that his or her actions were in violation of University regulations. While the failure to fulfill the general requirements for acknowledgment of sources in academic work may not necessarily involve academic fraud, any such failure will be considered an academic infraction and will normally result in a disciplinary penalty.

Violations

Jurisdiction. Violations of these regulations are under the jurisdiction of the Faculty-Student Committee on Discipline or the Office of the Dean of the Graduate School.

Student's Defense. The only adequate defense for a student accused of an academic violation is that the work in question does not, in fact, constitute a violation. Neither the defense that the student was ignorant of the regulations concerning academic violations nor the defense that the student was under pressure at the time the violation was committed is considered an adequate defense.

Seriousness of Offense. Academic fraud is always considered a serious matter, but will be considered especially serious if:

1. The student has submitted a paper prepared by another person or agency.
2. The student has on his or her record a previous conviction for an academic violation.
3. The academic fraud includes the theft of another student's work for the purpose of plagiarizing it. "Theft" shall be construed as meaning any unauthorized use of another student's paper—even if the paper is returned after use, or consulted without being removed from the student's room or from any public or private room where the paper has been placed.

Penalty. Normally, the penalty for academic fraud will be one year's suspension or required withdrawal from the University. For more serious offenses, the penalty will be required withdrawal for more than one year. In most serious cases, the penalty may be permanent separation from the University.

An Explanation of the Honor System (University of Virginia)

Philosophy

The Honor System is a changing standard of behavior required of students attending the University of Virginia by their fellow students. This standard of behavior promotes a spirit of community conducive to mutual trust among students, who are assumed to be honorable unless their conduct proves them to be otherwise. Serious and intentional acts of lying, cheating, and stealing are precisely those acts which cannot be tolerated in any community if its members are to live in close harmony together. Such strict standards are necessary to maintain a community where one has the right to keep what he has earned, to have his word taken as true, and to compete fairly in the classroom.

Student Responsibility

Throughout its history the Honor System has been administered and enforced entirely by the students. The success or failure of the System is determined by each student's willingness to abide by the System and to enforce it by investigating potential honor offenses and serving on honor trial juries when called upon.

Violations

An honor offense is an intentional act of lying, cheating, or stealing which is so reprehensible as to warrant permanent dismissal from the University. Reprehensibility is determined by current student opinion, and rests solely on the merits of each individual case. The criteria of act, intent, and reprehensibility must be proven beyond a reasonable doubt.

If, while under pressure, a student commits a dishonorable act, a conscientious attempt to rectify the situation, made before any knowledge of an investigation, shall be considered a complete defense.

Procedure

Any student believing that a breach of the Honor System may have been committed shall consult with an Honor Advisor as soon as possible. Honor Advisors are students selected and trained by the Honor Committee to provide information and advice to those students who are considering making an honor accusation or who are being investigated for an honor offense. The relationship between student and advisor is of a strictly confidential nature. The Honor Advisor can never reveal, in or out of a trial situation, the confidential information given to him by another student.

In making an investigation and accusation, a student should involve one or two fellow students to help him whenever possible. Through confidential investigation, these students attempt to establish the three criteria of an honor offense beyond a reasonable doubt. If, after a thorough investigation, they still have suspicions, they shall confront the person and ask that he explain his conduct. In case the investigating group is satisfied that the suspected student is not guilty of improper conduct, they shall proceed no further and nothing connected with the case shall be made public. If, after hearing his explanation (or after he has refused to make an explanation), the investigators are convinced of his guilt, they shall demand that he leave the University. Accusors may not drop a charge upon the agreement of the accused to resign from the University; if a breach of honor has occurred, the guilty student must be dismissed for it.

The accused student must either leave the University or request that an honor panel be convened to try his case. When the accused leaves without trial, the accusor shall inform the Honor Committee of the name of the student and the nature of the offense. The status of an accused student who leaves the University without trial is the same as though he had been found guilty in trial. A student who leaves the University before an accusation can be brought may be contacted by any means available to the investigating students. In the absence of satisfactory explanation, the accusors and the Committee shall proceed as though the accused had left after the accusation. Every effort will be made in such a case to ascertain that the accused understands the nature of the accusation and voluntarily refuses the opportunity to return for a trial.

An accused student who believes himself innocent of an honor violation may request a trial by an honor panel composed of either 7 to 11 Honor Committee members, or a mixed panel of between 5 and

8 randomly selected students and between 3 and 4 Honor Committee members. In trial, the burden of proof rests entirely with the accusors. Every effort will be made to safeguard the rights of the accused, which include the right: to be advised in writing of the nature of the accusation; to be informed of the nature of the evidence to be used against him; to have all proceedings against him held publicly or privately at his selection; to be given a reasonable time to prepare for a hearing before the panel; to be represented by counsel of his own choosing from the student body; to confront and to cross-examine witnesses against him; to present evidence and witnesses in his own defense; to be heard in his own defense; to refuse to testify against himself; and to challenge any conduct during the proceeding that may prejudice any of the foregoing rights.

If upon conclusion of the trial, four-fifths of the members of the panel are convinced beyond a reasonable doubt of the guilt of the accused, and shall so cast their votes in a secret ballot, the accusation is affirmed and the accused must leave the University immediately. Otherwise, the accused will be declared not guilty and all evidence and records of the hearing will be immediately destroyed.

Every student found guilty of an honor violation shall have access to a record of the proceedings against him and may appeal the panel's findings on the basis of new evidence affecting those findings or of a denial of a full and fair hearing in accordance with the Honor Committee Constitution.

All parties shall ensure that any and all proceedings concerning an honor violation will be kept strictly confidential. A violation of the confidentiality rule may result in disciplinary action by the Judiciary Committee for student misconduct and/or violation of University policies or regulations.

Honor Committee

The elected presidents of the ten schools of the University and the vice president of the College of Arts and Sciences serve on the Honor Committee. This group is in no way responsible to the faculty or administration; it is duly elected by students and represents student opinion. The Committee ensures that the Honor System covers only those offenses which the current student generation considers dishonorable and that the student who asserts his innocence receives a fair hearing. If an accused student requests a mixed panel trial, students must be willing to serve as jurors to guarantee a fair hearing.

The Honor Committee is responsible for implementing the Honor System. Yet the Honor system is not the Committee, it is the sum of each student's willingness to act honorably and to insist upon honorable conduct from his fellow students. The person who lives under the Honor System and enjoys the benefits must be willing to accept his responsibility without compromise or exception.

Scope of the System

A student is bound by the Honor System whenever he uses his identity as a University of Virginia student to induce reliance in someone affected by his actions. In Charlottesville and Albemarle County a student is presumed to induce reliance whether or not he specifically identifies himself as a student.

One of the greatest dangers to which an honor system can be exposed is that of being overloaded with offenses. It is essential that the Honor System concern itself solely with what the current student generation finds dishonorable. Students have been dismissed from the University, for example, for cheating in the classroom, for willfully issuing bad checks, for plagiarism, and for the use of a false telephone credit card. Such actions as illegal use of drugs, civil disorders, and breaking of administrative regulations fall under the jurisdiction of other areas of authority on the Grounds.

Students are earnestly discouraged from requiring another student's word of honor to regulate trivialities or non-academic matters of minor concern. At the same time, each student should exercise the greatest care to keep himself free from suspicion and misunderstanding.

Inevitably, the scope of the Honor System will come into question in borderline instances. A knowing misrepresentation intended to induce reliance in another constitutes lying under the Honor System. A spontaneous misrepresentation, if immediately and voluntarily withdrawn, is not considered to have been intended to induce reliance. Similarly, stealing is to knowingly deprive another of what is his, but does not include accidental benefit by a machine or computer malfunction when neither sought nor exploited. Cheating is any violation of the academic pledge. This pledge states that the work that the student submits to his professor is his own, and has been done in accordance with the requirements of the course laid down by the professor. In case of doubt as to the nature or extent of any pledge, the student should immediately request that the professor make the requirements clear to the entire class.

The Honor Committee publishes a list each year of Advisors who will assist any student, in confidence, in the practical applications of the Honor System to situations which arise.

Alcoholic Beverages and Other Drugs (St. Olaf College)

Use and Possession of Alcohol

The college maintains an alcohol education program planned and implemented jointly by students and the administration. The college also provides assistance and referral for those with alcohol problems. The possession or consumption of alcoholic beverages is prohibited on campus, in college-owned honor and language houses, and at college-sponsored functions. Anyone violating college policy regarding alcoholic beverages may be subject to disciplinary action.

Gatherings where alcoholic beverages are served, "keggers", or possession of excessive amounts of alcohol represent some of the most flagrant violations of this policy. An automatic $75.00 minimum fine will be assessed each of the "sponsor(s)" or the occupant(s) of the room (house) in which such a gathering takes place. ("Sponsors" include individuals responsible for planning, purchasing, delivering, and hosting.)

The fine may be increased, and damages, if any, assessed against those students. If the same individuals are involved in a second violation of this nature, their housing assignments will be cancelled and they will have to find housing off campus.

This policy exists out of concern related to the use and abuse of alcohol and other drugs in our present society, the particular age group involved, and the combined living/studying campus setting. The St. Olaf community encourages student-initiated alternatives to chemical use.

In keeping with the alcohol policy, students are also asked to not have empty alcohol containers in their rooms. Empty containers found in rooms during break inspections will be disposed of by the residence life staff. In addition, empty containers found in rooms where College alcohol policy is being violated will be included when determining the amount of alcohol consumption. Empty alcoholic beverage containers may also be considered evidence in and of themselves.

Use and Possession of Other Drugs

The college considers the use, possession, distribution, or sale of illegal drugs as contrary to the welfare of the college community.

217

To provide for a reasonable consequence for the use, possession, distribution, or sale of illegal drugs, the following procedures shall serve as a general guideline:

Distribution and/or Sale

A student who distributes or sells illegal drugs will be subject to immediate dismissal from St. Olaf College.

Use and Possession

A student who uses or possesses illegal drugs will be subject to immediate referral to the Counseling Center and may be subject to disciplinary action up to and including dismissal from St. Olaf College.

Conduct at Public Events

For reasons of public safety and public relations, the use of drugs, including alcohol, is prohibited at public events on campus, and smoking at public events is limited to places specifically designated.

Faculty Senate Policy Concerning Use of Alcoholic Beverages by Students (University of Delaware)

Policy rationale

The University of Delaware strives to offer members of the University Community the same rights and responsibilities as those afforded to members of the larger community. All members of the University community are responsible for making decisions about their behavior within the context of Delaware law and University regulations. The University sanctions neither the abuse of alcoholic beverages by any person nor the use of alcoholic beverages by those who are underage as defined by the Delaware code.

Policy regulation

Unauthorized possession, use, manufacture, distribution or sale of alcoholic beverages on or in University property is forbidden.

Explanation of regulation

I. "Unauthorized" use will involve:

a. Possession, use, manufacture or distribution in areas other than those enumerated in this policy; and/or

b. Illegal possession, use, manufacture or distribution under the provisions of federal, state and city law.

II. The University reminds all members of the University Community that violations of state and city laws regarding the consumption, sale, possession or manufacture of alcoholic beverages are subject to legal action which includes the following:

a. Delaware Code, Title 4, Section 904 makes it unlawful to purchase alcoholic liquor for or to give to a person under 21 years of age, and also makes it unlawful for persons under 21 years of age to consume alcoholic liquor or to have it in their possession.

219

b. Newark City Code, Chapter 19, Section 5 makes it unlawful for a minor to possess or consume any alcoholic beverage within the city except when the possession or consumption is part of a religious service or for medical purposes.

c. Newark City Code, Chapter 22, Section 22-83(e) makes it unlawful to possess any open container containing intoxicating beverages where prohibited by the property owner. This applies regardless of age.

The above offenses are punishable within the Student Judicial System and in the off-campus courts by a fine and/or imprisonment.

III. Alcoholic beverages may not be possessed, consumed, manufactured, or distributed in any University facility or property under the jurisdiction of the University unless the area has been designated by the President of the University or his designee as one where alcoholic beverages may be used.

IV. Individual transportation ("brown bagging") of alcoholic beverages is not permitted except in stadium parking areas on the days of home varsity football games. Beer kegs are prohibited at football games. Alcoholic beverages are not permitted in the stadium. Individuals are not permitted to possess any open container containing spirits, wine, or beer, or consume any spirits, wine, or beer in stadium parking areas while the football game is in progress.

V. Alcohol shall not be served at functions connected with academic programs or immediately preceding or during business meetings of any University organizations or those authorized to hold meetings on the campus.

VI. Open social functions involving the consumption of alcohol are not permitted. Open social functions are defined as open campus events where an invitation is extended to all or a significant segment of the University members.

VII. Violations of this policy shall be referred to the University Student Judicial System and/or civil authorities. . . .

Registered student organizations shall have the opportunity to serve alcoholic beverages at social functions held in approved University locations to those of legal age. The procedures listed below must be followed to obtain the use of University facilities for such functions.

1. Functions sponsored by registered University student organizations and held in University facilities at which alcoholic beverages are to be served must be registered. Such functions must be limited in attendance to members of the organizations and their invited guests.

2. Groups in good standing as sponsoring organizations (i.e., free

of censure or restriction that would prohibit that organization from sponsoring said function) who are thereby entitled to use University facilities and desire to serve alcoholic beverages at closed events scheduled in University facilities will be permitted to do so upon submitting written guarantee that the proper procedural safeguards have been adopted by them so that state and local beverage laws and University regulations will not be violated. At the time any reservation for service and consumption of alcoholic beverage is made, a person authorized to sign for the group making the reservation must complete and sign a notice form which states that the group is using the University facilities for a closed party or meeting limited in attendance to members or guests of the named person, group, association, or organization as authorized in conformance with federal, state, and city ordinances and University regulations.

C. Residence halls
1. Individual actions
a. Only students of legal age *and* their guests of legal age may possess and/or consume alcoholic beverages on an individual basis in the privacy of their residence hall rooms.
b. The possession and consumption of alcohol shall not infringe upon the privacy and peace of other individuals. Any such infringement shall be considered a violation of the Code of Conduct and shall be dealt with in the manner prescribed in the University Student Judicial System. In all such situations the consumption of alcoholic beverages will be considered as aggravating rather than mitigating the situation.
c. The Office of Housing and Residence Life shall continue to provide procedures for permitting students to select to live with someone who does not wish to use alcoholic beverages in his or her room.

J. Mandatory Alcohol Referral

Any student charged with an initial minor violation of the alcohol policy will be required to complete an Alcohol Education Program. Also, any student who is found guilty of a serious first offense alcohol violation or a second alcohol violation will be referred for a mandatory evaluation session with the Alcohol Abuse Counselor in the Student Health Center.

University Policy on Alcohol, Drugs, and Smoking (Columbia University)

In order to comply with federal, state, and city laws, and to promote the health and well-being of its community, Columbia has produced and distributed this publication to inform all students and employees (faculty and staff) about University policy on alcohol, drugs, and smoking. All members of the University community are expected to comply with this policy.

Alcohol

Legal and Disciplinary Issues

New York State law provides that:

"No person shall sell, deliver or give away or cause or permit or procure to be sold, delivered or given away any alcoholic beverages to
1. Any person, actually or apparently, under the age of twenty-one years;
2. Any visibly intoxicated person;
3. Any habitual drunkard known to be such to the person authorized to dispense any alcoholic beverages."

"Any person who misrepresents the age of a person under the age of twenty-one years for the purpose of inducing the sale of any alcoholic beverage. . . . to such person, is guilty of an offense . . ."

"No person under the age of twenty-one years shall present or offer to any licensee under this chapter [the alcoholic beverage control law], or to the agent or employee of such licensee, any written evidence of age which is false, fraudulent or not actually his own, for the purpose of purchasing or attempting to purchase any alcoholic beverage."

In addition, New York State law states that ". . . no person under the age of twenty-one years shall possess any alcoholic beverage . . . with the intent to consume such beverage."

It is the policy of Columbia University that all University affiliates (students and employees) comply with New York State and other applicable laws and regulations governing alcoholic beverages while at

222

the University's premises or participating in its activities. The violation of these laws may subject the violator to legal actions that range from confiscation of the beverage by a police officer to suspension of one's driving license to fine or imprisonment.

Within the University, the illegal or wrongful possession, provision, or consumption of alcohol will lead to proceedings in accordance with the procedures of the respective school or administrative unit, which can include the requirement for the student to receive psychological or medical assessment and/or counseling and appropriate treatment. Disciplinary action may result in expulsion or the referral of violators for criminal prosecution. Employees should also note that they may not report to work or be at work while under the influence of alcohol.

Policies Regarding the Consumption of Alcohol

In every case, the host or sponsor of a student event has the responsibility to insure that legal requirements and University policy are observed. The following rules must be observed in all instances where alcohol is served:

1. No alcohol may be served to a person who is disorderly or who is, or appears to be, intoxicated.

2. No person shall be sold, served or given or shall otherwise receive alcoholic beverages if that person is not 21 years of age.

3. No person shall misrepresent his or her age or identity, or assist another in such misrepresentation, in an attempt to obtain alcoholic beverages, or otherwise assist a person under 21 years of age to obtain alcoholic beverages.

4. The theme of the event must be social, cultural, or educational, not the type or quantity of alcohol.

5. Ample quantities of food and appealing non-alcoholic beverages must be continuously provided and visibly displayed.

6. Games of chance are not permitted.

7. There may be no drinking games, contests, or other activities that induce or encourage the consumption of alcoholic beverages.

8. Where there is reason to believe that the attendees include those under 21, individuals must be checked for proof of age before being served alcohol.

9. Consumption of alcoholic beverages on outdoor University property is prohibited except at events for which authorization to serve alcoholic beverages has been obtained.

10. Alcoholic beverages may not be dispensed or given away where

money changes hands (sales, admission charged, donations solicited, etc.) without a license or permit.

11. In licensed areas (such as the Plex and Faculty House), all individuals and groups must adhere to the provision of the license. *No unauthorized alcohol may be brought into a licensed area.*

12. Under no circumstances can alcoholic beverages other than beer or wine be sold in an unlicensed premise.

13. All events that have alcoholic beverages served must state in all promotions or advertising: "Double proof of age is required for the possession or consumption of alcoholic beverages." This must be in a reasonable proportion to the rest of the advertising. No other mention of alcohol or displays of alcohol are permitted in any promotional material (including T-shirts).

14. Grain alcohol may not be served at any function.

15. Only one drink at a time may be dispensed to each person. People may not accumulate drinks. . . .

Health Issues Related to Alcohol

According to the U.S. Department of Education, alcohol consumption causes a number of marked changes in behavior. Even low doses significantly impair the judgment and coordination required to drive a car safely, increasing the likelihood that the driver will be involved in an accident. Low to moderate doses of alcohol also increase the incidence of a variety of aggressive acts, including spouse and child abuse. Moderate to high doses of alcohol cause marked impairments in higher mental functions, severely altering a person's ability to learn and remember information. Very high doses cause respiratory depression and death. If combined with other depressants of the central nervous system, much lower doses of alcohol will produce the effects just described.

Repeated use of alcohol can lead to dependence. Sudden cessation of alcohol intake is likely to produce withdrawal symptoms, including severe anxiety, tremors, hallucinations, and convulsions. Alcohol withdrawal can be life-threatening. Long-term consumption of large quantities of alcohol, particularly when combined with poor nutrition, can also lead to permanent damage to vital organs such as the brain and the liver.

Mothers who drink alcohol during pregnancy may give birth to infants with fetal alcohol syndrome. These infants have irreversible physical abnormalities and mental retardation. In addition, research indicates that children of alcoholic parents are at greater risk than other youngsters of becoming alcoholics.

Columbia University provides a variety of counseling, treatment, and educational programs to identify and help those who abuse alcohol. These programs are listed at the end . . . Inquiries about this policy or the procedures it establishes should be directed to the appropriate Dean of Students' Office, Student Affairs Officer, or unit supervisor. . . .

Drugs

Columbia University recognizes the illegality and danger of drug abuse and accordingly strictly prohibits the possession, use, manufacture, or distribution of illicit drugs on University premises or as part of any University activity.

Columbia affiliates (students and employees) who violate the University's policies about illicit drugs will face discipline through their schools or administrative units, up to and including expulsion or termination of employment, which may include the requirement for completion of an appropriate rehabilitation program. Moreover, all students and employees should be aware that, in addition to University sanctions, they may be subject to criminal prosecution under federal and state laws which specify severe penalties, including fines and imprisonment, for drug-related criminal offenses. The seriousness of these crimes and the penalties imposed upon conviction usually depend upon the individual drug and the amount of it involved in the crime. Attachment A provides information concerning penalties and sanctions under Federal Law.

New York State also provides sanctions for unlawful possession or distribution of illicit drugs. For example, in New York State, unlawful possession of four or more ounces of cocaine is a class A-1 felony, punishable by a minimum of 15–25 years and a maximum of life in prison. Where appropriate or necessary, the University will cooperate fully with law enforcement agencies and may refer students and employees for prosecution.

Following the adoption of the federal Drug Free Workplace Act of 1988, the University announced these policies for all employees, which remain in effect:

1. The unlawful manufacture, distribution, dispensation, possession, or use of a Controlled Substance in a University Workplace by

any Columbia employee is prohibited. A "Controlled Substance" is any of those substances referred to in Schedule I through V of Section 202 of the Controlled Substances Act, 21 U.S.C. 812, and as further defined in regulation at 21 CFR 1308.11–1308.15. These include substances that have a high potential for misuse, or which if abused may lead to severe psychological or physical dependence. Among these are heroin and other opium derivatives, marijuana, cocaine, and mescaline and other hallucinogens. "University Workplace" means any site at which employees perform work for the University, whether or not such site is owned by Columbia University.

2. Employees may not report to work, or be at work (at a University Workplace) while under the influence of either a Controlled Substance or alcohol.

3. It is a condition of employment that each University employee will abide by the terms of this Policy. In addition, each employee must notify the University's Vice President for Personnel Management at 311 Dodge Hall, Columbia University, New York, New York 10027 in writing no later than 5 days after Conviction for a violation occurring in the University Workplace of any Criminal Drug Statute. A Conviction is a finding of guilt (including a plea of *nolo contendere*) or imposition of sentence, or both, by any judicial body charged with the responsibility to determine violations of the Criminal Drug Statutes. Such statutes involve the manufacture, distribution, dispensation, possession or use of any Controlled Substance.

4. Any employee who violates this Policy will be subject to serious disciplinary action up to and including termination of employment.

5. Within 30 days after receiving notice from an employee of a Conviction, the University will:

a) take appropriate disciplinary action up to and including termination of employment or

b) require the employee to satisfactorily participate in a drug assistance or rehabilitation program approved for such purposes by a Federal, State or local health, law enforcement or other appropriate agency.

Health Issues Related to Drugs

While adverse health effects can vary depending on the substance, most drugs can produce one or more of the following reactions: headache, nausea, dizziness, anxiety, damage to organs, addiction, and, in extreme cases, death. Interactions between drugs and alcohol can be especially extreme. Moreover, the use of drugs can result in asocial or violent behaviors and can have a severe negative effect on personal development, school work, and job performance.

Policy on Illegal Drugs and Alcohol (Wesleyan University)

Wesleyan University believes that illegal activity involving alcohol or illicit drugs, on campus or during University-sponsored activities, has the potential to damage the quality of campus life in the following ways:

1. by injuring the physiological and psychological well-being of individuals,
2. by disrupting and endangering the welfare of those in the immediate environment of the illegal activity,
3. by attracting criminal activity to the campus.

Wesleyan's response to illegal activity involving alcohol or illicit drugs is through educational and treatment programs and through the establishment and enforcement of explicit standards of conduct. The specific elements of the Wesleyan response are described below.

Standards of Conduct

The University prohibits the unlawful possession, use or distribution of illicit drugs and alcohol by students or employees on University property or while participating in any University-sponsored activity. The University will impose disciplinary sanctions on students and employees who violate the standards.

Disciplinary sanctions that may be imposed on students include warning, disciplinary probation, work-hours, suspension, expulsion, and dismissal. The University may also require a student who violates these standards to participate in a program of rehabilitation. Whenever the University determines that a student has violated one of the standards, it will consider as a possible sanction referral of the matter to law enforcement officials for prosecution.

The disciplinary sanctions that may be imposed on employees may include one or more of the following, in ascending order of severity: warning, reprimand, probation, suspension (with or without pay), and termination of employment. In some instances, the University may also require an employee who violates these standards to participate in a program of rehabilitation outside of the University. Whenever the University determines that an employee has violated one of the standards, it will consider as a possible sanction referral of the matter to law enforcement officials for prosecution.

Visitation Policy
(Southwestern College)

The University's visitation policy strives to provide students with the personal freedom which promotes self-regulation in recognition of the adult status of students while at the same time setting forth guidelines to promote a healthy community environment for living and learning. To prevent ambiguity in interpretation of the policy some terms must be defined:

A *resident* is defined as a member of the campus community who lives in the residence halls and has been asigned to live in the room in question. A *visitor* is defined as a non-member of the campus community or a resident who resides in a room other than the room in question. A *cohabitant* is defined as a visitor who adopts daily activities analogous to those of an assigned resident with respect to 24-hour use of the room in question. Examples include maintaining clothes and possessions in the room, staying in the room overnight for more than 3 nights, using the amenities of the hall such as the laundry room on a frequent basis, and any combination of these or similar activities.

Visitation is allowed in *upperclass residence halls,* in both individual student rooms and public areas, on a 24 hour basis. Visitation in freshman halls in both individual student rooms and public areas is permitted from 10 a.m. to 12 midnight, Sunday through Thursday, and 10 a.m. to 2 a.m. on Fridays and Saturdays.

The visitation policy is not meant to foster cohabitation, and a visitor may not become a cohabitant of a residence hall room.

Visitors are governed by the same rules and regulations set forth in the most recent *Student Handbook* or any supplements thereafter distributed to the student body. This includes, and emphasis is placed upon, the escort and quiet hours policies. The resident host is held responsible for informing the visitor of such rules and regulations, and of the visitor's conduct to the contrary of these rules and regulations.

Escort Policy

The University's Escort Policy strives to provide safety and privacy for those living in the residence hall community. The Escort Policy is tailored to the different types of residence halls on campus to be convenient and manageable.

In single gender residence halls, any person that is not a member of the Southwestern community (faculty, staff, and students) or any member who is of the opposite gender than that designated for that residence hall, must be escorted throughout the hall by a member of the community who is of the same gender as that hall. Exceptions to this are those University staff members who are entêring the hall for maintenance, cleaning, or security purposes, or persons who have secured permission from the Dean of Students.

In mixed gender residence halls, any person who is not a member of the Southwestern community (faculty, staff, and students) must be escorted throughout the hall by a member of the community. Exceptions to this are persons who have secured permission from the Dean of Students.

Students are discouraged from escorting persons whom they do not know into and about the halls.

Visitation Policy
(University of Richmond)

Co-educational visitation is regarded as an important part of the co-curricular educational experience in University residential facilities. However, the visitation privilege must respect students' rights to privacy, security and safety, which are directly related to the physical and social environment in which students reside. Therefore, it is the policy of the University of Richmond to restrict hours of visitation in the residence halls where the security and privacy of the residents is more difficult to secure.

Visitation Regulations

• **Responsibility for Visitors.** Individual residents must accept responsibility for the actions of their visitors.
• **Right to Free Access.** No resident shall, at any time, abrogate a roommate's right to free access to his/her room.
• **Rights to Privacy, Study, Sleep.** A resident will not deprive a roommate of his/her right to privacy, study time or sleep because of a visitor.
• **Westhampton College Residence Hall Main Doors.** Lora Robins Court main doors are locked 24 hours a day. All other Westhampton College residence hall main doors will be locked at 12 midnight daily for the protection of residents throughout the night. The card access system permits residents and their guests to continue to enter or leave the residence halls after 12 midnight.
• **Escorts for Male Visitors in Westhampton College Residence Halls.** After 12 midnight, any male visitor within the Westhampton College residence halls will be escorted by a female resident of that hall at all times to protect residents' rights and safety.

Visitation Hours

As long as the above rights and responsibilities are respected, the following visitation hours pertain:

232

Richmond and Westhampton College Residence Halls: Visitation regulations for the residence halls of RC and WC will allow visitors of the opposite gender to visit residents in accordance with the following hours:

Sunday through Thursday	10 AM to 2 AM
Friday and Saturday	10 AM to 3 AM

AIDS Policy
(Mount Holyoke College)

The Acquired Immune Deficiency Syndrome (AIDS) is a public health problem that is spreading rapidly throughout the world. Because AIDS is a contagious, apparently always fatal disease, it is appropriate to formulate AIDS guidelines for the entire Mount Holyoke College community. These guidelines are based upon recommendations of the American College Health Association, the Centers for Disease Control, the U.S. Public Health Service, and the American Council on Education.

These guidelines are consistent with existing Mount Holyoke College policies that prohibit discrimination against individuals with special needs. The guidelines are intended to promote the safety and well-being of infected individuals as well as the entire college community, to steer programs about AIDS on campus, and to be used to direct college decision-making where appropriate. Mount Holyoke College complies with applicable state and federal law prohibiting discrimination.

Guidelines

These guidelines apply to the entire Mount Holyoke College community; including faculty, staff, and students.

1. Mount Holyoke College is committed to adhering to the standards established by the federal Vocational Rehabilitation Act of 1973. Under this act, applicants for admission or employment will not be subject to handicap discrimination. Mount Holyoke recognizes AIDS to be a handicapping condition.

2. So long as an individual is capable, with reasonable accommodation, or performing her/his job duties or responsibilities as a student, an HIV-positive individual will not be precluded from advancement or promotion.

3. Mount Holyoke College will not require random, mandatory AIDS screening or testing. Applicants for employment will not be subjected to pre-employment screening tests.

234

4. Individuals who make it known that they are infected with the AIDS virus will not be prevented from attending classes, working, using any campus facilities, or participating in any aspect of college life as long as doing so will not pose a health risk to themselves or to others.

5. Confidentiality regarding AIDS, as well as all other health concerns, is protected by state and federal law. Information in an individual's Health Center medical record will not be shared without that individual's written consent.

6. Mount Holyoke College will observe state and federal public health requirements for reporting newly-diagnosed cases of AIDS.

7. The Health Center will assist with AIDS education. It will also counsel individuals about available AIDS-related services and testing sites.

Policy Statement on AIDS
(Saint Anselm College)

Saint Anselm College is a Catholic liberal arts college in the Benedictine tradition that strives to foster a community in which academic endeavor is complemented by opportunities for social, personal, and spiritual growth. As such, the College has a responsibility to address one of the major health problems confronting society—Acquired Immune Deficiency Syndrome ("AIDS"). Accordingly, the College adopts and promulgates this policy statement concerning the treatment of those persons who have AIDS, AIDS-related Complex ("ARC"), or a positive Human Immunodeficiency Virus (HIV) test. . . .

I. Non-Discrimination

A. The College shall not discriminate in enrollment or employment against any student or employee who has AIDS.

B. Members of the student body, faculty, administration, or staff of the College shall not be denied access to college facilities or campus activities solely on the ground that they have AIDS.

C. The College reserves the right to deny access to a person with AIDS to school facilities and functions if the College with professional advice makes a medically-based determination that the restriction is necessary for the welfare of the person with AIDS' and/or the welfare of the other members of the College community.

II. Confidentiality

A. The College shall comply with all pertinent statutes and regulations which protect the privacy of persons in the College community who have AIDS. The College shall ensure the procedural safeguards sufficient to maintain the strictest confidence about persons with AIDS are in effect in all offices of the College.

B. Information identifying members of the College community with AIDS shall be available only to the President of the College and the Director of College Health Services. Such information shall be divulged to other members of the College only on a clearly demonstrated need-to-know basis for the purpose of protecting all the members of the College community.

C. Except as provided in paragraph (B) above, specific information concerning any person with AIDS in the College community shall not be divulged to any faculty member, administrator, staff person, other institution, insurer, or parent without the express permission of the person with AIDS. All medical records of persons with AIDS shall be maintained in confidence.

III. Testing

As currently understood by competent medical opinions, the risks of transmitting AIDS in the college environment generally do not justify mandatory or discriminatory testing of applicants for admission, students, faculty, or staff of the College. They also do not generally support a requirement that such persons be asked to respond to questions concerning any test that they may have had for AIDS. The College shall neither require all members to be tested, nor shall identify persons in high risk groups and require that they alone be screened for AIDS.

IV. Responsibilities of the College

A. The College shall comply with all federal, state, and local laws and regulations that protect the welfare of persons with AIDS or the welfare of others within the College community who may come into contact with a person with AIDS. The College shall also comply with any law or regulation which requires that proven cases of AIDS be reported to public health officials (See N.H.R.S.A. Sections 136.6 and 141.1, 141.3).

B. The College shall develop and maintain a comprehensive education program about AIDS in conformity with the moral teaching of the Church for all members of the Anselmian community. The program shall address, among other things, current medical opinions about the nature of AIDS and its symptoms, methods of transmission, types of behavior which increase the risk of communication of the disease, and preventive measures for avoiding infection by the AIDS virus. The College will also undertake an education program about AIDS for residence hall staff (whether student or otherwise) because they often may be the first persons to confront and AIDS issue.

C. The College shall be prepared to refer members of the College community to sources of competent and confidential testing for AIDS upon their request for such screening. In addition, the College will be prepared to provide counseling services to those desiring to be tested or to refer them to qualified counselors outside of the College.

D. On the basis of current medical opinion, there appears to be no reason for the College to advise occupants of a residence hall of the presence in the hall of any person who has AIDS.

E. The College shall require persons with AIDS to secure qualified medical care for their affliction. When other contagious diseases are prevalent on campus, the College with professional advice may have to take steps to protect persons who have been immunologically compromised by AIDS.

F. The College shall implement practices for all settings in the College (e.g. laboratory, College Health Services, etc.) for safely handling and disposing of blood and body fluids.

G. If the College learns that a student or employee has AIDS, it shall have the discretion to take steps to protect the welfare of other members of the community including, among others, regularly monitoring the person's medical condition, counseling the person on the nature of the disease and the necessity of refraining from behavior that could transmit it to others, and, where qualified medical opinion concerning the individual's particular case so dictates, restricting the person with AIDS from close contact with other members of the College community.

H. Copies of this policy shall be made available to the Anselmmian Community through the offices of the Academic Dean, Treasurer, Dean of Students, College Health Services, and the Geisel Library.

Sexual Harassment
(Carleton College)

Policy Statement

When sexual harassment occurs at Carleton College, the standards of the community are violated. Sexual harassment of any student, faculty member, or employee by any other student, faculty member, or employee is prohibited and will not be tolerated.

Retaliation against a person who reports, complains about, or participates in the investigation of sexual harassment is also intolerable and prohibited.

Students, faculty, and staff are reminded that apparently consensual sexual relationships, particularly those between individuals of unequal status, may be or may quickly become violative of this policy. Anyone who engages in a sexual relationship with a person over whom he or she has any degree of power or authority must understand that the validity of the consent involved can and may be questioned, and must anticipate the closest scrutiny of his or her actions. The College particularly abhors the abuse potentially inherent in sexual relationships between faculty members and their students.

The essential importance of academic freedom is recognized and a standard of reasonableness will guide the College. Only when it is used to disguise, or as the vehicle for, prohibited conduct will be questioned. Carleton College believes that ideas, creativity, and free expression thrive—and indeed can only exist for the entire community—in an atmosphere free of sexual harassment or coercion.

Because sexual harassment may also constitute a violation of federal and state law, anyone who feels that she or he has been subjected to sexual harassment has the right to institute legal proceedings in addition to or in lieu of a complaint pursuant to this policy. . . .

Response and Procedure

Carleton College, in its effort to prevent and eliminate sexual harassment, will direct resources and energy to the following:

Education. The College will publish this policy in pamphlet form and

239

distribute it to every student, staff member, and faculty member. Students, faculty, and staff will be offered and encouraged to attend training sessions on the subject of sexual harassment. In addition, the College policy against sexual harassment will be reiterated at appropriate opportunities in classes, meetings, programs, and publications.

Counseling and Support. Counseling: The College provides counseling services which may be used by persons who feel that they have been sexually harassed. Students may seek counseling from the Counseling Center, while staff and faculty may use the Employee Assistance Program. In addition, the College Chaplain is available to all members of the community.

Support of Advocacy Groups: The College acknowledges the validity and importance of groups and activities devoted to the support of those who have been subjected to sexual harassment. Such advocacy groups and activities will be provided with appropriate support by the College. Support of these groups will include funds for training, organizational services, meetings, and communications to the community. Students, staff, and faculty may all volunteer to join advocacy groups. Participation in these advocacy groups should in no way deleteriously affect their status in the College. Whenever possible, supervisors should permit their staff members to participate.

Complaint Investigation and Responsive Action. Every complaint about sexual harassment made to the College by a student, faculty member, or employee will be promptly, thoroughly, and impartially investigated by an investigative officer employed by the College. The investigative officer will be appointed by the President in consultation with appropriate members of the College community including the Sexual Harassment Resource Committee. When investigation indicates that a violation of this policy may have occurred, prompt and appropriate responsive action will be taken by the appropriate College authority.[1] The investigative officer may recommend action and facilitate resolution of complaints, but may not impose any discipline or implement any resolution without the specific direction of appropriate College authorities.

A complaint is made to the College when it is communicated to the President, a Vice President, a Dean, a Department Chair, a Department Head, any member of the Sexual Harassment Resource Committee, or the investigative officer. If a complaint is made to anyone else, the complainant risks the possibility that it will not come to the attention of the appropriate authorities and may, therefore, not be acted upon.

When it appears that the safety or security of the College or of any individual student, staff member, or faculty member may be jeopardized, the President or his or her designee may take immediate action to prevent the occurrence or reoccurrence of sexual harassment.

Informal resolution of a complaint of sexual harassment may occur if recommended by the investigative officer and acceptable to the complainant, the person or persons accused by violating this Policy, and College authorities. Such informal resolution may be negotiated by the investigative officer but must be implemented by the appropriate College authority.

When an informal resolution is not possible or cannot be accomplished, the complaint and investigative results will be referred to the appropriate College authority as required by College policy and existing agreements with the faculty and staff. Additionally, if a complainant is unsatisfied with the investigative officer's action, she/he may ask the appropriate College authority to review the proceedings.

The timing and specific nature of the investigation of any complaint will be determined by the investigative officer, who may consult with appropriate College authorities. Generally, however, complaints will be investigated promptly. If more than one complaint is under investigation, the investigative officer will consider the seriousness and potential impact of the conduct complained of in determining the order in which complaints will be investigated. While investigations will be conducted with discretion and sensitivity, the nature of alleged actions may require questions about sensitive matters, and it may be impossible to ensure complete confidentiality. For example, if safety and security or the prevention and elimination of sexual harassment require it, investigative information will be communicated as appropriate to those with a need to know. Both a person making a complaint and one against whom a complaint is made may be accompanied during the investigation process and responsive action by an individual of his or her own choosing, with the understanding that those accompanying the person must respect the confidentiality of the proceedings. Complaints may, under certain circumstances, be investigated in the absence of cooperation or participation from the complainant. An incident or information which is not the subject of a complaint may form the basis of an investigation at the discretion of the investigative officer. Written reports and documentation related to each complaint will be produced or obtained as necessary for an adequate investigation, and will be permanently maintained by the investigative officer. Such reports and documentation as are necessary will be forwarded to the appropriate College authority when the investigative officer determines that a violation of the Policy may have occurred, and that the violation warrants action by that authority. The availability of investigative information to any other individual or group is subject to the discretion of the investigative officer, in consultation with the appropriate College authority.

Because the circumstances of every complaint of sexual harassment are different, the investigative officer has and will use discretion and flexibility to conduct an appropriate investigation of each complaint, and to recommend a response to each complaint to the appropriate College authority. Investigation and response will be consistent with the College policy against sexual harassment and with the goal of taking timely, appropriate, and effective action to eliminate sexual harassment and prevent its reoccurrence.

Note

[1]If the alleged harasser is a staff member, the matter will be referred to the Vice President and Treasurer for disposition. If the alleged harasser is a faculty member, the matter will be referred to the Dean of the College. If the alleged harasser is a student, the matter will be referred for handling in accordance with Part VI of the Statement of Student Rights and Responsibilities contained in the Student Handbook.

Statement on Sexual Harassment (Columbia University)

Sexual harassment is particularly reprehensible in an academic community. Columbia's basic integrity is threatened when professors misuse their authority and sexually coerce or intimidate students. Following guidelines from the Federal Equal Opportunity Commission, Columbia University developed the formal policy-statement on sexual harrassment reprinted on the following page.

Sexual harassment occurs when someone in a more powerful position attempts to coerce another, less powerful person into unwanted sexual activity, subjects that person to unwanted attention on the basis of sex or sexual preference, or makes that person's learning or working environment intimidating, hostile or offensive through sexual comments, suggestions, or pressures. It can range from coerced sexual relations or physical assault to constant joking or repeated generalized sexist remarks or behavior.

While harassment by "equals" (for example, your class or suite-mates) is not considered sexual harassment by strict legal definition of the University's Policy Statement, it, too, is unacceptable within the Columbia community.

Here are four specific forms sexual harassment can take:

• *Coercion into sexual activity by threats of punishment* such as lower grades, spreading rumors, etc. What is at stake goes far beyond one grade or a single recommendation or research opportunity. Frequently it is access to a particular discipline that is denied or a career that is jeopardized.

• *Solicitation of sexual activity or other sex-related behavior by promise of rewards.* This form of harassment neither directly states nor implies a threat but suggests there will be a reward for complicity. Put blatantly, it amounts to an attempt to purchase sexual behavior using promises such as higher grades, fellowships, or job opportunities as barter.

• *Inappropriate, offensive, but essentially sanction-free advances.* In this case, sexual harassment takes the form of request for social or sexual encounters, often accompanied by touching. The advances are unwelcome, make the student feel uncomfortable, but carry with them neither direct nor implied threats or rewards.

243

• *Generalized sexist remarks or behavior.* This type of incident is closest to racial harassment and may or may not be directed at a particular individual.

If you think you are being sexually harassed, the first step to take is to stop ignoring the problem. If you can, confront your harasser. Be polite, but firm. Present the facts as you see them, describe how you feel about what has happened, make clear that the harassment is unwelcome, and say that you want it to stop. If you're reluctant to have this conversation face-to-face, put it in a letter, preferably delivered by registered mail, and keep a copy.

If that doesn't work, or if you're reluctant to have any dealings at all with your harasser, you can—and **should**—go to your Dean of Students' Office, the Office of Equal Opportunity and Affirmative Action, or a member of the University Panel on Sexual Harassment.

Policy

Federal Law [Title VII of the Civil Rights Act of 1964] provides that it shall be an unlawful discriminatory practice for any employer, because of the sex of any person, to discharge without just cause, to refuse to hire, or otherwise to discriminate against that person with respect to any matter directly or indirectly related to employment. Harassment of any employee on the basis of sex violates this federal law.

To help clarify what is unlawful sexual harassment the Federal Equal Employment Opportunity Commission has issued Guidelines on the subject. While the EEOC Guidelines apply only to faculty and other employees, the University prohibits sexual harassment of any member of the Columbia community, whether such harassment is aimed at students, faculty, or other employees, and violators will be subject to disciplinary action. Unwelcome sexual advances, requests for sexual favors, and other verbal or physical conduct of a sexual nature will constitute sexual harassment when:

1. submission to such conduct is made explicitly or implicitly a term or condition of an individual's employment;
2. submission to or rejection of such conduct by an individual is used as the basis for academic or employment decisions affecting that individual; or,
3. such conduct has the purpose or effect of unreasonably interfer-

ing with an individual's academic or work performance or creating an intimidating, hostile, or offensive academic or working environment.

Any person who believes that he or she is being sexually harassed should seek a resolution of the problem through discussion with the person directly concerned. If this does not resolve the matter, or if there is a reluctance to deal directly with the person involved, the problem should be brought to the attention of a member of the University Panel on Sexual Harassment. Advice may also be sought from the Office of Equal Opportunity and Affirmative Action (305 Low Memorial Library, 854-5511). If these steps have not resolved the problem, the applicable University grievance procedure should be used, including the University Discrimination Grievance Procedure that is available if no other University grievance procedure is specifically applicable. No one at the University may retaliate in any way against a person who makes a claim of sexual harassment.

Discrimination and Academic Freedom
(Carleton College)

The following is a statement of policy as well as a statement of values. It is intended to help sustain a civil atmosphere of unfettered intellectual freedom at the College and to discourage discriminatory speech and actions by its members.

As an institution dedicated to learning and teaching, Carleton College is committed to the principle of free expression and exploration of ideas in an atmosphere of civility and mutual respect. The College therefore also embraces the related principle that all members of its community shall have access to its educational facilities, activities, and employment without regard to race, creed, age, sex, national origin, sexual or affectional preference, or non-disqualifying handicap. These principles guide the College's relationships with individuals and should guide the interactions of all members of the community.

A possible breach of the foregoing principles may be brought to the attention of the appropriate College officer: the Vice President and Treasurer, Dean of the College or Dean of Students, if the party responsible is, respectively, a staff member, teacher or student.

While the nature of an academic community is to provide a milieu for the expression, criticism and discussion (and for the tolerance) of the widest range of opinions, it does not provide a license for bigotry in the form of demeaning, discriminatory speech or actions. Thus, the presentation of a reasoned or evidenced claim about a societal group that offends members of that group is to be distinguished from a gratuitous denigrating claim about, or addressed to, an individual or group such as those enumerated above. The former is *bona fide* academic behavior while the latter may demean, degrade or victimize in a discriminatory manner and, if so, undermines the above principles.

Discriminatory speech and actions are especially abhorrent when they are made anonymously, for anonymity precludes the possibility of an exchange and exploration of ideas; moreover, such an anonymous message—by the very nature of its delivery—is a threat to the recipient. Discrimination by one person against another is also particularly abhorrent when the first person is in a position of power with respect

246

to the second, whether in the academic, administrative, political, or social hierarchy on the campus.

Although this policy attempts to eliminate certain behavior and actions on the campus, Carleton cannot guarantee that the environment will always be comfortable for all members of the community. Often, the educational process is disturbing and unsettling; when one's ideas are under attack and one's values are being challenged, the effect may be simultaneously painful and highly educational. Thus, behavior that is disturbing or unsettling to an individual or group is not necessarily discriminatory. In this regard, it is imperative that teachers and students be able to take controversial positions without fear, in accordance with the principle of academic freedom.

Students, faculty, and staff of Carleton College are asked to support this anti-discrimination policy through participation in discussions about it. The College will facilitate this by providing educational opportunities and forums for such discussions to take place and by making it possible for students, faculty, and staff to attend them. The policy will be distributed to all students, faculty and staff members each year. The College will actively encourage the discussion of issues raised by the policy in appropriate classes, meetings, symposia and college publications.

Adopted by the Board of Trustees June 21, 1990, upon recommendation of the College Council.

Appendix C

Survey Questionnaire and Respondents

The survey questionnaire whose results are summarized in Chapter 3, and cited elsewhere in this study, was mailed on November 26, 1990, to seventy-six colleges and universities across the United States. The sample was selected principally from a widely cited listing of the nation's leading colleges and universities, prepared annually by *U.S. News and World Report*. Institutions were selected from the magazine's list of leading national and regional institutions in various categories. To this list I added several institutions representing categories, such as regional church-related colleges, that would otherwise have been nearly absent from the sample.

As is stated in the text of Chapter 3, this survey population does not represent a randomly selected sample of U.S. colleges and universities but rather is intended to include institutions in various categories that are highly regarded by educators and the public and whose policies are likely to serve as examples for other institutions. It is weighted toward liberal-arts colleges for that reason but includes public and private universities as well.

The survey questionnaire was accompanied by a letter explaining the nature of my project, requesting copies of relevant handbooks and policy statements, and assuring the respondent that any information provided would be used solely as a basis for statistical reports and would not be disclosed in a way that would permit a reader to identify the institution. The last page of the questionnaire contained several narrative questions and requested permission to quote from any policies that were being provided to me.

The administrators who received the survey were generally eager to assist me. In response to an initial mailing and one follow-up reminder, I received a total of forty-nine completed questionnaires, representing an overall response rate of 64 percent. (I actually received responses from two institutions not included in the original mailing of 76: Barnard College and Westhampton College, the women's colleges administratively linked to Columbia University and the University of Richmond, respectively. There are, accordingly, 78 institutions, not 76, in the listings below. The response rate from a sample of 78 is 63 percent.)

A. Institutions returning a completed questionnaire

The following forty-four institutions returned completed questionnaires, with institutional identification.

A "yes" in the BOOK? column indicates institutions that submitted student handbooks or policies for my reference. These documents are listed in the bibliography (Appendix D).

A "yes" in the QUOTE? column indicates, among institutions that supplied written policies, those that granted permission to quote from them. Materials supplied by other institutions—those with a "yes" in the first column and a "no" in the second—were used, without specific attribution, to corroborate or disconfirm general policy features and trends noted in the text.

	BOOK?	QUOTE?
Barnard College (New York)	No	
Bates College (Maine)	No	
Berea College (Kentucky)	Yes	Yes
Bowdoin College (Maine)	Yes	No
Calvin College (Michigan)	Yes	Yes
Carleton College (Minnesota)	Yes	Yes
Claremont McKenna College (California)	No	
Columbia University (New York)	Yes	Yes
Cornell University (New York)	No	
Davidson College (North Carolina)	Yes	Yes
Duke University (North Carolina)	Yes	Yes
Evergreen State College (Washington)	Yes	No
Georgetown University (District of Columbia)	No	

Grinnell College (Iowa)	No	
Hamilton College (New York)	Yes	No
Illinois Wesleyan University	Yes	Yes
Middlebury College (Vermont)	Yes	No
Mount Holyoke College (Massachusetts)	Yes	Yes
Northwestern University (Illinois)	No	
Occidental College (California)	No	
Princeton University (New Jersey)	Yes	Yes
Richmond College (Virginia)	Yes	Yes
Saint Anselm College (New Hampshire)	Yes	Yes
Saint Olaf College (Minnesota)	Yes	Yes
Smith College (Massachusetts)	Yes	Yes
Southwestern University (Texas)	Yes	Yes
Spelman College (Georgia)	No	
Stanford University (California)	Yes	Yes
Trinity University (Texas)	Yes	No
University of Delaware	Yes	Yes
University of Virginia	Yes	Yes
University of Chicago (Illinois)	No	
University of Rochester (New York)	Yes	No
University of California at Los Angeles	Yes	Yes
University of North Carolina	Yes	Yes
Washington and Lee University (Virginia)	Yes	No
Washington University (Missouri)	No	
Wellesley College (Massachusetts)	Yes	Yes
Wesleyan University (Connecticut)	Yes	Yes
Westhampton College (Virginia)	Yes	Yes
Westminster College (Missouri)	Yes	Yes
Williams College (Massachusetts)	Yes	Yes
Wittenburg University (Ohio)	Yes	No
Yale University (Connecticut)	Yes	Yes

B. Institutions not responding or responding anonymously

I received five completed questionnaires submitted anonymously, mailed—whether intentionally or simply through oversight I could not determine—without any institutional identification. (I did not anticipate that my providing a postage-paid envelope would make institutional identification more difficult!) They represent five of the thirty-four institutions listed below. From the remaining twenty-nine institutions on the list I received no response.

Alfred University (New York)
Amherst College (Massachusetts)
Bard College (Massachusetts)
Brown University (Rhode Island)
Bryn Mawr College (Pennsylvania)
California Institute of Technology
Carnegie Mellon University (Pennsylvania)
Colby College (Maine)
Colgate University (New York)
Converse College (South Carolina)
Dartmouth College (New Hampshire)
Harvard University (Massachusetts)
Haverford College (Pennsylvania)
Hiram College (Ohio)
Johns Hopkins University (Maryland)
Massachusetts Institute of Technology
Michigan Technological University
Oberlin College (Ohio)
Ohio Wesleyan University
Pacific University (Oregon)
Pomona College (California)
Rice University (Texas)
Saint Norbert College (Wisconsin)
Santa Clara University (California)
Swarthmore College (Pennsylvania)
University of Pennsylvania
University of Michigan
University of California at Berkeley
University of Puget Sound (Washington)
Vassar College (New York)
Villanova University (Pennsylvania)
Wake Forest University (North Carolina)

Wofford College (South Carolina)
Worcester Polytechnic Institute (Massachusetts)

C. Text of the survey instrument

The following is the text of the questionnaire distributed to the institutions listed above. In brackets after each response I have indicated the number of respondents who chose it. Numbers of total responses differ, because not all respondents answered all questions. Multiple responses (which occurred on questions 1, 3, 4, and 5 only) were counted more than once. See the tabulations in Chapter 3 for a summary of responses to selected questions, expressed in percentages as well as raw numbers.

1. Please indicate which of the following characterizes the residence halls on your campus:
   A. Single-sex men's and women's residence halls (men only or women only in each building) [5]
   B. Some or all buildings are mixed, by floor (men only or women only in each building) [19]
   C. Some or all buildings are mixed, by floor or by room [24]
   D. Not applicable: no residence halls [0]
   E. Not applicable: single-sex institution [1]
   F. Other (please describe) [3]

2. If your answer to #1 was B or C: May students choose single-sex residence halls instead?
   A. Yes; more than 50% of students select single-sex buildings [3]
   B. Yes; 25–49% of students select single-sex buildings [5]
   C. Yes; 10–24% of students select single-sex buildings [4]
   D. Yes; fewer than 10% of students select single-sex buildings [8]
   E. No [16]

3. Which of the six descriptions in #1, above, characterized your campus ten years ago, in 1979–80?
   Responses: A. 10   B. 18   C. 16   D. 0   E. 4   F. 3

4. Which of the six descriptions in #1, above, characterized your campus twenty years ago, in 1969–70?
   Responses: A. 24   B. 6   C. 1   D. 1   E. 12   F. 1

5. Which of the following best characterizes your institution's stated policy regarding social use of alcoholic beverages by students?

A. Prohibited under all circumstances during term [0]
B. Prohibited on campus [7]
C. Permitted on campus, with extensive restrictions (e.g., only at functions with faculty, staff, or other chaperones present; only at designated sites) [7]
D. Responsible use by students of legal age is permitted [35]
E. No stated policy [0]
F. None of the above (please explain briefly) [1]

6. Is use of alcoholic beverages permitted in residence halls?
   A. Yes, in private rooms and in common areas [19]
   B. Only in private rooms of students of legal age [24]
   C. Only in designated common areas [0]
   D. No [5]

7. In the academic year 1989–90, how many students at your institutions were subject to formal disciplinary proceedings for alleged violation of alcohol policies?
   A. None [9]
   B. 1–5 [6]
   C. 6–9 [4]
   D. 10–19 [10]
   E. 20–39 [7]
   F. 40 or more [12]

8. Which of the following most accurately characterizes your institution's stated policy regarding student use of tobacco products?
   A. Prohibited under all circumstances [0]
   B. Permitted only in designated areas [27]
   C. Responsible use by students of legal age is permitted [5]
   D. No stated policy [13]
   E. None of the above (please explain briefly) [1]

9. In the academic year 1989–90, how many students at your institutions were subject to formal disciplinary proceedings for alleged violation of tobacco-use policies?
   A. None [43]
   B. 1–5 [4]
   C. 6–9 [0]
   D. 10–19 [0]
   E. 20–39 [0]
   F. 40 or more [0]

10. Which of the following most accurately characterizes your institution's policy regarding student use of controlled substances such as marijuana, cocaine, amphetamines, and other drugs?
   A. Prohibited under all circumstances [47]
   B. Responsible use of some such substances is permitted [0]
   C. No stated policy [0]
   D. None of the above (please explain briefly) [0]

11. In the academic year 1989–90, how many students at your institutions were subject to formal disciplinary proceedings for alleged use of illegal drugs?
   A. None [17]
   B. 1–5 [22]
   C. 6–9 [5]
   D. 10–19 [2]
   E. 20–39 [1]
   F. 40 or more [0]

12. Which of the following most accurately characterizes your institution's stated policy concerning sexual relations among unmarried students?
   A. Prohibited [2]
   B. Strongly discouraged [4]
   C. Permitted [37]
   D. No stated policy [3]
   E. None of the above (please explain briefly) [1]

13. Are there any restrictions on visiting hours in residence halls for guests of the opposite sex?
   A. Yes, in all residence halls [12]
   B. Only in some residence halls [3]
   C. No [32]

14. Are there any restrictions on visiting hours in residence halls for guests of the same sex?
   A. Yes, in all residence halls [1]
   B. Only in some residence halls [0]
   C. No [45]

15. Does your institution's residence-hall policy permit a student to invite a person of the opposite sex as an overnight guest?
   A. Yes [17]
   B. Yes, with restrictions (e.g., explicit permission of other students sharing a room or suite) [13]

C. No [16]

D. None of the above (please explain briefly) [1]

16. Does your institution's residence-hall policy permit a student to invite a person of the same sex as an overnight guest?

A. Yes [24]

B. Yes, with restrictions (e.g., explicit permission of other students sharing a room or suite) [22]

C. No [0]

D. None of the above (please explain briefly) [0]

17. In the academic year 1989–90, how many students at your institutions were subject to formal disciplinary proceedings for alleged violation of residence-hall rules?

A. None [20]

B. 1–5 [14]

C. 6–9 [3]

D. 10–19 [4]

E. 20–39 [3]

F. 40 or more [4]

18. Does your institution have a stated policy prohibiting racist or antihomosexual speech and writing?

A. Yes; it was first adopted in the last two years [14]

B. Yes; it was adopted more than two years ago [12]

C. No, but such a policy is under active consideration [4]

D. No, and no such policy is under active consideration [15]

19. In the academic year 1989–90, how many students at your institution were subject to formal disciplinary proceedings for allegedly racist or antihomosexual speech or writing?

A. None [32]

B. 1–5 [11]

C. 6–9 [1]

D. 10–19 [1]

E. 20–39 [0]

F. 40 or more [0]

20. In the academic year 1989–90, how many students at your institution were subject to formal disciplinary proceedings for alleged violation of rules regarding plagiarism and academic dishonesty? (Include only incidents brought before an administrator or committee for adjudication; exclude those dealt with solely by the instructor in the relevant course.)

A. None [3]
B. 1–5 [18]
C. 6–9 [8]
D. 10–19 [7]
E. 20–39 [6]
F. 40 or more [4]

21. At your institution, who has the responsibility of formulating and revising rules governing student behavior in the areas mentioned above? (Choose A, B, or C even if others are present as observers; choose D, E, or F if others have a vote.)
    A. An administrator or a committee of administrators [12]
    B. The faculty or a committee of the faculty [0]
    C. Student government or a committee of students [2]
    D. A committee on which administrators are a majority [1]
    E. A committee on which faculty members are a majority [5]
    F. A committee on which students are a majority [4]
    G. A committee in which none of these groups is a majority [12]
    H. None of the above (please explain) [6]

22. Using the same choices as in #21: Who initially adjudicates violations of such rules?
Responses: A. 19   B. 0   C. 3   D. 0   E. 3   F. 4   G. 4   H. 9

23. Using the same choices as in #21: To whom may a student appeal a judgment that he or she has violated behavioral rules?
Responses: A. 10   B. 0   C. 1   D. 1   E. 9   F. 5   G. 12   H. 6

24. In your personal judgment, which of the following best characterizes your institution's implementation of alcohol policies? (I will treat the information provided strictly in confidence and will not report it in any way that permits identification of your campus.)
    A. They are enforced strictly and consistently [14]
    B. Minor violations are frequently overlooked; flagrant violations are dealt with strictly [27]
    C. Enforcement is irregular and arbitrary [0]
    D. They are not enforced [0]
    E. Not applicable; there is no stated policy [1]
    F. None of the above (please explain) [2]

25. Using the same choices as in #24: How would you characterize your institution's enforcement of its policy regarding drug use? [*Note: A typographical error in this and the following question referred*

respondents to #13, whose responses could not possibly apply to this question, instead of #24. The distribution of responses suggests that respondents used the choices enumerated for #24, as was intended.)
Responses: A. 28   B. 12   C. 1   D. 0   E. 0   F. 2

26. Again, using the same choices as in #24: How would you characterize your institution's enforcement of its policy regarding sexual relations among students?
Responses: A. 4   B. 2   C. 3   D. 1   E. 29   F. 1

27. Compared with ten years ago (1979–90), are your campus's policies regarding alcohol use
    A. More restrictive now [39]
    B. Essentially the same [6]
    C. Less restrictive now [1]

28. Compared with ten years ago (1979–90), are your campus's policies regarding drug use
    A. More restrictive now [15]
    B. Essentially the same [30]
    C. Less restrictive now [1]

29. Compared with ten years ago (1979–90), are your campus's policies regarding sexual relations
    A. More restrictive now [3]
    B. Essentially the same [39]
    C. Less restrictive now [3]

30. Compared with ten years ago (1979–90), are your campus's policies regarding plagiarism and academic dishonesty
    A. More restrictive now [2]
    B. Essentially the same [42]
    C. Less restrictive now [1]

31. Does your institution require entering students to sign a document that commits them explicitly to abide by the institution's behavioral rules?
    A. Yes [10]
    B. No [35]

32. Has your institution been subject to legal action in the past five years challenging its authority to enforce behavioral rules?
    A. Yes, on more than one occasion [7]
    B. Yes, on one occasion [4]

C. No [35]

33. Has your institution been subject to legal action in the past five years alleging negligence in overseeing student behavior?
   A. Yes, on more than one occasion [6]
   B. Yes, on one occasion [4]
   C. No [36]

The following questions are intended solely for demographic purposes.

34. Your university is
   A. a research university [15]
   B. a liberal-arts college [29]
   C. Other [2]

35. The number of full-time undergraduate students at your institution is:
   A. Fewer than 1000 [2]
   B. 1000–1999 [15]
   C. 2000–3999 [14]
   D. 4000–7999 [10]
   E. 8000 or more [5]

36. Your campus is located:
   A. In a major city (population greater than 1 million) [8]
   B. In a suburban area of a major city [9]
   C. In a city of moderate size (population 250,000 or more) [4]
   D. In a small city (population 50,000 or more) [7]
   E. In a small town or rural area [18]
   F. Other (please explain) [0]

37. Your institution is:
   A. A state university or college [6]
   B. A private university or college [38]
   C. A church-related institution whose sponsoring church plays a significant role in its governance [2]
   D. Other (please explain) [0]

The remainder of the questions invite narrative answers. Please answer as briefly or as extensively as you wish.

38. What is the most significant change that has occurred in the rules and procedures governing student conduct on campus in the past few years?

39. What in your judgment is the area in which your institution is now most successful in encouraging responsible student conduct?

40. What is the area in which, in your judgment, your institution is now least responsible?

41. In what ways has the threat of legal action compelled changes in rules of conduct and modes of enforcement?

42. Are you satisfied with the way in which the faculty at your institution participate in the formulation and enforcement of student rules?

43. Are you satisfied with the ways in which students have influenced the formulation and enforcement of behavioral rules?

Appendix D

Bibliography

Works Cited

"Recent Developments in the Law." 1989. *Journal of Law and Education.* 18(1, Winter):143–60.

"Recent Developments in the Law." 1989. *Journal of Law and Education.* 18(2, Spring):319–20.

"Recent Developments in the Law." 1989. *Journal of Law and Education.* 18(3, Summer):457–79.

"Recent Developments in the Law." 1989. *Journal of Law and Education.* 18(4, Fall):622–27.

American Civil Liberties Union. 1970. *Academic Freedom and Civil Liberties of Students in Colleges and Universities.* New York: ACLU.

Austin, J. L. 1962. *How to Do Things With Words.* Cambridge, Mass.: Harvard University Press.

Bernstein, Richard J. 1983. *Beyond Objectivism and Relativism: Science, Hermeneutics and Praxis.* Philadelphia: University of Pennsylvania Press.

Black, Henry Campbell. 1979. *Black's Law Dictionary.* 5th ed. St. Paul, Minn.: West

Blackstone, William. 1886. *Commentaries on the Laws of England, in four volumes.* Edited by T. Cooley. Philadelphia: Lippincott.

Blackwell, Thomas E. 1961. *College Law.* Washington, D.C.: National Association of College and University Attorneys.

———. 1974. *The College Law Digest, 1935–1970.* Washington, D.C.: National Association of College and University Attorneys.

Bok, Derek. 1990. *Universities and the Future of America.* Durham, N.C.: Duke University Press.

Bolmeier, Edward. 1976. *Legality of Student Disciplinary Practices.* Charlottesville, Va.: Michie.

Bolton, Charles D. 1967. *The University Student: A Study of Student Behavior and Values.* New Haven: College and University Press.

Chickering, A. 1981. *The Modern American College: Responding to the New Realities of Diverse Students and a Changing Society.* San Francisco: Jossey-Bass.

Dutile, Fernand N. 1986. *Sex, Schools and the Law.* Springfield, Ill.: Charles C. Thomas.

Fulton, Maurice Garland. 1926. *College Life: Its Conditions and Problems.* New York: Macmillan.

Gadaleto, Angelo F., and David S. Anderson. 1986. "Continued Progress: The 1979, 1982, and 1985 College Alcohol Surveys." *Journal of College Student Development* 27(November):499–509.

Gaffney, Edward McGlynn, Jr., and Philip R. Moots. 1982. *Government and Campus: Federal Regulation of Religiously Affiliated Higher Education.* Notre Dame, Ind.: University of Notre Dame Press.

Gibbs, Annette, and James. J. Szablewitz. 1988. "Colleges' New Liabilities: An Emerging New *In Loco Parentis.*" *Journal of College Student Development* 29(March):100–105.

Gifis, Stephen H. 1984. *Law Dictionary.* 2nd ed. Woodbury, N.Y.: Barron's Educational Series.

Gonzalez, Gerardo. 1986. "Trends in Alcohol Knowledge and Drinking Patterns Among Students: 1981–1985." *Journal of College Student Development* 27(November):496–499.

Goodwin, Leonard. 1989. "Explaining Alcohol Consumption and Related Experiences Among Fraternity and Sorority Members." *Journal of College Student Development* 30(September):448–458.

Gregory, Dennis E. 1985. "Alcohol Consumption by College Students and Related Liability Issues." *Journal of Law and Education* 14(1, January):43–53.

Hauser, Gregory F. 1990. "Social Fraternities at Public Institutions of Higher Education: Their Rights Under the First and Fourteenth Amendments." *Journal of Law and Education* 19(4, Fall):455–480.

Hildebrand, M., and S. Abramowitz. 1984. "Sexuality on Campus: Changes in Attitudes and Behaviors in the 1970s." *Journal of College Student Personnel* 25:534–546.

Hoekema, David A. 1980. "What Makes Church Colleges Distinctive?" *The Christian Century* 97(32, September): 972–974

———. 1990. "Beyond *In Loco Parentis?* Parietal Rules and Moral Authority." 177–194. In *Studies in Academic Ethics,* edited by Steven M. Cahn, Philadelphia: Temple University Press.

Hollander, Patricia A. 1978. *Legal Handbook for Educators*. Boulder, Colo.: Westview Press.

Hudgins, H. C., Jr., and Richard S. Vacca. 1979. *Law and Education: Contemporary Issues and Court Decisions*. Charlottesville, Va.: Michie.

Kaplan, William A. 1985. *The Law of Higher Education*. 2nd ed. San Francisco: Jossey-Bass.

Kemerer, Frank R., and Kenneth L. Deutsch. 1979. *Constitutional Rights and Student Life: Value Conflict in Law and Education: Cases and Materials*. St. Paul, Minn.: West.

MacIntyre, Alasdair. 1981. *After Virtue: A Study in Moral Theory*. London: Duckworth, 1982.

———. 1988. *Whose Justice? Which Rationality?* Notre Dame, Ind.: University of Notre Dame Press.

Millington, William G. 1979. *The Law and the College Student: Justice in Evolution*. St. Paul, Minn.: West.

Moffatt, Michael. 1989. *Coming of Age in New Jersey: College and American Culture*. New Brunswick, N.J.: Rutgers University Press.

Navasky, Victor. 1980. *Naming Names*. Harmondsworth, Sussex: Penguin.

Nussbaum, Martha. 1986. *The Fragility of Goodness: Luck and Ethics in Greek Tragedy and Philosophy*. New York: Cambridge University Press.

———. 1990. *Love's Knowledge: Essays on Philosophy and Literature*. New York: Oxford University Press.

Piele, Philip K. *Yearbook of School Law 1983*. Topeka, Ks.: National Organization on Legal Problems of Education.

Prosser, William L. 1971. *Handbook of the Law of Torts*. 4th ed. St. Paul, Minn.: West.

Ray, Laura Krugman. 1981. "Toward Contractual Rights for College Students." *Journal of Law and Education* 10(2, April):163–189.

Richmond, Douglas R. 1989. "Group Billing for University Residence Damages: A Common But Questionable Practice." *Journal of Law and Education* 18(3, Summer):375–409.

———. 1990. "Institutional Liability for Student Activities and Organizations." *Journal of Law and Education* 19(3, Summer):309–344.

Rudolph, Frederick. 1962 (rev. 1990). *The American College and University: A History*. Edited by John H. Thelen. Athens, Ga.: University of Georgia Press.

Smith, Michael Clay. 1989. "Students, Suds, and Summonses: Strategies for Coping with Campus Alcohol Abuse." *Journal of College Student Development* 30(March):118–122.

Spees, Emil R. 1987. "College Students' Sexual Attitudes and Behaviors,

1974–1985: A Review of the Literature." *Journal of College Student Development* 28(March):135–140.

Strange, Carney. 1986. "Greek Affiliation and Goals of the Academy." *Journal of College Student Development* 27(November):519–527.

Szablewicz, James J. and Annette Gibbs. 1987. "Colleges' Increasing Exposure to Liability: The New *In Loco Parentis.*" *Journal of Law and Education* 18(4, Fall):453–465.

Thomas, Nancy L. 1991. "The New In Loco Parentis." *Change* 23(5, September/October):33–39.

Thomas, Stephen B. *Yearbook of Education Law 1988.* Topeka, Ks.: National Organization on Legal Problems of Education.

———. *Yearbook of Education Law 1985.* Topeka, Ks.: National Organization on Legal Problems of Education.

Valente, William D. *Law in the Schools.* 1987. 2nd ed. Columbus, Ohio: Merrill.

Wilder, David H., Arlyne E. Hoyt, Beth Shuster Surbeck, Janet C. Wilder, and Patricia Imperatrice Carney. 1986. "Greek Affiliation and Attitude Change in College Students." *Journal of College Student Development* 27(November):510–519.

Yamamotu, Kaoru. 1968. *The College Student and His Culture: An Analysis.* Boston: Houghton Mifflin.

College Disciplinary Handbooks

The disciplinary handbooks and policy statements sent to me by college administrators, with permission to reprint, and cited in abbreviated form in the text, are listed below. The listing is alphabetical by institution.

Berea College Handbook for Students. 1990.

Calvin College, *Residence Hall Living, 90/91.*
Official Handbook of the Calvin College Knight, 90–91.

Carleton College, *Student Handbook 1990–91.*

Columbia University, *Facts About Columbia Essential to Students, 1990–91 Guide to Living,* Autumn 1990.
"University Policy on Alcohol, Drugs, and Smoking" (photocopy of newly adopted policies), September 1990.

Davidson College, *The Honor Code; Drugs and Alcohol* (pamphlets). 1990–91
"The Honor Code and the Code of Responsibility and Code of Disciplinary Procedure (1991)" (photocopy).

Bulletin of Duke University, 1990–91: Information and Regulations.

Illinois Wesleyan University, *Student Handbook 1990–91.*

Mount Holyoke College, *Student Handbook, 1989–91.*

Princeton University, *Rights, Rules, Responsibilities: 1990 Edition.*

Saint Anselm College, *Student Handbook 1990–91.*

Saint Olaf College, *1990–91 Student Handbook.*

Smith College, *1990–91 Handbook.*

Southwestern University, *1990–91 Student Handbook.*

Stanford University, *Student Conduct Policies,* 1990.
"The Legislative and Judicial Charter of 1968 (as amended)" (photocopy).
"Policy on Controlled Substances and Alcohol," October 1990 (photocopy).
"Report for 1989–90 from the Judicial Affairs Office" (photocopy).

University of California at Los Angeles, *Student Conduct Code of Procedures,* January 1987.
Activity Guidelines: Services and Facilities; Regulations, 1986.
1990–91 UCLA On Campus Housing Handbook.
Policies Applying to Campus Activities, Organizations, and Students, 1983 (adopted by the University of California system).

University of Delaware, *The Official Student Handbook* (undated).

University of North Carolina at Chapel Hill, *The Instrument of Student Judicial Governance, 1990.*

University of Richmond, *Living in the Web: A Handbook for Richmond College Students, 1990–91.*
Westhampton College Handbook 1990–91.

University of Virginia, *The Honor System* (undated).
The Judicial System (undated).
"On my honor. . .": Philosophy and Guidelines of the Honor System (undated).

Wellesley College Student Handbook, 1990–91.

Wesleyan University, *The Blue Book: Documents of Interest to Members of the Teaching Staff and the Student Body, 1990–91.*

Westminster College, *Student Life Handbook 1990–91.*

Williams College Bulletin: 1990–91 Student Handbook.

Yale University, *Undergraduate Regulations, 1990–91.*

Index

About the Author

DAVID A. HOEKEMA is a professor of philosophy and an academic dean at Calvin College in Grand Rapids, Michigan. He served previously on the philosophy faculty at the University of Delaware and as Executive Director of the American Philosophical Association, and prior to his appointment to those positions was a member of the philosophy department and the Paracollege faculty at St. Olaf College. His previous publications include a book on political philosophy, *Rights and Wrongs: Coercion, Punishment and the State* (Selinsgrove, Penn.: Susquehanna University Press, 1986), and numerous articles in philosophy journals and general periodicals on a variety of topics in political justice, the morality of war and peace, and the legitimacy of institutional moral codes. He received the A.B. from Calvin College and the Ph.D. from Princeton University.